Get the Most Out of Retirement

Checklist for ☑Happiness, ☑Health, ☑Purpose, and ☑Financial Security

SALLY BALCH HURME

Real Possibilities

Defending Liberty
Pursuing Justice

AMERICAN BAR ASSOCIATION

20 19 18 17   5 4 3 2

Library of Congress Cataloging-in-Publication Data

Names: Hurme, Sally Balch, author.
Title: Get the most out of retirement / by Sally Balch Hurme.
Description: Chicago : American Bar Association, [2016]
Identifiers: LCCN 2016029674 | ISBN 9781634256513 (print : alk. paper)
Subjects: LCSH: Pensions—Law and legislation—United States. | Pension trusts—Law and
    legislation—United States. | Retirement income—United States—Planning. | Finance, Personal—
    United States. | Retirement—United States—Planning.
Classification: LCC KF3510 .H86 2016 | DDC 332.024/01402434—dc23
LC record available at https://lccn.loc.gov/2016029674

Discounts are available for books ordered in bulk. Special consideration is given to state bars, CLE programs, and other barrelated organizations. Inquire at Book Publishing, ABA Publishing, American Bar Association, 321 N. Clark, Chicago, Illinois 60610-4714.

www.ShopABA.org

Contents

About the Author   xi

Introduction   xiii

**Chapter 1 Ready . . . Set . . . Retire! 15 Key Steps to Getting the Most Out
of Your Retirement**   1

   1. Reflect on the broad strokes of your life up to now   1

   2. Take stock of who you are   2

   3. Peek ahead   2

   4. Reimagine your life   2

   5. Think outside your box   2

   6. Choose how you spend your time   2

   7. Get going   3

   8. Be connected   3

   9. Stay centered   3

   10. Expect the unexpected   3

   11. Keep talking   3

   12. Get organized   3

   13. Revel in unstructured time   4

   14. Continue to be vital member of community   4

   15. Plan for Plan B   4

Ready . . . Set . . . Retire! Action Checklists   5

Who I Am   6

What Will Be Different a Year into My Retirement   8

My Legacy   9

Chapter 2 Adjust to Changing Relationships   **11**

My To-Do Checklist   12

Prepare your work for your departure   12

Coordinate with your partner on retirement plans and activities   13

Maintain—and enhance—your current relationships   15

Grow new relationships   16

Nurture your caregiving relationships   17

Understand the scope and limits of legal relationships   18

Changing Relationships Action Checklists   23

My Social Network   24

Widening My Circle   27

Financial Agent   28

Health Care Agent   30

Representative Payee/VA Fiduciary   32

Guardian/Conservator   33

Chapter 3 Get Organized and Clean Out the Clutter   **35**

My To-Do Checklist   36

Record basic facts about yourself   36

Pull together key papers   36

Know how long to keep records   38

Take care of special possessions   39

Get rid of what you don't need   40

Inventory your digital assets   42

List all income and expenses   42

Get Organized Action Checklists   43

    Personal History   44

    Education   48

    Residences   50

    Employment   52

    Memberships   54

    Awards   56

    Biography   57

    Where I Put It   59

    Personal Property   63

    Digital Assets   66

    Income   68

    Expenses   69

    Public Benefits   71

Chapter 4 Work with Your Retirement Team   **73**

   My To-Do Checklist   74

    Touch base with the human relations department   74

    Keep track of all who provide personal services   74

    Develop your roster of health professionals   74

    Know the different types of financial professionals   75

    Rely on a team of insurance agents   76

    Find the right legal professionals   76

   My Team Action Checklists   77

    Employer Retirement Coordination   78

    Personal and Home Services Contacts   80

    Health Contacts   86

    Financial Contacts   93

    Insurance Contacts   96

    Legal Contacts   98

Chapter 5 Welcome Your New Adventure   **101**

My To-Do Checklist   102

Find or expand volunteer opportunities   102

Learn something new   102

Make a travel bucket list   103

Work your way into a new job   106

Start your own business   107

New Adventure Action Checklists   109

Volunteer Opportunities   110

Things I'd Like to Learn   111

Education Opportunities   112

Travel Bucket List   115

Back to Work Inventory   118

Business Start Up   119

Chapter 6 Decide Where to Live   **121**

My To-Do Checklist   122

If you're staying put, make your home the home of your dreams   122

Compare the livability of the communities you are considering   123

Determine what's important about where you live   123

Consider dividing your time between two locations   123

Live with family   124

Investigate "villages" in your community   125

Explore whether an active living community is right for you   126

See if a continuing care retirement community (CCRC) is what you want   127

Understand what is and isn't provided in an assisted living facility   128

Look into skilled nursing facilities   130

Understand the differences in how property can be titled   131

Prepare for emergencies   134

Where to Live Action Checklists   134

Home Safety   135

What's Important About Where I Live   138

Living Together   140

Continuing Care Retirement Community (CCRC)   141

Assisted Living Facility Contracts   144

Skilled Nursing Facility Contracts   146

Emergency Preparedness   149

Chapter 7 Retiring Abroad   **151**

My To-Do Checklist   151

Set your priorities   152

Narrow down ideal retirement destinations   153

Ask the embassy about residency requirements   153

Figure out how you'll manage your finances   154

Consider how to handle your legal affairs   155

Check access to and coverage for health care   155

Prepare to leave   156

Retiring Abroad Action Checklists   158

Choosing My Destination   159

Pre-departure Preparation   163

Chapter 8 Take Control of Financial Matters   **165**

My To-Do Checklist   166

Organize information about how you bank   166

Review how financial accounts are titled   168

Check to make sure your savings bonds are still a sound investment   169

Keep original documents that are valuable or irreplaceable
in a safe deposit box   169

Make sure your investments match your investment objectives   170

Pay attention to investment fees   172

Document the terms of any personal debts or loans   175

List credit and debit cards   175

Recognize the signs of scams and financial exploitation   175

Financial Action Checklists   178

    Checking Accounts   179

    Savings Accounts   181

    Certificates of Deposit   182

    Credit Unions   184

    Savings Bonds   185

    Safe Deposit Boxes   186

    Stocks and Bonds   188

    Treasury Bills, Notes, and Bonds   189

    Municipal Bonds   190

    Mutual Funds   191

    Money Market Funds   192

    Personal Debts and Loans   193

    Credit and Debit Cards   195

    Signs of Scams and Financial Exploitation   197

Chapter 9 Manage Retirement Plans and Benefits   199

My To-Do Checklist   200

    Document all retirement plans and accounts
to understand the withdrawal rules   200

    Track down all pension benefits   202

    Understand Social Security benefits and how to navigate the system   203

    Take advantage of benefits available to veterans and their caregivers   205

Retirement Plans and Benefits Action Checklists   207

    Retirement Plans   208

    Pensions   211

    Social Security Benefits   212

    Veterans' Benefits   213

Chapter 10 Insure a Sound Retirement   215

My To-Do Checklist   216

    Locate all insurance policies   216

Go over the terms of all insurance policies 216

Update the beneficiaries on your life insurance 218

Review your health, disability, and Medicare insurance 219

Review insurance coverage for residences 223

Keep vehicle insurance current 224

Weigh the pros and cons of long-term care insurance 224

Insurance Action Checklists 229

Annuity 230

Life Insurance 231

Health, Disability, and Medicare Insurance 232

Medical Claims Tracker 235

Homeowners and Renters Insurance 236

Umbrella Insurance 237

Vehicle Insurance 238

Long-Term Care Insurance 240

Chapter 11 Deal with Legal Matters **243**

My To-Do Checklist 244

Document your health care preferences 244

Prepare an organ donor card 248

Plan the disposition of your body 249

Let family know your funeral wishes 249

Consider options for paying for your funeral 250

Know your veterans' burial benefits 251

Create or review your estate plan 252

Identify a source of funding for the costs to close your estate 257

Select an agent to manage your financial affairs 258

Discuss your advance planning with those who need to know 260

Legal Matters Action Checklists 260

Health Care Directives and Medical Orders 261

Final Wishes Summary 262

Organ and Tissue Donation   263

Whole Body Donation   264

Cremation   265

Burial   266

Entombment   267

Funeral/Memorial Service   268

Veterans' Burial Benefits   270

Will   271

Codicils   272

Living Trust   273

Pet Care   274

Letter of Instruction   275

Financial Power of Attorney   276

Chapter 12 Take Care of Yourself   **277**

My To-Do Checklist   277

Exercise to stay strong   278

Eat the good (for you) stuff   279

Keep your spirits up and your stress low   280

Take advantage of preventive services   281

Carry with you a personal medication record   282

Know your family medical history   282

Take Care of Yourself Action Checklists   283

Getting or Staying Fit   284

Eating Well   286

Personal Medication Record   287

Medicare-Covered Preventive Services   289

ACA-Covered Preventive Services   290

Family Medical History   292

ABOUT THE AUTHOR

Sally Balch Hurme, J.D., has led the national conversation on many of the legal issues of concern to older people and their families. Whether the issue is how to plan for what comes next, make decisions for others, or avoid fraud, she's been in the forefront. During her almost 25 years with AARP, she advocated on a wide range of issues including financial security, advance care planning, surrogate decision making, consumer fraud, financial exploitation, and elder abuse. Throughout her professional career she has focused on explaining the law so everyone can understand it.

Hurme is quoted frequently in national media, including the Wall Street Journal, USA Today, the New York Times, Money, Kiplinger's Retirement Report, CNN.com, NPR, and Fox Business News. She has lectured on elder abuse and guardianship in Australia, Czech Republic, Germany, Great Britain, Italy, Japan, Moldova, the Netherlands, and Spain. She is in demand as a speaker, having given more than 100 presentations on elder law topics in at least 40 states.

Get the Most Out of Retirement: Checklist for Happiness, Health, Purpose, and Financial Security is the fourth in the ABA/AARP Checklist series, which includes the bestselling *Checklist for My Family: A Guide to My History, Financial Plans, and Final Wishes; Checklist for Family Survivors: A Guide to Practical and Legal Matters When Someone You Love Dies;* and *Checklist for Family Caregivers: A Guide to Making It Manageable.*

For the past two decades, Hurme's volunteer commitment has focused on the rights of adults with diminished capacity and the reform of guardianship policy and procedures. She has served multiple terms on the boards of the National Guardianship Association and the Center for Guardianship Certification, where she has been instrumental in developing standards for guardians and criteria to improve professional competency. She's been an adviser to the Uniform Law Commission in drafting the uniform guardianship jurisdiction act and revising the uniform guardianship act. Hurme is a past chair of the National Guardianship Network, a collaboration of 11 national organizations working to improve guardianship. As a member of U.S. State Department delegation, she participated in the drafting of the Hague International Convention on the Protection of Incapacitated Adults. In 2008, she was honored by the National College of Probate Judges with the William Treat Award for excellence in probate law.

Hurme started her legal career as a partner in a private law firm, gained valuable experience serving older clients as a legal services attorney, and served as a city magistrate in

Alexandria, Virginia. She spent three years as an attorney adviser with the U.S. Department of Justice Office of Intelligence Policy and Review. She then returned to elder law advocacy as an assistant staff attorney with the American Bar Association Commission on Law and Aging before moving to AARP. Hurme taught elder law as an adjunct professor in elder law at the George Washington University Law School for eight years, honing her ability to explain the law. She is a long-term member of the American Bar Association, National Academy of Elder Law Attorneys, and the Virginia and District of Columbia bars. Hurme was a member of the Discipline and Ethics Commission of the Certified Financial Planners Board of Standards. She is also vice-chair of the board of governors of Stuart Hall School in Staunton, Virginia.

She received her B.A. from Newcomb College of Tulane University, New Orleans, Louisiana, and received her J.D. cum laude from the Washington College of Law, American University, Washington, D.C. After retiring from AARP she moved to Bridgewater, Virginia, so she could spend more time with her grandchildren and enjoy all that the Shenandoah Valley offers.

INTRODUCTION

Congratulations! You're ready to retire—or thinking of it enough to pick up this book.

Just about everyone dreams of retiring someday. Who doesn't want to ditch the commute, slow the pace down, and enjoy our families and hobbies more? You probably have a vision in your mind of what it will look like. Take a moment to close your eyes and savor that dream.

You may be feeling excitement, anticipation, trepidation. You may be wondering: How can I make my vision a reality? Do I need to modify my dream to make it work? What do I need now—and what will I need in 5, 10 years? How can I prepare?

I have to tell you: The big step of actually retiring involves lots of details and decisions. You'll want to think about medical, financial, and legal matters; your home, your family, and friends; vacations, hobbies, volunteer opportunities.

And then it takes some getting used to.

Retirement, it turns out, involves quite a lot of, well, work. I know from firsthand experience. I just retired.

Having just gone through the process, I have a better understanding of how to plan, the details and decisions you'll need to make, and ways to ease the adjustment. I'm here to share that experience with you. With this book, I hold your hand as you walk through the process. It may take a lot of work, but this book offers a straightforward and easy path. I promise.

And I'm hoping you can learn from my journey—including the mistakes and tweaks I've made along the way. For example, when to retire? Retiring at 70 had always seemed right for me: I was in good health, loved my work, and would max out on my Social Security benefits. (You've probably heard that before, but I'll repeat it: If you can, it's best to wait until 70 to get the most benefits.) Yet when my boss took a new job and the company offered a buyout, I decided the time was ripe for me to go out the door, too. I'm so glad I did, but my accelerated retirement date modified some of my plans (though I still intend to hold off starting Social Security until I turn 70).

Then there's the question of working in retirement. I always though it sounded like an oxymoron, but you might want to consider it for a variety of reasons—money, mental challenge, social outlet. The first thing I did when I retired was rent office space where I could continue to write. I'd been getting up and going to work every day for 40 years and didn't want to break that habit. A desk, chair, and computer were all I needed, and my new work space was just 10 minutes from home, with plenty of parking. In case it didn't work the way I had planned, I negotiated a month-to-month lease. That turned out to be a wise decision. A couple of months into retirement, my husband became seriously ill. Never mind writing away in my sensible little office; I was spending all my time camped out in the hospital and rehabilitation facility. He's doing fine now, but we've moved, at least temporarily, to our daughter's. I cancelled the lease to my office but found another one in our new town with twice the space at half the rent.

Another aspect of retirement is the paperwork. I quickly learned that no, it's not that much different from when I worked, but keeping track of all my husband's medical bills, co-payments, insurance claims, and medications opened my eyes about how essential it is to have an effective system to keep organized. One doctor billed us twice for the same co-payment. I caught the mistake before I paid double because I had good records of when he saw which doctor. With another statement, I noticed that Medicare hadn't been billed, so I called the lab to ask that it file a Medicare claim. That bill went in the "on hold" file until I could match the doctor's billing with the Medicare statement of claims paid. I've discovered you have to stay vigilant and use a record system that readily tracks what was done when, which claims have been filed, and what's been paid, along with contact information for when there's a question. Throughout this book, I give you tips on how not to drown in paper.

Then there's our home. The place we bought 15 years ago as our retirement haven is not going to fit our needs at all. We chose an old stone house on a beautiful farm near historic Harper's Ferry, West Virginia. As much enjoyment as we've gotten out of it so far, it takes too much work to keep it up. I love working in the yard, but spending three hours to just mow the grass is taxing. And it's too far from family, the grocery store, and doctors' offices. It's definitely not an age-friendly place, either, with steep and narrow stairs to the bedroom and bath. So our haven is now on the market. We were disappointed at first, sure, but we're happy where we ended up. In this book, you'll find guidance and checklists to carefully work through where you're going to be living for the next decade or more.

So, you see, there's lots to do. "Plan" may be a four-letter word, but you need to plan for retirement like you do other things. Fun things to plan might be dinner with friends: coordinating schedules, honing the guest list, setting the menu. Or a vacation: where to go, what to do, how to get there, how much to spend. We've all learned that whatever the occasion, with a good dose of planning, we have more options and can stay in control over what happens when the event occurs. At the same time, it helps to be flexible or have some wiggle room in those plans.

Planning for retirement is one valuable step, but living in retirement takes some getting used to, no matter how carefully we plan. Retirement is changing what you do every day. For most, it's a new schedule. Instead of getting up at a set time each morning to get to the office on time, you now can control what you have to do every day. Cheers to no more morning commute, the race to get to the train or bus on time, awful traffic jams. No more long meetings and bosses who set the agenda.

The 9-to-5 is gone, but you still have the hours between 9 and 5 to fill. You'll want to look at the reality of how you will spend your days. Will you volunteer? Go on long bike rides? Take that trip you never had time for? Start a business? I found that a good portion of my new "free time" is spent on paperwork and caregiving, not the volunteering and travel I envisioned. But I still find time to kayak and keep in touch with former colleagues. I can easily hop in the car to pick up the grandkids from sports practice or chaperone my granddaughter's field trip.

You may have more time but less income. For many, retirement means moving from getting a regular paycheck to adjusting to new ways of paying for everyday expenses. You may incur fewer work-related expenditures, but you may also encounter new costs. My health insurance eats up a bigger portion of my budget, now that I no longer have my employer paying part of it. Rent for my office takes a small chunk, as does sharing the grocery bill now that we have a three-generation household. Having a clear idea of what expenses you need to cover cuts down on sleepless nights. The recommendations and checklists in the book are designed to get you organized right at the start of retirement so you can enjoy your new lifestyle.

As Yogi Berra said, "When you come to a fork in the road, take it." Retirement is one of those forks in the road of your life. When you come to this point, you'll want to be prepared for the path that lies ahead.

What's Ahead

This book is definitely not something to rush through. Don't try to read it in one or two sittings. Skim through to see what jumps out at you. Stick it on your end table or night stand—wherever you like to read. Dip into different sections as they become relevant. If there's a detail that doesn't apply, just skip it.

Chapter 1 gives you, neatly and concisely, the 15 steps I've discovered are critical to getting the most out of your retirement. Take stock of what you've done and who you are. Take some time to dream a little. What sort of life can you reimagine for yourself? What do you need to do to get to where you want to be socially, emotionally, and financially?

Chapter 2 covers your relationships. Relationships often change during retirement. You're not chatting daily at the coffee pot or joining colleagues for lunch. How can you maintain a satisfying social life? As the scouting camp song advises, "Make new friends, but keep the old; one is silver, the other is gold." Perhaps you've retired, but your partner hasn't, or you need to spend time caregiving; you'll want to prepare for that as well.

Chapter 3 helps you get organized and clean out the clutter. What papers do you need to keep—and toss? Take the time now to gather and sort. I also give you tools to track bills, statements, and claims so when you, too, get duplicate bills, you'll spot it. In addition to organizing papers, I offer tips on how to inventory your special possessions and then get rid of the stuff you no longer have a use for. And to keep you organized, this chapter goes into creating and staying on budget and check for any public benefits you might be eligible for.

In Chapter 4, you'll pull together your team of professionals that you rely on for any medical, investment, insurance, or legal questions you need answers to. You probably already have contact information for medical professionals, insurance agents, HR staff, and even lawyers and financial planners; you just want it in one place.

Chapter 5 explores your new 9 to 5. We look at the many options for what you are going to do to spend your newly acquired independence from a regular work schedule. You now can set your own time line for what you do each day. Now that you don't have to go to work, do you want to concentrate on your hobbies, volunteer, learn something new, hit the road in your RV, explore a new career, or start your own business? Use the checklists to make sure you have a good foundation for your what's next.

Chapter 6 is about where you're going to live for the foreseeable future. Many retirees want to stay right where they are and "age in place." Look around your home and make sure it is the home of your dreams. Also look at safety: If your mobility declines, what changes will you need? If you're considering a move, you'll find information about all of the many options available, including that luxury of snow birding. And if you're looking at independent living, continuing care retirement communities, assisted living, or skilled nursing facilities, I help you understand the legal contracts you'll need to sign. Of course, you should always have a local lawyer review and explain all contracts before signing.

Chapter 7 is for the adventuresome who are thinking about making the really big move to retire abroad. Here I help you pick the best place for you and make the transition. Yes, you can continue to receive your Social Security benefits, but you need to pay special attention to health insurance, residency requirements, and how you'll manage your long-distance finances.

Chapter 8 helps you take control of all your financial matters. Here's where you can take stock of your assets and investments so you can comfortably complete your plans for the future. This chapter also covers the fees to help you safeguard your nest egg and how to spot scammers and fraudulent investment schemes. Be sure to get independent investment advice from your financial adviser.

In Chapter 9, you'll pull together your retirement accounts. You'll find valuable information about how and when to apply for Social Security, how to switch from saving for retirement to drawing from your investment accounts, and what benefits are available if you are a military veteran.

Chapter 10 is about insurance, designed to protect us from the unexpected. I help you assess the insurance coverage you have and what you may need to change or acquire. Whether it is life insurance, long-term care insurance, annuities, vehicle insurance, or homeowners insurance, you want to make sure you are appropriately covered and you know what the policies do and do not include. Understanding health insurance and all the various parts to Medicare is essential. Make sure you get the most out of your coverage and know what medical expenses are covered and what health care costs you need to plan for.

If you have both retiree health insurance and Medicare, you'll find information about how coverage is coordinated.

Chapter 11 covers advance planning in the event something should happen to you. Your plans for how you want to distribute your wealth need to be set out in proper legal documents. You'll find information about the difference between a will and trust and what to include in either or both. In addition to an estate plan for your finances, you need an advance care plan for the medical care you want. I go into the importance of the conversations you have with loved ones about your medical preferences and how to put your wishes into writing. If your loved ones don't know your plans and wishes, they cannot carry them out.

Chapter 12 is all about you. Is it time to re-assess your fitness regime? With more free time, are you dipping into the cookie jar (literally) too often, or cooking healthful meals? Are you taking care of yourself emotionally and spiritually—whatever that means to you? Are you up-to-date with your vaccines and immunizations? Does your family have a record of your health history: allergies, surgeries, and prescriptions? I also give you some tools to plan and track your medications and walk you through those free preventative checkups you get, compliments of the Affordable Care Act and Medicare.

A Few Tips

Fill in the paper checklists with a pencil or erasable pen. This book is made to be written in. As you gather more information as time goes by, it will be easy to update what you have previously written.

Download the electronic files from http://ambar.org/RetirementChecklists. As you complete a chapter, you may want to print out a copy and place the pages in a three-ring binder. You may also want to add plastic pages to slip in documents you come across. You'll want to keep a hard copy (and a backup file) of these documents in your filing system. Be sure to note where you have those copies stored so you don't waste time looking for them later.

Keep the information up to date. As changes occur, you'll want to note them.

A word of caution: You are assembling a great deal of very personal information you don't want to get into the wrong hands. Be cautious about where you store it and with whom you share it.

> **PDF versions of these checklists can be found at http://ambar.org/RetirementChecklists.**

CHAPTER 1

READY . . . SET . . . RETIRE!
15 KEY STEPS TO GETTING THE
MOST OUT OF YOUR RETIREMENT

Whether you're in the planning stages or have already retired, get ready for an adventure! Maybe you chose the date, or perhaps you weren't quite expecting it due to downsizing or other changes at work, your own health issues, or your family's needs. No matter how near or far away your retirement is, you may be wondering what to expect. And how to be best prepared for the best years of your life.

Let's face it: there will be changes. Changes can be unsettling, but we've been dealing successfully with change for decades. We're pros at it! We have wisdom gained from experience and that experience has value. In the words of President Kennedy, "Change is the law of life. And those who look only to the past or present are certain to miss the future."

This is your chance to go after opportunities to live your best life. As Jo Ann Jenkins, AARP's CEO, says in her book *Disrupt Aging*, "We are a generation of makers and doers who have a desire to continue exploring our possibilities, to celebrate discovery over decline. When we disrupt aging and embrace it as something to look forward to, we can begin to discover the real possibilities for becoming the person we've always wanted to be."

Get ready, get set: Start your retirement journey now. Here are the 15 key steps down that path.

1. Reflect on the broad strokes of your life up to now

Reflect on your past and the legacy you'll leave behind. How did you get to where you are now? What things gave you the most satisfaction? Complete this sentence: I am so glad that I decided to _____. I'd fill in that blank with "go to law school"; yours could be any decision, big or small, that made an important difference in your life.

2. Take stock of who you are

A good way to take stock is with a personality profile such as the Who I Am Checklist in this chapter. Who are you right now? What do you consider to be your strengths and weaknesses? Pick ten words you'd use to describe yourself today. Think about how your sense of identity changes upon retirement. Some may find it hard to reorient from worker to retired. I've not yet figured out what to put on my business cards. When I do media interviews or fill out speaker proposals, I'm not sure what say about who I am. "Former employee" has no pizzazz! For me, the label "retired" says more about what I'm not doing, rather than who I am. Yes, I'm struggling a bit with an identity crisis. Nevertheless, I'm still a lawyer, writer, spouse, mom, grandmother, volunteer, and friend. Those identities haven't and won't change.

3. Peek ahead

Looking forward, what is most important to you? What part of the answers in the Who I Am Checklist do you most want to work on changing as you enter retirement? How much of a new you do you want to be? Who do you want to be next year? What choices are you likely to face in the years ahead? What changes do you want to make about how you spend most of your time? What possibilities would you most like to pursue? What do you want your new mission in life to be? What in your life do you want to say no to?

4. Reimagine your life

It's a time to reimagine your life. Here's your chance to fulfill the dreams you've had all your life. Embrace the changes your new lifestyle brings. Spend more time doing something you really love and are fascinated with. Need guidance? Visit LifeReimagined.org.

5. Think outside your box

Think of retirement as an adventure when you can try new things, meet new people, have a different schedule. Explore new ideas and activities. Do something you've never done before. This might be reading a different section of the newspaper, going to a musical performance or movie that's never appealed to you, or exploring a different cuisine. These small explorations into the new you can set you up for larger journeys of life discovery. Experience the wonder and joy of trying new things and developing skills and even expertise you never imagined was possible. Deliberately taking small steps down multiple paths is a way to test and try out something that's new to you. Take action and see what happens. Then adapt your next steps as things unfold. When you act, doors open. Chapter 5 has lots of ideas and tools to help you think outside your box.

6. Choose how you spend your time

Think strategically about how you spend each day. Choose to do fewer things you don't like or enjoy and more things that make your heart sing. Whenever you can, don't say yes when you want to say no. Say no and do what you want to do instead. Spend more time with the people you enjoy and less time with the people you don't.

7. Get going

Get out of doors. Begin your day with a walk. Exercise for at least a few minutes every day. Go dancing. Make a garden. Adopt a pet. Travel around your town, state, and country— and, if you have the means and inclination, beyond.

8. Be connected

Introvert or extrovert—it doesn't matter. Stay involved with your old friends. Reconnect with acquaintances from the past. Add new friends to your support network. Put forth the effort to meet new people. Get to know someone much younger than you. Spend time with someone much older than you. Write a letter. Send a thank you note.

9. Stay centered

Turn off the gadgets. Turn down the volume. Try yoga. Meditate. Attend a house of worship. Purchase a bouquet of flowers for yourself. Get enough sleep. Eat well. Write a poem or paint a picture. Sing in the shower.

10. Expect the unexpected

Your retirement may last 20 or more years. You don't have to accomplish everything you set out to do in the first year you're retired. Be flexible if what you try first doesn't work out to your satisfaction. Think back to all the changes that happened in your life between ages 20 and 40, or between 40 and 60. Some plans were fulfilled; others got diverted due to events you couldn't foresee. It's OK to take detours or explore by-ways that seem attractive as you transition through retirement. You can always come back to the familiar path if you want to. Do a reality check from time to time: Are you doing too much or not enough? Be flexible so you can adjust your sights when needed.

11. Keep talking

Talk with your spouse, friends, and family about your retirement vision and your expectations for them. Mutually negotiate when priorities don't mesh. Speak up when you see a need to change course. Let others know when you need help. Tell key people what quality of life you want now and in the future and how they can help you get what you want. Chapter 2 has more tips on how to manage your relationships as they change during retirement.

12. Get organized

Different people have differing ideas of what "being organized" means. It can range from just this side of hoarding to picky neat-nik. Wherever your comfort zone lies within that continuum, at a minimum know where your important documents are located so you can find them when you need them. Prepare the key planning documents: health care power of attorney, financial power of attorney, and estate plan. Document your special personal possessions and write down who you want to get them. Share your family history and your personal legacy. It's easier to talk about your own funeral wishes now than later. Procrastinating on these sometimes hard topics limits your options and leaves your family in a quandary about the right thing to do. Find more help on getting organized and cleaning out the clutter to start your retirement afresh in Chapter 3. Chapter 11 walks you through the legal matters you need to put in place.

13. Revel in unstructured time

Even though retirement is not a rest-of-my-lifetime vacation, it does usually offer us the chance to slow down from a frantic work pace. Have a leisurely breakfast, enjoy the sunset, or savor the opportunity to spend more time with the folks you care about. Leave time to do the unexpected or to just hang out. As longevity expert Dr. Bill Thomas suggests, experience the energy that results from spontaneous, unstructured play. If you need help figuring this one out, find a child to guide you. Everyone lives better when they have enough unstructured playtime.

14. Continue to be vital member of community

Dr. Thomas's prescription: Get involved in your community—however you define it. Enjoy the fact you have abundant time to devote to others. Give of yourself to help others and you will strengthen the bonds between you and other people in your community. Leave a mark by passing your values on to those who follow you. Leave a legacy by mentoring a high school or college student, starting a nonprofit with a mission you are passionate about, making a video reflecting a key cause or important event in your life, or writing poetry or a memoir. I offer other suggestions for volunteer opportunities in Chapter 5.

15. Plan for Plan B

Retirement means being open to opportunities and taking the actions you need to achieve your vision. Sometimes though, plans don't quite go as planned, as you well know from your personal experience. Do you have a Plan B? Build in some options and don't be hard on yourself if Plan A doesn't work out. Your plans for retirement are not something you set and forget. Goals change as life changes. There are some downsides to retirement. Illness and death are part of life's journey. My first plan for what I'd do in retirement lasted two months. Then my husband got sick and I became a full-time caregiver, which was not in my original plan. He's much improved and we are back on track for Plan A for now. When the next bump in the road comes along, we are better prepared to make adjustments.

These 15 steps are positive strides you can take toward a satisfying retirement. In the following chapters you'll find more detailed guidance on how to get the most out of your retirement. Happy trails!

Ready . . . Set . . . Retire! Action Checklists

The following Action Checklists are included in Chapter 1:

❑ *Who I Am*

❑ *What Will Be Different a Year into Retirement*

❑ *My Legacy*

Who I Am

Ten words that describe me today:

_____   _____

_____   _____

_____   _____

_____   _____

_____   _____

My personal strengths:

_____

_____

_____

People most important to me:

_____

_____

_____

Activities that give me the most satisfaction:

_____

_____

_____

What frustrates me:

_____

_____

_____

I am good at:

_____

_____

_____

I manage stress by:

_____

_____

_____

Key influences on my life:

_____

_____

_____

Key decisions I'm glad I made:

_____

_____

_____

Key decisions I wish I'd made differently:

_____

_____

_____

Things about me I'd most like to change:

_____

_____

_____

I spend too much time doing:

_____

_____

_____

I spend too much money on:

_____

_____

_____

What Will Be Different a Year into My Retirement

I will spend my time with:

_____

_____

_____

_____

_____

I will spend my time doing:

_____

_____

_____

_____

_____

I will have started:

_____

_____

_____

_____

_____

I will have stopped:

_____

_____

_____

_____

My Legacy

Accomplishments I'm proud of:

_____

_____

_____

_____

_____

_____

_____

_____

Memories I want to pass on:

_____

_____

_____

_____

_____

_____

_____

_____

Values I wish to share:

_____

_____

_____

_____

_____

_____

_____

_____

Goals I strive for:

_____

_____

_____

_____

_____

_____

_____

_____

_____

_____

Family history to remember:

_____

_____

_____

_____

_____

_____

_____

_____

_____

_____

CHAPTER 2

ADJUST TO CHANGING RELATIONSHIPS

Retiring is a time of shifting relationships. We have lots more time to spend with family and friends—a retirement goal of many, according to research. But we may be leaving the circle of people we spent our working hours with. No more chatting over the coffee machine. If you want to keep in touch with colleagues, you'll have to make a concerted effort to do so. I often reach out by e mail and Facebook to catch up or make a date for lunch the next time I'm in the city.

When you retire and what you are going to do after you retire involves all those around you: your colleagues, partner or spouse, family members, others who live with or near you, as well as all the other people you engage with on a daily basis. Your new adventures, schedules, and activities are inevitably going to bring changes—and perhaps even challenges—to those around you. You and your spouse may need to align expectations about personal time and space. You may be moving to a new location and need to create a new circle of friends. Making new friends is not always easy, but the big plus is that it's more fun to share interests and good times with others. And it has a side benefit: Having friends can keep us mentally fit and physically active.

You may also experience a shift in your relationships because someone else needs your help. At some point in your retirement, you may join the 43.5 million caregivers providing unpaid care to a loved one. Becoming a caregiver adds an extra dimension to your relationship with the person you care for. Being both a daughter and caregiver for aging parents, or a husband and caregiver for your wife, can deepen your sense of fulfillment and bring you closer, but it can also stress that relationship. Your time spent as a caregiver can also reduce the time, energy, and attention you can give to other family members and friends. I offer some tips to help you nourish all those relationships.

You may be asked to enter into new legal relationships with your spouse or family members. Taking on the responsibility to make personal, financial, or medical decisions for someone else can be a big job. These legal relationships have significant ramifications as to how you relate to the person on whose behalf you are making decisions.

My To-Do Checklist

Done   **Need to Do**

❑   ❑   Prepare your work for your departure

❑   ❑   Coordinate with your partner on retirement plans and activities

❑   ❑   Maintain—and enhance—your current relationships

❑   ❑   Grow new relationships

❑   ❑   Nourish caregiving relationships

❑   ❑   Understand the scope and limits of important legal
                          relationships

✓ Prepare your work for your departure

Once you have decided to retire, you need to think about the impact leaving your job is going to have on your employer and co-workers. Whether you've been at your current place of employment for a year or a decade, someone is going to have to take on your responsibilities. You may be easy to replace or nearly indispensable. However big the hole you are leaving in the company's organizational chart, you have the responsibility, at a minimum, to give your employer sufficient notice of your planned departure. (In Chapter 3 you'll learn more about all the other things you need to do to log out with the human relations department.)

Consider what your colleagues will do without you. While you've been thinking about retirement, perhaps you've been mentoring a successor or coaching someone else in your work group to learn your responsibilities. The option of phased retirement, where you gradually reduce your work hours and responsibilities before a final exit, is a way to focus on training others to take over.

Between your retirement announcement and your departure is the time to get your files and folders—paper and electronic—in order. You'll need to spend some time cleaning up or organizing the stuff you are leaving behind so those who come after you can locate key information. Be sure you understand company policy on the information you need to archive, save, or transfer to common files, and what you can or cannot take with you. Proprietary information must remain with your employer. Be judicious about how much you bring home as you clean out your work space. I carted home several boxes of books and papers that I thought would be invaluable; they sit in my garage untouched.

Let colleagues outside your office, too, know of your new adventure. You'll want your professional network to know how to stay in contact with you. Sign up for a new e-mail address before your work computer shuts off and your business e-mail vanishes. Set up or update your LinkedIn account. Send an e-mail to all your contacts letting them know your new e-mail address, mailing address, and phone number. Capture contact information on the My Social Network Checklist for all the people you want to be able to get in touch with.

My husband, who has been retired for more than 10 years, still keeps in touch with more than a dozen office mates on a regular basis. You may also want to get in touch with former managers for recommendation letters for any new job—or new career.

If you have a business, are self-employed, or are in a partnership, you will need to take many steps to wind down that work. A succession plan should be in place that determines when, to whom, and for how much your business will be sold or transferred to family members or key employees. Work with your financial adviser to determine the fair value of your business and to identify strategies for you to continue to get income after you retire, avoid lingering liabilities, and save on taxes. You'll need to communicate with clients, customers, suppliers, and creditors that you are going out of business; determine what to do with business assets, inventory, accounts receivable, and liabilities; and notify licensing authorities.

If your business structure is that of a limited liability company (LLC) or partnership, you need to follow the dissolution procedures set out in your organizational documents. Make sure your decision to dissolve is recorded in business minutes or by written consent of all required individuals or entities involved in the LLC or partnership. Notify the state corporation commission or other state government office that you have gone out of business and fill out the appropriate forms. In some states you may need to get clearance from taxing authorities to make sure all business taxes have been paid. Cancel your business licenses, permits, and name so you don't incur additional tax or other liabilities. Check with your county clerk for any other steps you need to take or forms to fill out. Let your insurance company know of your closing; give timely notice to your landlord; stop utilities, phone, Internet, and any other services in your business name; file a change of address with the post office; cancel business credit cards; and pay any taxes that still may be due. Work with your legal adviser to ensure that you have appropriately minimized your risk of liabilities. More information about LLCs is in Chapter 5.

When the final day arrives, celebrate! It might be a big office party, recognition reception, lunch with favorite colleagues, or quiet good-byes and hugs. My last day was festive and a little bit sad, shared with many others who were departing at the same time. No gold watch, but wonderful photos recorded our team's farewells.

✓ Coordinate with your partner on retirement plans and activities

For couples, especially if both work outside the home, retirement has a big impact on their relationship with each other. Not only do you need to agree on when each of you is going to retire, but also you need to work out what both of you are going to do with your time in retirement. New schedules, lifestyles, and finances come into play that can alter each partner's roles and responsibilities.

In my family, my husband was ready to retire 10 years ago while I was still going strong with my work. His retirement was fine with me because I had a long "honey-do" list of things I wanted him to accomplish. I put job slips in a bowl with the expectation he would pick one out each morning and have it done by the time I came home. Anyone can guess how that worked out! To him, retirement meant not having to do what others wanted him to do on a fixed schedule. My expectations and his plans did not mesh, but we compromised.

So my advice to you: Be clear on your expectations and be open to compromise. Start the conversation long before you retire.

Ditto if you will both now be retired. Be sure you share your mental picture of retirement with your spouse. Your mindsets and priorities need to coincide, or at least be brought out into the open for discussion and negotiation. What if one is ready to travel while the other wants to start a new career? Or, one thinks retirement means moving to warmer climes and the other wishes to stay close to the grandkids? Both of you should prepare your own Who I Am Checklist in Chapter 1 and then resolve any differences in priorities. If priorities don't match, one solution is to take small steps and agree to try one path for a short time. You could rent in a different location for six months, take a part-time seasonal job, or enroll in one course. Experiment and keep an open mind to new possibilities that you may not have thought about.

Separately prepare your travel dreams in Chapter 5 and then together map out which trips are most doable. Maybe plan on one big trip this year to celebrate retirement and then schedule shorter trips for other years. Or a celebratory long weekend now, while you save and plan for the cross-country excursion a couple of years later. You have time to spread out your trips. You don't have to do everything you've been planning in the first month, or even the first year. Take time to adjust to being retired.

One key issue to work out is how much togetherness is right for your relationship. If you've both been working, you haven't been spending all day every day in each other's company. You've been focusing on work and childrearing, and now, as empty nester retirees, the focus is on each other. Will both of you enjoy that companionship, or should you have separate schedules and activities? What things will you do together—will you have the same volunteer commitments and foreign language class, but different gym times and book clubs?

Keep in mind that you will need to help each other adjust to new lifestyles as you are settling into your retirement adventures. It's important to communicate how much time you want to spend together and apart. Positive communication skills and healthy boundaries will go a long way in keeping the marriage on strong footing. Don't be offended if your spouse wants some personal time and space. Day after day in close proximity can stress the best marriage.

Some words of advice, from personal experience, on how to have smooth waters rather than ruffled feathers, as you work through retirement relationships:

- Share expectations. If you expect your spouse to do more chores around the house, speak up before hard feelings develop. Comments like, "But I thought you knew what I wanted" go nowhere in strengthening your relationship.
- Talk about how you are going to disagree. Do this by setting rules for how you agree to disagree.
- Acknowledge that negotiation and compromise are key ways to avoid driving each other crazy.
- Make space in your days for "alone time" and "doing my own thing."

- Maintain separate friendships and activities. Your spouse is not your social director or event planner.

- Honor the fact that each of you has a unique identity that may grow and change in the new retirement environment.

- Have separate territories so you both have personal space. It's okay—and even healthy— to have his and her spaces where you can each retreat and have your own stuff.

It takes work to create a mutual lifestyle that takes each other's feelings into account. The goal should be finding what both of you enjoy doing and what meets each other's emotional needs. But even if you have trouble adjusting, keep the faith. Research shows that retirees successfully manage this transition into retirement, and their relationships don't suffer—and even sometimes improve.

Couples entering retirement have important financial relationships to consider. Decisions you make about your retirement significantly impact your spouse's retirement security. As I explain in Chapter 9, the decision to start Social Security benefits can affect the amount your spouse receives for the rest of his or her life, in either spousal or survivor benefits. The risk of losing health insurance benefits for a spouse who was covered under an employee health plan was a reason many workers continued employment until the spouse turned 65 and could start Medicare. Now, with the Affordable Care Act, the spouse who loses coverage as a dependent under an employee health plan can shop for insurance in the Health Insurance Marketplace. There's more about health insurance in Chapter 10.

Most pension plans require the spouse's consent if the retiree does not set aside a portion of the payout as a survivor benefit. When both spouses have pensions, a key decision is whether one or both members of the couple should elect survivor benefits for the other partner. This financial relationship calls for mutual consideration of other assets saved, the difference in ages and health between the couple, the size of the pension, and some good number crunching with an experienced financial adviser. Read more about retirement plans in Chapter 9.

✓ Maintain—and enhance—your current relationships

Spending more time with family and friends is what many dream about for their retirement. Adults over 50 tell AARP they want to be a part of their children's or grandchildren's lives and be close to and do activities with family and friends. Your retirement gives you the opportunity to do just that.

My retirement allowed me the freedom to move closer to my daughter and spend time every day with my grandkids: taxiing them to school when they missed the bus, helping with homework, building snow forts, and reading bedtime stories. That's my choice and I love it. If that's not your choice, be sure your preferences match your family's expectations. If you live close to your kids and you really would like to be responsible for your grandkids' afterschool care every day until their parents come home from work, speak up. If you need to set limits on your babysitting duties, be clear.

Include your family in discussions about whether you are considering moving closer to them or farther away, how much travel you plan to do, what financial support you may need, and what financial support you may no longer provide. You'll also want to share your health care preferences, your estate planning goals, and other important information you've recorded in this book's checklists.

If you're not near your kids and grandkids, one of your new adventures in retirement could be to build or use your tech skills to be more involved with them as a willing ear, history teacher, and role model. The Internet is fast becoming a key way for grandparents and grandkids to stay in touch. Research by AARP and Microsoft found that 83 percent of parents, grandparents, and teenagers consider going online to be a helpful form of communication among family members, with a third of the teens and grandparents saying texting and e-mail helps them better understand each other.

✓ Grow new relationships

Staying socially connected is key to a vibrant retirement. In fact, scientists are finding links between loneliness and illness. So even if you consider yourself an introvert and think you could spend your retirement years cozy in your easy chair reading good books, make an effort to maintain or build new social connections.

Although you may be planning to stay in touch with your work colleagues—those people you've spent most of your waking hours with—they are probably not going to remain your primary social circle. You may stay in touch for a year or two, but then interest generally wanes. They are working; you are not. They move to a different job; your activities shift. Old friends are valuable, but the changes brought by your retirement may require developing a new circle of friends.

For social butterflies, making new friends can be an exciting part of retirement. Others may be more reticent about building a new social circle. You may need to do something you've never done before: Be proactive to find new people with common interests. Don't be daunted, though. One of the easiest pieces of advice I can give you is to think of the things you enjoy doing and find ways to do them with others.

For example, you may enjoy walking. It definitely can be a solo activity and that may be just the way you like it. But if you're looking for new friends, strike up a conversation with a neighbor you see regularly on your morning route, then make plans to meet on a regular basis. Reach out to the person at the dog park whose puppy is romping with yours.

Exploring groups that center on your favorite hobby is a great way to get to know people who share your interests. Like to read? Turn that solitary activity into a social activity by joining a book club or attending a program at the public library. Talking about your stamp collection with someone at a stamp swap meet is an easy way to start a conversation. Groups traveling to the places you like to go or focusing on the special things you like to do is another way to bring you into contact with others with similar interests; operas in Santa Fe, Broadway shows in New York, wine tasting in Napa Valley, Civil War sites—it's easy to find groups who share your interests. Websites like nationalgeographicexpeditions.com, sierraclub.org/outings, and smithsonianjourneys.org are just a few of the many companies that host themed travel groups to exciting places.

You may want to reconnect with old college or work buddies. Attend a reunion to find out what everyone you went to school with is now doing. Make plans to see that former colleague from two jobs ago who still sends you birthday cards. Reminiscing about that difficult assignment can rekindle a friendship.

Volunteering is another option. Not only do you gain personal satisfaction from helping out, but it's also a way to meet and connect with people who share your values. A local place of worship—even if it is not your denomination—may have activities that help you find new friends in your neighborhood. Senior centers, libraries, and the local coffee shop are other casual places to find new friends. Read the billboards, sign up for e-mail, and check the local newspaper for events.

Chatting online may not be the same as face-to-face contact, but social media such as Facebook, LinkedIn, Twitter, forums, chat rooms, and other social networking sites on the Internet are the newest tools to meet people. Try out the chat rooms at community.aarp.org to connect with others with similar interests. AARP/Microsoft research found that staying in touch with friends and family we do not see regularly is our number one reason for using social networking sites.

If you're looking to meet that special someone, get a copy of AARP's *Dating After 50 for Dummies*, by Pepper Schwartz, available online and at brick-and-mortar bookstores.

✓ Nurture your caregiving relationships

At some point in your retirement you may become a caregiver. Many people find they need to retire because of their caregiving responsibilities. Others confront that responsibility once they retire. When I retired, I wasn't thinking about becoming a full-time caregiver, but just two months later my husband became seriously ill. If I hadn't been retired when he got sick, I would have had to do so.

Caregiving is a very special relationship. The person you care for could be your spouse, parent, sibling, adult child, grandchild, or friend. Caregiving becomes an added dimension to whatever relationship you have with the person you care for. You're still the daughter for your dad you're caring for, the husband of your wife in the nursing home, or mother of your son with muscular dystrophy. Your caregiving may include driving to doctor's appointments periodically and grocery shopping each week. Or you could help every day with bathing or getting dressed, preparing meals, and making sure medications are taken. You may be the one who steps up to pay the bills, locate legal documents, and track medical claims. In addition to these tasks, you also may take on the roles of health advocate, care coordinator, and decision maker for the person you care for.

All these roles and responsibilities can get complicated. I've learned that the sum of spouse plus caregiver plus health advocate can add up to relationship complications. When I shift into caregiving high gear, my husband reminds me that I'm his spouse, not his mother. The take-away: Respect the person and the underlying relationship.

Caregiving can strengthen the bond you have with those in your care, but at the same time it can strain other relationships. People you used to spend time with may feel neglected; friends may drift away because you just don't have energy to focus on them. It's true: Studies consistently confirm that caregiving does take time away from other people in our lives. Because caregiving can stress you and strain your relationships with other family members and friends, follow the wisdom of Amy Goyer, author of AARP's *Juggling Life, Work and Caregiving*: Your relationships with your friends, spouse or partner, children, grandchildren, siblings, and other loved ones are part of who you are. Do your best to stay in touch, prioritize time together, take breaks or even vacations together, and be there for these important people. When caregiving comes to an end, you'll want them in your life. To ease your role, see my book, the *AARP/ABA Checklist for Family Caregivers: Making It Manageable*. Find Amy's and my books in retailers nationwide, or at AARP.org/CaregivingBooks.

✓ Understand the scope and limits of legal relationships

As a caregiver, you may make many decisions about the person you care for. But even if you are the person's spouse, child, grandchild, grandparent, or sibling, there will be times when being a caregiver does not give you the authority to make important decisions. As important and responsible as the role of caregiver is, that title may need to be supplemented with other titles that give you legal authority to make decisions. Banks, care facilities, government agencies, and other third parties that you need to work with may expect or require that your authority be based on more than being a concerned and loving caregiver.

The core legal reason for this is the right of every person to make his or her own decisions. Those decisions could be bad, foolish, harmful, or irrational. We all have made decisions that turned out to be pretty stupid or not well thought through. Still, individually and as a society, we cherish our independence, personal autonomy, and right to make our own decisions.

Of course, we often look to others to help us make decisions. We seek advice from our friends, family, faith leaders, and professionals and even the Internet or social media to help us decide what to do. Few of us make decisions totally on our own without any input from others, but our decisions are still our own.

At other times, we do want someone else to make decisions for us. We may want a friend to order our dinner at a restaurant when we're unfamiliar with the menu. We could ask a neighbor to decide if our lawn needs watering while we're away on vacation. Those sorts of decisions don't need any legal authority; verbal permission is sufficient. More important decisions, such as accessing money to pay bills or signing a resident agreement at an assisted living facility, require legal authority.

The most common way to delegate decision-making authority is through legal documents called powers of attorney. A power of attorney is a flexible, convenient, and effective way to say I want you, my agent, to do these things or make these decisions for me. Agents use the written power of attorney to document the authority given to them to make whatever personal, medical, or financial decisions are assigned to them. Chapter 11 covers these legal documents in detail. In this chapter I help you understand the legal relationship that is created when the title of "agent" is added to your other roles as spouse, child, or caregiver.

If someone has selected you to be their *financial agent*, you have big responsibilities ahead. Making decisions on behalf of someone else (called the principal) and managing someone else's financial affairs is far more difficult than making your own decisions. Depending on the responsibilities the principal delegated to you, your job description could include serving as a good financial manager and being totally trustworthy, well organized, detail oriented, and experienced with dealing with bankers, insurance agents, government officials, real estate agents, financial advisers, and tax preparers.

You must understand the scope and limits of your legal relationship. For example, you can only do those things mentioned in the power of attorney. If authority to sell a home isn't given, you can't do it. After the principal dies, your authority ends. A "durable" power of attorney means you can act even after the principal become incapacitated.

As a financial agent, you are a fiduciary with fiduciary duties. This means you must do the following:

- Respect the principal's wishes and act only in his or her best interests.
- Involve the principal in the decision making as much as possible.
- Realize that any money you are managing is not your own—it's not your money!
- Manage all assets carefully, even more carefully than your own.
- Keep good records of everything you spend or receive.
- Separate the principal's funds from yours.

Given all the responsibilities you have as a financial agent, your job may not be easy. Like Rodney Dangerfield, you may feel like you "don't get no respect." By this I mean that some businesses or banks may be reluctant to honor your authority, even if you have a power of attorney in hand.

If your loved one wants you to have access to bank accounts, be sure you both go to the bank to sign the bank's authorization forms and signature card. Typically, a bank has its own forms to fill out before you will be able to access a particular account. This can be a problem if your loved one has lost the capacity to consent, so it's best to get things squared way at the bank as soon as possible. If a business refuses to accept the power of attorney, ask to speak to a supervisor. Some state laws require businesses to accept powers of attorney unless there is a good reason to not do so.

You'll need to make multiple copies of the power of attorney. It's a good idea to keep track of every place you've given a copy. Whenever you sign any document, you should sign as "(my name), as agent for (your loved one)." Don't sign the person's name (that's forgery!) and don't just sign your own name. You need to make sure those seeing your signature understand you are signing on behalf of your loved one.

If you've been asked to serve as the *health care agent*, it is vitally important that you know and understand the individual's wishes about medical treatments. You will need to feel comfortable talking about end-of-life care and be willing to follow those wishes, even if they are not the same as your own. You need a thorough understanding of what is important to that person for his or her quality of life and the kind of medical care he or she does or does not want to have.

As a health care agent, you'll need to be able to talk with health care providers about changing medical conditions and consent to treatment or have it stopped as circumstances change. You may need to be assertive when to begin talking with health care professionals. In the sometimes bewildering medical system, you should be a strong advocate who can stand up for what you know the patient would want and take any other necessary steps to see that those wishes are honored, including changing doctors or hospitals if necessary.

For those who receive Social Security or VA benefits but are unable to manage those funds, you will need to apply for specific authority to handle the benefits. Being a caregiver, agent with powers of attorney, guardian, joint owner on the bank account, or even a spouse does not give you any authority to spend those benefits. Other federal benefit programs, such as veterans or railroad retirement, and some state government benefits also have similar requirements for a specifically designated representative to manage payments for a beneficiary. The Social Security Administration can give limited decision authority through the title of *representative payee*. Similarly, the Department of Veterans Affairs (VA) can give limited financial management authority through the title of a *VA fiduciary*.

You need to apply to Social Security to be designated the representative payee, or for short, rep payee. Before beginning the application process, it's a good idea to call Social Security at 800-772-1213, read the *Guide for Individual Payees*, and check out the Frequently Asked Questions at socialsecurity.gov/payee. You will need to submit an application form (SSA-11) along with a doctor's report stating that the person is unable to manage Social Security benefits and have a face-to-face interview with a Social Security representative at a local Social Security office.

Once you are appointed, the benefit payments come to you. You'll need to set up a separate bank account where the benefit will be directly deposited. The bank account must be in the beneficiary's name and show that you are the representative payee. You can use the money only for the beneficiary's needs, such as rent, food, and clothing. Any money left over after paying expenses should be saved in an interest-bearing savings account or savings bonds for future expenses. Representative payees do not have authority over any other money, property, or medical decisions. That's why it is important to have a bank account just for the Social Security payments that you use to pay only the beneficiary's bills.

As a representative payee handling someone else's money, you are a fiduciary. All fiduciaries must follow specific standards: You must act in the best interests of the beneficiary, use the money to meet the beneficiary's needs, keep the funds separate from your own or any other money, and report how you have used the money. You cannot lend the money to anyone else or sign leases or contracts, and you cannot pay yourself for managing the funds. Have bills sent directly to you, pay the bills on time, and review the bank statements carefully.

You must keep accurate records of the money you receive and spend, and each year you must file an accounting to the Social Security Administration. Its *Guide for Individual Payees* has a worksheet you can use to keep track of the money. The reporting form is at socialsecurity.gov/payee/form/index.htm. You also need to inform Social Security about any changes in address or circumstances that would affect benefit eligibility.

The VA has a similar process to select federal fiduciaries, with the same requirements on how to manage the veteran's benefits. Check out *A Guide for VA Fiduciaries* at benefits. va.gov/fiduciary/Fid_Guide.pdf.

In most circumstances, the so-called guardianship alternatives, such as financial and medical powers of attorney, are all the legal tools needed to make decisions and manage resources on behalf of those who do not have the ability to do so on their own. But powers of attorney need to be set up while the person has the capacity to do so. If there's been no advance planning to put these options in place before the person loses capacity, it's too late to rely on them.

If someone doesn't have the ability to pick who has the authority to make decisions on his or her behalf, courts can pick who will. Those titles would be *guardian* or *conservator*. *Guardianship* (or *conservatorship*) should only be considered as a last resort, but if your loved one becomes unable to make decisions and doesn't have in place the appropriate legal decision-making documents, obtaining guardianship may be necessary for his or her protection and safety. If your loved one doesn't have the capacity to make decisions and important decisions need to be made, you would ask a court to appoint you or someone else as guardian. Before making the leap to petitioning for guardianship or conservatorship, consider the following questions:

- What can I do to help support the person I care for in making decisions on his or her own, by including input from his or her circle of friends, family, or advisers?

- What alternatives to guardianship are available, such as powers of attorney for financial and medical decisions, representative payeeship, VA fiduciary, or living trust?

- If alternatives are available, why have they not been used or failed to work?

- What are the specific areas of decision making where he or she has such a deficit that his or her right to make those decisions needs to be taken away by the court?

- What rights or powers should remain with him or her, such as the right to vote, to drive, or to decide where to live?

The procedural details to obtain guardianship vary from state to state, so you'll need to consult with an elder law attorney to find out the process in your state. Also, the terms used vary: Some states use the words guardian of person and guardian of property; in others, the title for someone with authority over property may be called a conservator. I use the word guardian to refer to any fiduciary appointed by a court.

In general, someone who believes a loved one needs a guardian files a petition with the court setting out the reasons why a guardianship is necessary. That individual is called the petitioner. A medical, mental, or functional assessment must accompany the petition. The petition must be served on the person (called a respondent or alleged incapacitated person) with notice of the reason for the petition and the date of the hearing. In most states, a lawyer will be appointed to represent the respondent, if the respondent doesn't already have one. Most likely a guardian ad litem, court visitor, or other third party selected by the court will interview the petitioner, prospective guardian, and the respondent to review the facts of the petition and to report to the court if there is a way to avoid or limit the guardianship. The hearing before the judge may be brief or extensive, depending on the circumstances. The respondent has the right to attend and offer testimony or witnesses. In a few states, a jury may decide.

The judge or jury needs to determine three things: 1) whether the respondent's condition meets the state's definition of incapacity; 2) what decision-making powers to remove from the respondent and delegate to the guardian; and 3) who should be appointed as guardian. The judge then issues an order setting out the guardian's powers. The powers granted may be broad or limited to specific decision areas, such as making medical decisions or placing the person in a nursing facility.

If a court has appointed you as a guardian, you are legally responsible for following the court's order and state guardianship laws. Depending on the order, you may be a guardian of the person with responsibilities to make decisions about personal matters, such as where to live or what medical treatment to receive. If you are appointed as guardian of property (called conservator in some states), you are responsible for managing the individual's assets, paying bills, making investments, and filing taxes. As a guardian over financial matters, you are a fiduciary, with fiduciary duties. This means you must act only on behalf of the individual under guardianship, manage the money wisely, keep your money separate, and keep good records so you can report to the court how you have been managing the money. Ask your lawyer if you have any questions about what you can or cannot do.

While the court order tells you what you can do, most guardians get little guidance about how to make those decisions. A good place to start is the National Guardianship Association's *Standards of Practice* (guardianship.org). Experienced guardians from around the country developed these standards. You'll find step-by-step guidance on what you need to consider as you go about making a decision on behalf of someone else. The standards explain, for example, how to ethically consent to medical treatment, change a residence, or decide whether to sell property. Another resource is the NGA's *Fundamentals of Guardianship*.

Keep in mind the decisions you need to make for someone else may not be the decisions you'd make for yourself. Although you remain the spouse/daughter/nephew, your additional relationship as a guardian requires that you make decisions in a special way. You may have to ignore your own interests and resist pressure from others because it is your duty to do what is best for your loved one. You should also involve her in the decisions as much as possible. She may have difficulty making important decisions—you wouldn't have been appointed guardian if that wasn't the case—but with your help and encouragement, she should participate in as many decisions as possible.

Managing someone else's money is never easy. One cardinal rule for guardians of property to always keep in mind: It's not your money! Other points flow from this rule:

- Identify all income and property that belong to your loved one that you are responsible for managing.
- Report all of these assets (and any debts) to the court by the due date.

- Protect all property. This may mean changing locks, obtaining a safe deposit box or a secure storage unit, moving money to bank accounts with lower fees, or getting insurance to protect property.

- Create separate guardianship accounts for the funds you are managing. The account should show that it is your loved one's money and you are the guardian with authority to make deposits and withdrawals.

- Don't borrow, lend, or give away any money that you are managing on behalf of your loved one.

- Make gifts only if approved by the court and if the gift is like gifts your loved one gave in the past.

- Avoid any conflicts of interest, such as paying your family members or business partners to do work for your loved one.

- Create a budget so you'll know how much you'll need to spend to pay for your loved one's needs for food, clothing, shelter, medical care, medications, and insurance.

- Keep detailed records, statements, and receipts for everything you receive and spend as a guardian.

- Report to the court all income and expenses. Most courts require guardians to file an accounting at least annually.

- Pay yourself for time spent serving as guardian only if the court permits you to do so and only after the court has approved the amount. Keep detailed records of what you did, when you did it, how much time it took, and why you did it.

The Consumer Financial Protection Bureau has a series of guides, *Managing Someone Else's Money,* to help agents with powers of attorney, representative payees, VA fiduciaries, and guardians at consumerfinance.gov/blog/managing-someone-elses-money.

These are all complex legal issues. When necessary, be sure to consult a lawyer who can walk you through any decisions that need to be made and draw up the necessary paperwork.

Changing Relationships Action Checklists

The following Action Checklists are included in Chapter 2:

- ❑ *My Social Network*
- ❑ *Widening My Circle*
- ❑ *Financial Agent*
- ❑ *Health Care Agent*
- ❑ *Representative Payee/VA Fiduciary*
- ❑ *Guardian/Conservator*

My Social Network

People I want to stay in touch with:

Manager/Supervisor: _____

Phone: _____ E-mail: _____

Website: _____

Address: _____

_____

Office administrator: _____

Phone: _____ E-mail: _____

Website: _____

Address: _____

_____

Name: _____

Phone: _____ E-mail: _____

Website: _____

Address: _____

_____

Name: _____

Phone: _____ E-mail: _____

Website: _____

Address: _____

_____

Name: _____

Phone: _____ E-mail: _____

Website: _____

Address: _____

_____

Name: _____

Phone: _____ E-mail: _____

Website: _____

Address: _____

_____

Name: _____

Phone: _____ E-mail: _____

Website: _____

Address: _____

_____

Name: _____

Phone: _____ E-mail: _____

Website: _____

Address: _____

_____

Name: _____

Phone: _____ E-mail: _____

Website: _____

Address: _____

_____

Name: _____

Phone: _____ E-mail: _____

Website: _____

Address: _____

_____

People I want to better get to know:

Name: _____

Phone: _____ E-mail: _____

Website: _____

Address: _____

_____

Name: _____

Phone: _____ E-mail: _____

Website: _____

Address: _____

_____

Name: _____

Phone: _____ E-mail: _____

Website: _____

Address: _____

_____

Name: _____

Phone: _____ E-mail: _____

Website: _____

Address: _____

_____

Name: _____

Phone: _____ E-mail: _____

Website: _____

Address: _____

_____

Name: _____

Phone: _____ E-mail: _____

Website: _____

Address: _____

_____

Widening My Circle

Places I can find new friends and acquaintances:

- ❑ Book club
- ❑ Civic organization
- ❑ Class reunion
- ❑ Community college classes
- ❑ Dog park
- ❑ Exercise class
- ❑ Hobby club
- ❑ Homeowners association
- ❑ Library
- ❑ Local eatery/coffee shop
- ❑ Musical group
- ❑ Online
- ❑ Place of worship
- ❑ Pool
- ❑ Recreation center
- ❑ Senior Center
- ❑ Sports team
- ❑ Travel tour
- ❑ Volunteer activity
- ❑ Other: _____
- ❑ Other: _____

Financial Agent

❑ My loved one has a power of attorney for financial management.

❑ The following person (if not me) is the financial agent:

Agent's name:_____

Phone: _____ E-mail: _____

Address: _____

_____

❑ I have been named as the agent to manage financial affairs.

❑ I have a copy of the power of attorney.

❑ The power of attorney is durable:　❑ Yes　❑ No

❑ My loved one has discussed his or her expectations with me and I understand what he or she wants me to do as agent.

❑ The power of attorney gives me the responsibility to make the following decisions:

_____

_____

_____

_____

_____

_____

❑ The co-agent(s) are:

_____

❑ I have talked with the co-agent(s) about how we will work together.

❑ My responsibilities begin _____.

❑ My responsibilities will last until _____.

❑ I can receive the following compensation for serving as agent: _____

❑ I have completed all necessary paperwork with financial institutions to have the powers given to me recognized.

❑ I have set up a record-keeping system to keep track of all transactions I make, which includes what I've done, when I did it, how much time I spent, and why I did it.

❏ The lawyer advising me on power of attorney matters is:

Name: _____

Phone: _____ E-mail: _____

Address: _____

_____

❏ The following agencies, financial institutions, or other entities have been given copies of the durable power of attorney:

Name: _____

Phone: _____ E-mail: _____

Address: _____

_____

Name: _____

Phone: _____ E-mail: _____

Address: _____

_____

Name: _____

Phone: _____ E-mail: _____

Address: _____

_____

Name: _____

Phone: _____ E-mail: _____

Address: _____

_____

Name: _____

Phone: _____ E-mail: _____

Address: _____

_____

Health Care Agent

❑ My loved one has a health care power of attorney.

❑ The following person (if not me) is the health care agent:

Name: _____

Phone: _____ E-mail: _____

Address: _____

_____

❑ I have been named as the health care agent.

❑ I have a copy of the health care power of attorney.

❑ My loved one has discussed his or her expectations with me and I understand what he or she wants me to do as a health care agent.

❑ The health care power of attorney gives me the responsibility to make the following decisions:

_____

_____

_____

_____

_____

_____

❑ The following health care providers have been given copies of the health care power of attorney:

Hospital: _____

Phone: _____ E-mail: _____

Address: _____

_____

Hospital: _____

Phone: _____ E-mail: _____

Address: _____

_____

Doctor: _____

Phone: _____ E-mail: _____

Address: _____

_____

Doctor: _____

Phone: _____ E-mail: _____

Address: _____

_____

Doctor: _____

Phone: _____ E-mail: _____

Address: _____

_____

Doctor: _____

Phone: _____ E-mail: _____

Address: _____

_____

Assisted living facility: _____

Phone: _____ E-mail: _____

Address: _____

_____

Nursing facility: _____

Phone: _____ E-mail: _____

Address: _____

_____

Health care agency: _____

Phone: _____ E-mail: _____

Address: _____

_____

Other: _____

Phone: _____ E-mail: _____

Address: _____

_____

Representative Payee/VA Fiduciary

- ❑ The Social Security Administration has selected me as the representative payee.
- ❑ The Veterans Administration has selected me as the VA fiduciary.
- ❑ The benefit amount is _____.
- ❑ I have created a fiduciary bank account for the benefit payments.
- ❑ I have set up electronic deposit of the benefit.
- ❑ I have created a budget to pay for expenses including food, housing, clothing, and medical needs.
- ❑ I have set up a record keeping system to keep track of all expenses paid.
- ❑ Date my first accounting report is due: _____

Guardian/Conservator

❑ The court has appointed me guardian of the person.

❑ The court has appointed me guardian of property (or conservator).

❑ The court has given me the responsibility to make the following decisions:

_____

_____

_____

_____

_____

_____

_____

❑ The order was granted on _____.

❑ I have obtained bonding as ordered by the court in the amount of _____.

❑ My personal status report is due to the court on _____.

❑ I have done an inventory of all assets, property, and debts that I'm responsible for.

❑ My inventory is due to the court on _____.

❑ My first accounting is due to the court on _____.

❑ I have created a guardianship/conservatorship bank account.

❑ I have set up electronic deposit of income and automatic payment of bills.

❑ I have secured and insured all property that I'm responsible for.

❑ I have applied to be the representative payee or VA fiduciary for any Social Security or veterans' benefits.

❑ I have set up a recording keeping system to keep track of all decisions I make, including what I've done, when I did it, how much time I spent, and why I did it.

❑ I have created a plan of care.

❑ I have created a budget to cover expenses.

❑ I have applied for any eligible benefits.

❑ I have a current photograph.

❑ I have notified the following agencies or individuals of my appointment:

_____

_____

_____

_____

_____

_____

CHAPTER 3

GET ORGANIZED AND CLEAN OUT THE CLUTTER

Entering retirement is a great time to take stock of what you have and to get organized. With a new schedule, you may have more time to sort through accumulated papers and boxes, organize old files, and clear out lots of clutter, whether hard copies or digital. Think of it as a fresh start on your new way of living. (Be sure to shred and recycle any papers that have personal information!)

As you are going through the old stuff to get ready for the new, figure out what you need to keep and where you are going to keep it. Now's a good time to make an inventory of the important information about you, put it in some sort of order, and track down what's missing. When you're done, you'll have a system that's easy to maintain. And, should your family members want to know something about your history, or where you got that keepsake, they'll be able to find it.

In addition to organizing all the paper you've accumulated, now's a good time to organize your digital life. I have at least 50 electronic accounts, rewards programs, or apps with profiles, user IDs, and passwords. Keeping them all straight can be a nightmare, so have a secure way to record them.

This chapter also helps you pull together a basic budget. What's coming in? What's going out? If you're never done this before, relax—I make it a painless process for you.

With the rest of the chapter, just have fun. Sift through your old academic records, gloat as you go through those awards you've won, and reminisce over (and label!) those old photo books. Find (and, yes, label!) those long-lost keys.

Have too much stuff or need to downsize? I also offer suggestions for getting rid of things you no longer need.

My To-Do Checklist

Done   **Need to Do**

❑   ❑   Record basic facts about yourself

❑   ❑   Pull together key papers

❑   ❑   Know how long to keep records

❑   ❑   Take care of special possessions

❑   ❑   Get rid of what you don't need

❑   ❑   Inventory your digital assets

❑   ❑   List all income and expenses

✓ Record basic facts about yourself

This chapter is all about you. Use it as a convenient place to record pertinent information. As you go through the checklists, you'll see that some entries are very obvious, like your birth date and current address. Other lines ask for perhaps more obscure information: your military service number, voting precinct, and blood type. One bit of information I had to dig for was my blood type. You'd think I would know it, but I had to ask my doctor. Now I have it recorded in case I need it in an emergency.

Some of the checklists help you organize your educational background, where you have lived and worked, organizations you have belonged to, and awards you have received. Don't be modest! Brag a bit about what you've accomplished so far and use it as a foundation for what you are going to do next.

If you are thinking about a new career or part-time job, you'll want to have a list of former employers and the commendations you've received. Be sure to include any special recognition you've received for your volunteer activities and all the other things you do away from your work place. In listing the groups you belong to, you can think about the networking and volunteering that will keep you connected to the things you love to do. I've even included space for you to write your own biography. Be generous about all the things you've accomplished.

Another reason to make a list of past employment: You can double check to make sure you have received all benefits, pensions, retirement accounts, insurance benefits, or even unpaid leave. The Employment Checklist is the start to creating the resume of your past experiences for your new career opportunities.

✓ Pull together key papers

Retirement brings on a new slew of paperwork that you are going to have to keep track of. Start off your new life with the old information in places you can readily find and be ready to make room for the new stuff.

If you don't have or don't know where you've put very important documents, such as birth certificates and marriage licenses, you need to track them down now. Locate and record where you have stored them or start the process to obtain copies. You may also want to obtain copies pertaining to your family members so they'll be on hand whenever needed.

Where can you find them? The vast majority of births, deaths, and marriages are reported to the proper local authorities to maintain a lasting record. For a number of reasons, however, you may have difficulty or encounter delay obtaining them. For example, in the not too distant past, many births occurred in private homes and went unrecorded. Occasionally, fire destroys courthouses or other record depositories. Records may be incorrect because of misspellings, changes in spelling, illegible handwriting, misunderstanding of names, and other errors.

Each state has its own method of maintaining these records. Birth and marriage certificates can usually be obtained from the county clerk, registrar, or recorder of the county in which the birth or marriage took place. Many states have a central clearinghouse generally called the Department of Vital Statistics. The Centers for Disease Control and Prevention has a useful website with information on how and where to write to obtain these records in each state at cdc.gov/nchs/w2w.htm.

Fees generally range from $2 to $20 for each certificate. Additional copies may be available at reduced rates. Once you know the cost, to speed up the process you can enclose the necessary payment when you write for the copies you need.

Many states will not issue copies of birth or marriage certificates unless the requestor is closely related to the person named in the certificate. Therefore, if you're requesting someone else's papers, it is important to identify yourself as the spouse, parent, or child when requesting records for someone else in your family. You should obtain copies of any adoption papers, too. In some instances, it may be rather complicated to get information about some adoptions, depending on the circumstances. If you have lost or can't find your naturalization/citizenship documents, you can request replacement copies from the US Citizenship and Immigration Service. You'll need form N-565. Download it at uscis.gov/n-565.

Do yourself and your family a favor by making sure you have certified copies of judgments of divorce or annulment. Your family will need these to apply for Social Security death or survivor benefits, veterans benefits, and private pension plans. You can obtain these copies from the clerk or registrar of the court that granted the divorce or annulment. Once again, the fee for obtaining copies varies in each state and may also depend upon the number of pages in the document.

Write a letter to the court that granted the decree or judgment to ask about the cost of obtaining a copy of the document. You'll need to give the names of the parties, the case number (if you know it), and the date and year the divorce or annulment was granted. Enclose a self-addressed, stamped envelope along with the payment.

Keep in a safe-deposit box two *certified* copies each of birth and marriage certificates and adoption papers for you, your spouse, and your children. To be a "certified copy," your document must have a statement by an official that it is a true copy of an original. Once you've located all your important information, will you remember where you put it?

Use the Where I Put It Checklist in this chapter to list where you are keeping many of your records, lists, and documents. Note on the checklist where you've stored the documents: in your desk drawer, in a fireproof box in the den, or in the filing cabinet in the basement. You don't want to turn finding papers into a scavenger hunt.

You can check off the items that are in your safe deposit box or note where you are storing other information, including copies of all the checklists in this book. Keep only the most important documents—not what you need to update frequently or readily access—in your safe deposit box. Refer to Chapter 8 for more information about safe deposit boxes.

Wondering what to do with all those past tax files? Keeping them in one place helps you prepare your next year's tax return. Past tax returns with supporting documentation for any schedules or itemized deductions will also be a valuable source of information that your executor or personal representative may need to know. Your executor will be responsible for filing your income tax return for the year of your death and any estate tax returns.

I keep each year's tax return and all the supporting documents in a portable file box, with separate folders for donations, bills, mortgage statements, and W-2 forms. You need to keep tax returns for seven years. After that, you can go through all the supporting documentation and shred what's no longer important. As one box gets emptied, I use it to collect the current year's tax information

✓ Know how long to keep records

You'll want to save some records. Here are some guidelines for how long to do so.

Forever

These documents should be safely stored forever:

- Academic records, if needed for employment applications
- Adoption papers
- Baptismal certificates
- Birth certificates
- Death certificates (these may be needed for tax purposes or applying for survivor's benefits)
- Divorce orders
- Employment records (any separation papers, disciplinary files, and performance reviews)
- Health care power of attorney
- Marriage certificates
- Medical records
- Military records (DD-214)

- Retirement and pension records
- Social Security cards
- Trusts
- Wills and codicils

It Varies

The storage life of the following documents depends on their purpose:

- **Bank statements**: One year or until after tax returns are filed.
- **Bills**: For high-value items, for as long as you have the item to prove value for insurance purposes; one year for anything tax or warranty related; all other bills should be shredded as soon as they have been paid.
- **Credit card statements**: Shred once the statement has been reviewed for any errors or tax-related documentation and paid.
- **Home improvement receipts**: Until the home is sold. The amount spent on major improvements is important to establish cost basis of the home at the time of sale.
- **Home insurance policy**: As long as the home is owned.
- **Investment records/IRA statements/brokerage statements**: Keep monthly or quarterly statements until you get the annual statement, compare, and then shred. Keep annual statements for seven years for tax purposes.
- **Leases**: Seven years after the lease has expired.
- **Life insurance policy**: Life of the policy plus three years.
- **Mortgage statements**: Until paid off plus seven years.
- **Passport**: Until expired.
- **Paychecks/pay stubs**: One year or until W-2 received.
- **Sales receipts**: The life of the warranty on major purchases such as appliances or electronics; otherwise, toss after compared against the credit card statement or when you're sure it won't be needed for a return.
- **Tax documents**: Seven years including annual returns and all accompanying documents like W-2s and charitable and medical receipts.
- **Utility bills**: One year for tax purposes.
- **Vehicle records**: Until it is sold.

✓ Take care of special possessions

Now is a good time to inventory your special possessions. One way to do this is to walk through your rooms, closets, and cabinets recording what's there. Don't forget the attic, garage, and basement.

As you make this list, take the time to make a visual record—still or video—as well. This is simple to do with today's smartphones, tablets, or digital cameras. What I did was go room to room taking pictures of what was in each room, capturing the paintings on the walls, the knickknacks, and the furniture. Then I opened the cabinets and snapped what was on the shelves. When I got to the bedroom, I put important jewelry on a black cloth and took a close-up of each item. Where I could, I included the receipts or appraisals.

Once you have documented what you have, store a copy of the digital pictures or the videotape in cloud storage or on a thumb drive you put in your safe deposit box or other fireproof storage. This documentation will be invaluable if you should have a home fire, storm damage, or house burglary. Having these pictures will make it so much easier to file an insurance claim for loss or theft.

After you have taken the inventory, go the extra step to tell any interesting stories about how you acquired special items. You could make an audio recording, take notes in hand or on the computer, or dictate the stories to a family member. Only you will be able to pass on the history of the silver bowl you got as a wedding present from Aunt Tully or how you haggled with a street merchant for the painting in the dining room. Be sure your family knows that the opal ring came from your maternal grandmother, while the pocket watch was Great Uncle Randolph's.

List any furniture, paintings and artwork, coin or stamp collections, jewelry, and musical instruments that have great value or are of special interest. Receipts or appraisals are important in establishing the value of your special possessions.

Years from now your grandkids won't be able to remember if the family portrait hanging on the bedroom wall is from your mother's side of the family or your spouse's. A note you put on the back of the frame that says when and where it was taken and who is in the picture will be greatly appreciated. If you are not sure, check with others who might help you to get the facts captured now. The next generation will have an even harder time tracking the information down.

The same advice applies to those boxes and albums where you have stored family photographs. You'll have fun and raise some fond memories as you go through to label who's in the pictures and where they were taken. If you can't identify who's in the picture, you can be sure your kids won't have a clue. I've just gone through a cedar chest full of my in-laws' framed family photos. Even my husband doesn't know the family stories behind most of them.

✓ Get rid of what you don't need

As you sort through old papers and documents and as new paperwork comes in, you need to decide what to toss and how best to get rid of it. If there's something you don't need to hang on to, don't just throw it in the waste basket or paper recycle bin. Identity thieves search through trash for anything with personal information they can use to open new accounts. These thieves value cancelled checks or bank statements with bank account numbers, anything with a Social Security number or credit card information, utility bills, old credit cards, driver's licenses, and any card with a picture identification. One option is to invest in a durable paper shredder. If you need industrial strength shredding done, look in the newspaper or online for local shredding events. Libraries and shopping centers frequently host events where you can safely and securely shred large quantities of paper.

What do you do with anything else you don't want? The approach you can take depends on how much you want to get rid of. Downsizing to a smaller place? One option is to engage professionals to get rid of a whole house full of possessions. Items may be auctioned off in the home, hauled away to an auction site, or tagged with a price. The company will take a percentage of the proceeds and may even agree to dispose of things no one purchases. Be sure to get a signed contract that clearly explains what the company will do, how much it will take in commission and fees, costs of advertising, liability for accidents at the site, and disposal of unsold items.

Another option is to have auctioneers come to the house to bid on specific items they want. To make sure you get the best price, you may want a couple of different companies to view the items and make competitive bids.

You might want to hold a garage or yard sale. You get all the proceeds, but you have to do all the work yourself to set up, negotiate prices, and take care of the leftovers. Check with consignment shops to see what type of items they prefer to sell. Consignment shops typically give you a small percentage of any items they sell. Vintage clothing and furniture in sound condition can bring a good price in the right location.

Explore other groups that may be interested in special collections or items. A train museum may be interested in a donation of antique model trains. Books may be donated to a library or local fund-raising used book sale, or may be sold to second-hand bookstores. I've unloaded books I'll never read at a book recycling box in the parking lot of my grocery store.

Speaking of recycling, check the Internet for ways to recycle most anything: paint, tires, scrap metal, electronics, you name it. I successfully got rid of some old computers at a brand-name computer store. Many television and computer components can be salvaged and reused, which is much better than putting them in the trash. Your county government may have special days and locations to drop off hazardous materials that shouldn't go into a landfill.

Cars, boats, and planes can be donated to charities, although you need to follow the IRS rules on how much you can deduct. If you claim a deduction between $250 and $500 you need a written acknowledgement of the donation with a description of the car from the charity. If you claim more than $500 the charity needs to provide you with Form 1098-C, and you need to file Form 8283, which includes the vehicle identification number (VIN), dates the car was donated and sold, and the gross proceeds of the sale. The deduction is limited to the gross amount of the sale of the car to a third party. More details are available at irs.gov, search "car donation."

Other donations of appliances, furniture, and household items can be made to places like AMVETS, Catholic Charities, Goodwill, ReStore (run by Habitat for Humanity), and the Salvation Army, to name a few. These are just a few of the charities that will take donations of usable, used items. Some will pick up at your house, some won't. Call to find out. Be sure to keep receipts or acknowledgements for all charitable donations for tax deduction purposes.

A good resource for downsizing and decluttering is Marni Jameson's *Downsizing the Family Home: What to Toss, What to Keep* (AARP/Sterling, 2016), at AARP.org/Downsizing.

✓ Inventory your digital assets

In this digital age, user IDs and their associated passwords are essential to gain access to e-mail, electronic banking, online bill paying, bitcoins, iTunes files, e-books, games, Facebook, LinkedIn, Twitter, blog posts, movies, videos, digital photo storage, and shopping sites, to name just some of the most obvious. You may have a user name and password to access your benefit information at MyMedicare.gov and MySocialSecurity.gov, or a TreasuryDirect account. Many of our business and personal records and files are found or stored online. Even the forms in this book can be downloaded from http://ambar.org/Retirement Checklists so you can access, update, and store your checklists on your computer.

Have you ever thought about what would happen to all that information if you suddenly become unable to use your computer or device, or when you die? Most websites and social media, as well as federal and state privacy and computer fraud laws, make it very difficult for anyone other than you to access your digital accounts and records. You probably want those protections now, too, but in an emergency or after death, they can be huge barriers to your family or those you want to have access. Most current laws now criminalize, or at least penalize, unauthorized access of computers and digital accounts. Many digital providers are prohibited from disclosing most account information to anyone without the account holder's consent. And most sites aren't very clear, or are silent, about how you might go about giving consent to someone else.

You can, in your durable power of attorney or will, authorize your agent or your executor to have access to your online accounts. Of course, if there are certain accounts you don't want anyone else to access, put that in your document, too. Read the privacy or access policies of key websites to learn what they allow. Each site may have different procedures and steps you need to take.

Be sure to have a secure list of your online accounts with user names and current passwords. Without having a secure list of passwords, your family will waste many hours trying to figure out basic information, such as if your utility bill is on automatic bill payment, or if your credit card bill has been paid, or even how to unlock your computer or smartphone.

A word of caution: As valuable as this information is for you and your family, it is a gold mine for identity thieves! Keep this information in a very secure place. You may want to tell just one or two trusted family members where it is located. But also remember that you need to keep it updated. We all need to change our passwords frequently to keep them secure. This means you may want to enter the information in pencil so it can be easily changed, or keep an electronic file that you can update.

✓ List all income and expenses

After 30 or 40 years of saving, it's going to take some getting used to shifting your mindset from saving to spending. Instead of working hard to make sure your nest egg is growing, you need to work at protecting your money from market down swings, inflation, and spending too much in the early years of retirement. This is where the family budgeting becomes critical. You'll need to pin down all of your anticipated income streams: Social Security, employment, pensions, and other retirement investments.

Next you'll need to estimate all your expenses. How much are you paying each month for utilities, rent or mortgage, insurance premiums, credit card debt, out-of-pocket medical expenses, groceries, and more? Use the Expense Checklist in this chapter to track down how much you need monthly to cover your living expenses. If there's not enough money to pay current expenses, you may need to find ways to cut back. Are there cheaper phone plans? Can you save money on prescriptions by ordering by mail? If your home were better insulated, could you lower the fuel bill? Are you eligible for other benefits? A good source for information about saving money, cutting costs, and budgeting is aarp.org/money.

Once you have figured out what income you have and what you'll need, you can figure out what percentage of your savings you can spend each year. A traditional rule of thumb is to withdraw no more than 4 percent of your savings each year to make sure you don't outlive your money. That means if you have saved $500,000, you could safely withdraw $20,000 a year to cover the difference between income and expenses. This is not a hard-and-fast rule, but a guideline you could use while working with your financial professional to effectively manage your money. Chapter 8 includes more details about managing your retirement accounts.

Need additional money to close the gap? Use the Public Benefits Checklist in this chapter to get an idea of the various programs that you may be eligible for. Each of these programs has different eligibility requirements; take the time to check each one out. The tool at aarp.org/quicklink has explanations and applications for most public benefit programs in your area. To find services and programs especially for seniors in your community, use the Eldercare Locator at eldercare.gov or contact your area agency on aging to find out what's available locally.

Get Organized Action Checklists

The following Action Checklists are in Chapter 3:

- ❏ Personal History
- ❏ Education
- ❏ Residences
- ❏ Employment
- ❏ Memberships
- ❏ Awards
- ❏ Biography
- ❏ Where I Put It
- ❏ Personal Property
- ❏ Digital Assets
- ❏ Income
- ❏ Expenses
- ❏ Public Benefits

Personal History

Name: _____
              First   Middle   Last

Name at birth: _____
              First   Middle   Last

Place of birth: _____
              City   State   Country

Date of birth: _____

Date of adoption: _____

Legal name change: _____
               First   Middle   Last

Legal name change date: _____

Legal name change court: _____
               Court   City   State

****

Current address: _____

How many years: _____

Phone: _____Cell phone: _____

E-mail: _____Fax: _____

****

Citizenship: _____

    ❑ By birth

    ❑ By naturalization

Date of naturalization: _____

Naturalization place: _____
              City   State   Country

****

Military veteran:

❑ Yes

❑ No

Branch of service: _____

Dates of service: _____

Serial # (DD-214): _____Rank: _____

Type of discharge: _____

****

Social Security #: _____

Medicare #: _____

Passport #: _____Expiration: _____

Country of issue: _____

Driver's license #: _____Expiration: _____

State of issue: _____

****

Where I am registered to vote: Precinct: _____County: _____State: _____

****

Faith/Denomination: _____

Place of worship: _____

Address: _____

Pastor/Priest/Rabbi/Spiritual leader: _____

Phone #: _____E-mail: _____

****

My blood type: _____

****

Marital Status:

❑ Divorced

❑ Married

❑ Never married

❑ Widowed

First Spouse

Name of spouse at birth:_____

Name at present: _____

Date of birth: _____

Place of birth:_____

Date of marriage: _____

Date of divorce: _____

Date of death: _____

Spouse is buried at: _____

Cause of death: _____

Phone #: _____E-mail: _____

Address: _____

_____

Second Spouse

Name of spouse at birth:_____

Name at present: _____

Date of birth: _____

Place of birth:_____

Date of marriage: _____

Date of divorce: _____

Date of death: _____

Spouse is buried at: _____

Cause of death: _____

Phone #: _____E-mail: _____

Address: _____

_____

Third Spouse

Name of spouse at birth:_____

Name at present: _____

Date of birth: _____

Place of birth:_____

Date of marriage: _____

Date of divorce: _____

Date of death: _____

Spouse is buried at: _____

Cause of death: _____

Phone #: _____E-mail: _____

Address: _____

_____

Education

I have attended these schools:

Elementary or Grade Schools

Name of school: _____

Location: _____

Grades attended: _____Dates attended: _____

Name of school: _____

Location: _____

Grades attended: _____Dates attended: _____

Middle/Junior High and High Schools

Name of school: _____

Location: _____

Grades attended: _____Dates attended: _____

Name of school: _____

Location: _____

Grades attended: _____Dates attended: _____

Preparatory schools

Name of school: _____

Location: _____

Grades attended: _____Dates attended: _____

Name of school: _____

Location: _____

Grades attended: _____Dates attended: _____

Colleges and Universities

Name of school: _____

Location: _____

Degree/Certificate: _____

Dates attended/Graduated: _____

Name of school: _____

Location: _____

Degree/Certificate: _____

Dates attended/Graduated: _____

Name of school: _____

Location: _____

Degree/Certificate: _____

Dates attended/Graduated: _____

Additional Schools and Training Programs

Name of school: _____

Location: _____

Degree/Certificate: _____

Dates attended/Graduated: _____

Name of school: _____

Location: _____

Degree/Certificate: _____

Dates attended/Graduated: _____

Residences

I have lived at these locations:

Address: _____

City: _____ State: _____ Dates: _____

Address: _____

City: _____ State: _____ Dates: _____

Address: _____

City: _____ State: _____ Dates: _____

Address: _____

City: _____ State: _____ Dates: _____

Address: _____

City: _____ State: _____ Dates: _____

Address: _____

City: _____ State: _____ Dates: _____

Address: _____

City: _____ State: _____ Dates: _____

Address: _____

City: _____ State: _____ Dates: _____

Address: _____

City: _____ State: _____ Dates: _____

Address: _____

City: _____ State: _____ Dates: _____

Address: _____

City: _____ State: _____ Dates: _____

Address: _____

City: _____ State: _____ Dates: _____

Address: _____

City: _____ State: _____ Dates: _____

Address: _____

City: _____ State: _____ Dates: _____

Address: _____

City: _____ State: _____ Dates: _____

Address: _____

City: _____ State: _____ Dates: _____

Address: _____

City: _____ State: _____ Dates: _____

Address: _____

City: _____ State: _____ Dates: _____

Employment

I have had these jobs:

Employer: _____

Address: _____

Contact: _____

Type of work/Job title: _____

Dates of employment: _____

Employer: _____

Address: _____

Contact: _____

Type of work/Job title: _____

Dates of employment: _____

Employer: _____

Address: _____

Contact: _____

Type of work/Job title: _____

Dates of employment: _____

Employer: _____

Address: _____

Contact: _____

Type of work/Job title: _____

Dates of employment: _____

Employer: _____

Address: _____

Contact: _____

Type of work/Job title: _____

Dates of employment: _____

Employer: _____

Address: _____

Contact: _____

Type of work/Job title: _____

Dates of employment: _____

Employer: _____

Address: _____

Contact: _____

Type of work/Job title: _____

Dates of employment: _____

Dates of retirement: _____

These accomplishments and interesting projects concerning my employment may be of interest:

_____

_____

_____

_____

_____

_____

Memberships

I belong to these organizations:

Membership organization: _____

Phone: _____Website: _____

Address: _____

_____

Involvement: _____

Interesting facts: _____

_____

_____

Membership organization: _____

Phone: _____Website: _____

Address: _____

_____

Involvement: _____

Interesting facts: _____

_____

_____

Membership organization: _____

Phone: _____Website: _____

Address: _____

_____

Involvement: _____

Interesting facts: _____

_____

_____

Membership organization: _____

Phone: _____Website: _____

Address: _____

_____

Involvement: _____

Interesting facts: _____

_____

_____

Membership organization: _____

Phone: _____Website: _____

Address: _____

_____

Involvement: _____

Interesting facts: _____

_____

_____

I have these season tickets: _____

Sports: _____

Contact phone: _____Website: _____

Address: _____

_____

Seat numbers: _____

Theater: _____

Contact phone: _____Website: _____

Address: _____

_____

Seat numbers: _____

Awards

I received the following work-related awards and commendations:

_____

_____

_____

_____

_____

_____

_____

_____

I received the following awards and recognition for my non-work-related activities:

_____

_____

_____

_____

_____

_____

_____

_____

Biography

Highlights to include in my biography:

_____

_____

_____

_____

_____

_____

_____

_____

_____

_____

_____

_____

_____

_____

_____

_____

_____

_____

_____

_____

_____

_____

_____

_____

_____

_____

_____

_____

_____

_____

Where I Put It

For each document or item, indicate where it is, such as in your safe deposit box, a fire-proof box, a filing cabinet, an electronic file, or with this book. Obviously not everything needs to be, or even should be, stored in a safe deposit box. Many items wouldn't even fit.

My safe deposit box is located at: _____(bank name),

_____(address), _____(box number).

Record Type	Location (cloud storage, safe deposit box/bank, fire-proof box, filing cabinet, electronic file, with this book)
Personal History	
Academic records	
Adoption papers	
Alimony settlement agreement	
Animal care information	
Annulment decrees or judgments	
Appointment book or calendar	
Award certificates	
Baptismal certificates	
Birth certificates	
Change of name certificates	
Citizenship papers	
Cohabitation agreement	
Digital photos	
Divorce decrees or judgments	
Durable power of attorney for finances	
Driver's license	
Educational transcripts	
Employment records	
Keys to home	
Keys to post office box	
Keys to safe deposit box	
Keys to storage units	
Keys to vehicles	
Lock combinations	
Mental health power of attorney	
Military separation papers	

Record Type	Location (cloud storage, safe deposit box/bank, fire-proof box, filing cabinet, electronic file, with this book)
Music/CD catalog	
Naturalization papers	
Passport	
Photo albums	
Prenuptial agreement	
Postnuptial agreement	
Property settlement agreement	
Qualified domestic relations order (QDRO)	
Security system information	
Storage unit locations	
Tax returns and records	
Timeshare records	
Video/movie catalog	
Family History	
Adoption papers	
Birth certificates	
Family tree	
Marriage certificates	
Newspaper articles and mementos	
Photo albums	
Portraits	
Insurance Policies	
Annuities	
Boat	
Health insurance card	
Homeowners	
Life	
Long-term care	
Medical	
Medicare card	
Medicare Part D card	
Medicare supplemental	
Pre-need funeral contract	
Renters	
Umbrella	

Record Type	Location (cloud storage, safe deposit box/bank, fire-proof box, filing cabinet, electronic file, with this book)
Benefits	
401(k) statements	
IRA statements	
Keogh plan statements	
Medicare summary notices	
Military separation papers	
Pension agreements	
Simplified employee pension (SEP) statements	
Social Security benefit statement	
Social Security card	
Workers' compensation	
Banking and Savings	
Checking account statements	
Credit union account statements	
Savings account statements	
Investments	
Brokerage account statements	
Certificates of deposit	
Savings bonds	
Real Estate	
Home improvement records	
Leases	
Mineral rights	
Mortgages	
Real estate deeds	
Reverse mortgage	
Tax records	
Timeshare agreements and records	
Other Assets and Debts	
Business records	
Computers	
Credit card numbers and contracts	
Heirlooms and collectibles	

Record Type	Location (cloud storage, safe deposit box/bank, fire-proof box, filing cabinet, electronic file, with this book)
Jewelry appraisals	
Jewelry inventory	
Vehicle certificates of title	
Warranties	
Estate Planning	
Durable power of attorney	
Letter of instruction	
Trust agreements	
Will and codicils	
Final Wishes	
Advance directives	
Body bequeathal papers	
Celebration of life prearrangements	
Cemetery/mausoleum deed	
Cremation prearrangement agreement	
Ethical will/legacy documents	
Funeral prearrangement agreement	
Health care power of attorney	
Living will	
Medical records	
Obituary	
People to contact	
Pet continuing care	
Physician orders for life-sustaining treatments	
Uniform organ donor card	

Personal Property

I have the following special possessions, including antiques, jewelry, art, furniture, silver, and musical instruments:

Item description: _____

Value: _____ Location: _____

Interesting facts: _____

Item description: _____

Value: _____ Location: _____

Interesting facts: _____

Item description: _____

Value: _____ Location: _____

Interesting facts: _____

Item description: _____

Value: _____ Location: _____

Interesting facts: _____

Item description: _____

Value: _____ Location: _____

Interesting facts: _____

Item description: _____

Value: _____ Location: _____

Interesting facts: _____

Item description: _____

Value: _____ Location: _____

Interesting facts: _____

Item description: _____

Value: _____Location: _____

Interesting facts: _____

Item description: _____

Value: _____Location: _____

Interesting facts: _____

Item description: _____

Value: _____Location: _____

Interesting facts: _____

Item description: _____

Value: _____Location: _____

Interesting facts: _____

Item description: _____

Value: _____Location: _____

Interesting facts: _____

Item description: _____

Value: _____Location: _____

Interesting facts: _____

Item description: _____

Value: _____Location: _____

Interesting facts: _____

Item description: _____

Value: _____Location: _____

Interesting facts: _____

Item description: _____

Value: _____Location: _____

Interesting facts: _____

Item description: _____

Value: _____Location: _____

Interesting facts: _____

Item description: _____

Value: _____Location: _____

Interesting facts: _____

Location of my letter of instruction on how and to whom these personal items are to be distributed:

_____

Location of photos or videos of these personal items:

_____

Digital Assets

I have designated: _____to serve as my fiduciary or agent to have access to my digital assets.

Word of caution: Carefully secure this list of passwords!

I have these user names and passwords:

Facebook profile name/Password: _____

Twitter profile name/Password: _____

MySpace profile name/Password: _____

Instagram profile name/Password: _____

Computer password: _____

Smartphone password: _____

Tablet password: _____

E-reader password: _____

iCloud: _____

Apple ID: _____

Website/App: _____

User Name: _____Password: _____

Website/App: _____

User Name: _____Password: _____

Website/App: _____

User Name: _____Password: _____

Website/App: _____

User Name: _____Password: _____

Website/App: _____

User Name: _____Password: _____

Website/App: _____

User Name: _____Password: _____

Website/App: _____

User Name: _____Password: _____

Website/App: _____

User Name: _____Password: _____

Website/App: _____

User Name: _____Password: _____

Website/App: _____

User Name: _____Password: _____

Website/App: _____

User Name: _____Password: _____

Website/App: _____

User Name: _____Password: _____

Website/App: _____

User Name: _____Password: _____

Website/App: _____

User Name: _____Password: _____

Website/App: _____

User Name: _____Password: _____

Website/App: _____

User Name: _____Password: _____

Website/App: _____

User Name: _____Password: _____

Website/App: _____

User Name: _____Password: _____

Website/App: _____

User Name: _____Password: _____

Website/App: _____

User Name: _____Password: _____

Income

Source	Amount	Frequency (weekly, monthly, occasionally)
Annuity		
Consultant Fees		
Disability		
Investments		
Pension		
Retirement plan		
Self-employment		
Social Security		
Supplemental Security Income (SSI)		
Veteran's benefit		
Wages		
Total income		

Expenses

Item	Monthly Amount	How Paid (autopay, check, credit card)
Housing		
Rent		
Mortgage		
Line of credit (HELOC)		
Home repair		
Housckeeping		
Yard care		
Homeowners insurance		
Household supplies		
Security system		
Homeowners association/condo fee		
Utilities		
Gas		
Electric		
Water/sewer		
Phone (land)		
Phonc (mobile)		
Fuel oil		
Internet access		
Cable		
Medical		
Medical insurance premium		
Medicare Part B premium		
Medicare Part D premium		
Medicare Advantage premium		
Medications		
Medical co-payments/deductibles		
Medical alert		
Home care/caregiver		
Long-term care insurance premium		

Transportation		
Car payments		
Car insurance		
Car repair/maintenance		
Car registration		
Parking		
Gasoline		
Public transit		
Taxes		
Federal		
State		
Personal property		
Lifestyle		
Clothing		
Dining out		
Entertainment		
Gifts		
Groceries		
Hair care		
Laundry/dry cleaning		
Membership dues		
Pet care		
Subscriptions		
Travel		
Toiletries		
Debt		
Credit card		
Student loans		
Personal loans		
Total Monthly Expenses		

Public Benefits

Public benefits to investigate:

- ❑ Earned Income Tax Credit (EITC): Reduced taxes for low income workers (irs.gov/Credits-%26-Deductions/Individuals/Earned-Income-Tax-Credit)

- ❑ Food benefits (SNAP): Help with grocery costs (fns.usda.gov/snap/supplemental-nutrition-assistance-program-snap)

- ❑ Lifeline: Help with cost of telephone services (fcc.gov/consumers/guides/lifeline-affordable-telephone-service-income-eligible-subscribers)

- ❑ Low Income Home Energy Assistance Program (LIHEAP): Help with weatherization, heating, and cooling costs (acf.hhs.gov/programs/ocs/programs/liheap)

- ❑ Medicaid: Help with medical expenses through local social services office (healthcare.gov/medicaid-chip/getting-medicaid-chip)

- ❑ Medicare Part D Extra Help: Help with prescription drug costs (ssa.gov/medicare/prescriptionhelp)

- ❑ Medicare Savings Plans: Help with Medicare premiums, co-pays, and deductibles (ssa.gov/medicare/prescriptionhelp/cms.html)

- ❑ Social Security Disability Insurance (SSDI): Income support for persons with disabilities (ssa.gov/disabilityssi)

- ❑ State Pharmaceutical Assistance Programs (SPAP): Help with prescription drug costs (medicare.gov/pharmaceutical-assistance-program/state-programs.aspx)

- ❑ State Property Tax Relief: State programs to lower property taxes (lincolninst.edu/subcenters/significant-features-property-tax/Report_Residential_Property_Tax_Relief_Programs.aspx)

- ❑ Supplemental Security Income (SSI): Income support for persons over 65, blind or disabled with very limited income (ssa.gov/disabilityssi/ssi.html)

- ❑ Veterans' benefits: Benefits for veterans of the US military service (va.gov)

CHAPTER 4

WORK WITH YOUR RETIREMENT TEAM

This chapter helps you identify the support you have—or need. Getting ready for and living in retirement takes teamwork. As the team's quarterback you need to know who to call for support, answers, and services on a multitude of different issues that you are about to face. As with any winning team, the players work together to support the quarterback and execute the game plan as the quarterback directs.

I know I sometimes think I can do it all—after all, I'm retired! I have *time*, that precious commodity I never had before. But I've come to realize that I can't do everything, and it's good to call for help. The first person I called when I set my retirement date was my financial adviser, because I realized I was going to have some big financial adjustments to make. Next, I called my lawyer to go over my estate plan. Yes, even though I'm a lawyer, I still rely on my legal colleagues for advice before preparing any new legal documents. Now that I'm dividing my time between two homes, having a ready list of whom to call in each city when something breaks is a time saver. I've got dentists in both places, different hairdressers, and lawn maintenance services in each city. Listing in one convenient place all the names and numbers for all the people I rely on sure helps simplify my life. Sometimes it's hard to delegate responsibility, but doing so can save your sanity.

Use the checklists in this chapter to keep track of your team. With these checklists, you can more easily schedule appointments with doctors or contact the appropriate lawyer to review contracts, draft documents, help you apply for benefits, and advise you on any legal issues that develop. You'll be able to immediately access the financial professionals to help you manage your investments, prepare taxes, and find assets to pay for care. And if you need someone to shovel your driveway, mow the lawn, clip the dog's nails, or help with caregiving tasks, the contact information is at your fingertips.

My To-Do Checklist

Done   **Need to Do**

❏   ❏   Touch base with your employer's human relations department

❏   ❏   Keep track of all who provide personal services

❏   ❏   Develop your roster of health professionals

❏   ❏   Know the different types of financial professionals

❏   ❏   Rely on a team of insurance agents

❏   ❏   Find the right legal professionals

✓ Touch base with the human relations department

Long before you've picked your retirement date, you'll want to touch base with your employer's human relations department. There you'll find information about all the things you need to do before you actually walk out the door. You'll need to know if you need to give advance notice and how much. Do you need to set your exit date to coincide with a pay period? What severance pay or leave balances are due to you? When will you receive your final check? How do you enroll in any retiree health plan or sign up for COBRA benefits? How do you start withdrawals from your 401(k) or pension? What are the options for how you receive your retirement benefits and does your age make any difference? The sections in Chapter 7 on retirement plans and pensions explain some of your options, but you'll need to get the specifics from your employer.

✓ Keep track of all who provide personal services

Lots of people and companies can help you get the most out of your retirement. Use the Personal Services Checklist to note how to reach the veterinarian, lawn service, property manager, housekeeper, car mechanic, and many others you may need to contact. Be sure to include contacts for your home security and personal emergency response systems.

✓ Develop your roster of health professionals

Another long contact list that you want to have on hand is for the medical professionals you may need. The Health Contacts Checklist includes primary care and specialty doctors, as well as any therapists, physical trainers, pharmacists, dentists, and audiologists. I've left space for you to list any specific conditions those professionals are treating, where relevant.

Next to all your medical providers, you may want to record the mileage to their offices (which you can look up on Google Maps or mapquest.com, or note the next time you drive there), because the cost of driving to and from medical appointments may be deductible as a health care expense. When it comes time to do taxes, all you need to do is multiply the mileage by the number of trips to that office you made that year. If you itemize your deductions, you can deduct out-of-pocket medical expenses for you, your spouse, and dependents if the amount exceeds 10 percent of your adjusted gross income, or 7.5 percent if you are age 65 or older. The 7.5 percent rate ends in 2016. Find the list of expenses you can deduct at irs.gov/taxtopics/tc502.html.

✓ Know the different types of financial professionals

Many different types of financial professionals can assist you in managing your retirement savings, developing an investment strategy, or setting up a withdrawal plan from pensions or other retirement accounts. Which type of professional you should consult depends on what financial help you need.

Accountants may offer a variety of accounting services including tax preparation, financial audits, business valuations, and succession planning for small businesses.

Daily money managers help with budgeting and bill paying, typically on an hourly basis.

Estate planning attorneys can draft legal documents, including a will and power of attorney, or develop wealth transfer strategies for tax efficiencies.

Fee-only advisers are paid a specific fee for each financial or investment service.

Financial planners generally take a broad view of a client's financial affairs. What they offer varies from provider to provider. Some create comprehensive plans that delve into every aspect of your financial life, including investments, insurance, retirement, taxes, and estate planning. Others have a more limited focus, such as insurance or securities. Some only prepare plans, while others also sell investments, insurance, or other products.

Insurance agents can help with health, long-term care, and life insurance, among others, as well as annuities.

Investment advisers generally focus on managing investments. Most are paid by taking a percentage of the assets they manage.

Stockbrokers buy and sell stocks and bonds and are paid by commissions on the trades they make. Some brokers also provide financial planning services.

Before hiring any financial professionals, always ask what licenses or certifications they hold, the types of services they offer, the typical clients they work with, and how they will be compensated. Get in writing how and how much you are going to pay for services, whether you are paying a retainer fee upfront, being charged a set fee for each service, or having a percentage or commission deducted from any transaction. Ask for, and talk to, references.

In addition to checking references, know what certifications the experts hold. Ever notice all those initials financial professionals list on their business cards? Some of those initials represent credentials reached through specialized training and examination; others may be meaningless or easily obtained. To find out what's behind the letters, use the Financial Industry Regulatory Authority's credential look-up tool at finra.org/investors/professional-designations. There you'll find the experience and education requirements to earn any credential.

Depending on the services they provide, financial professionals may be certified by a national organization and also may need to be licensed in their state. Professionals who sell investments or insurance must have a state license. You should always verify licensing information with your state's regulators. To get contact information for the insurance regulator in your state, go to naic.org. Contact information for your state securities regulator is at nasaa.org/about-us/contact-us/contact-your-regulator.

You can get information about the background and any disciplinary history of some financial professionals using these online resources:

- Certified Financial Planners: letsmakeaplan.org
- Certified Professional Daily Money Managers: aadmm.com/certification.htm
- Certified Public Accountants: aicpa.org/forthepublic
- Investment Advisers: adviserinfo.sec.gov
- Stockbrokers: finra.org/brokercheck

Use the Financial Contacts Checklist so you can contact your financial advisers and have a record that you checked the background on each you use and know how you will pay for their services.

✓ Rely on a team of insurance agents

There are about as many types of insurance professionals as there are types of insurance. Some may specialize in just one type of insurance, such as life insurance or farm equipment. Others help you with all your insurance needs, including health, vehicle, homeowners, renters, life, annuity, and travel. Some represent a specific insurance company, while others are independent agents who can make recommendations across a range of insurance companies and offerings. To make it efficient to know which agent to call about which policy, list all of the insurance agents you work with on the Insurance Contacts Checklist. In Chapter 4, you'll record more specifics about the policies you have.

✓ Find the right legal professionals

You may want to have a lawyer on your retirement team for a variety of different needs. You may want someone to advise you about any legal issues that you face. You may need one to draft legal documents, such as a power of attorney or a will. You many need legal assistance to review contracts from assisted living and other residential facilities. Use the Legal Contacts Checklist to record lawyers you use and the steps you took to hire them.

When thinking about hiring a lawyer for any type of legal service or advice, you have to answer two related questions: What do you want the lawyer to do, and who is most qualified to perform that service for you? Of key importance is finding a lawyer who has experience in that area of the law and in the proper jurisdiction. Cousin Tim who went to law school may not be the best choice if you want to review a contract from a facility and he does not have experience with elder law matters. The experienced lawyer in Michigan may not be sufficiently familiar with Texas law to answer a Texas Medicaid question. You'll want to find a lawyer who is licensed to practice and concentrates a substantial part of her or his practice in the state where you live.

A good way to find a lawyer is to ask friends and family members who have recently used a lawyer on a similar matter for their recommendations. Another way is to contact the local or state bar association's lawyer referral service. The American Bar Association has a directory of lawyer referral services available in each state at apps.americanbar.org/legals-ervices/lris/directory. You may also want to consult the list of elder law attorneys who are members of the National Academy of Elder Law Attorneys at naela.org or fellows who are members of the American College of Trust and Estate Counsel at actec.org/fellows/search.

You'll want to interview several lawyers to learn of their expertise, talk about what you think you want the lawyer to do for you, and find out how the lawyer will charge for those services. Lawyers charge for their services in a variety of ways. They can charge an hourly rate or a set fee for providing specific services. Some ask for a lump sum retainer before beginning any work. The lawyer would then draw down disbursements from the retained amount at the hourly rate as work is accomplished. It may be that at first the lawyer cannot calculate the total fee until gaining a better understanding of the problems that might develop. You should, however, expect a detailed and frequent statement of services so you can keep tabs on what has been done and what is being charged.

It is essential that you and the lawyer have the same expectations about what services are to be provided. You may want the lawyer to walk you through the steps you need to take to handle the issue on your own but be available to call from time to time for guidance when you run into a question. On the other hand, you may want the lawyer to handle all details so you don't have to worry about getting everything done. You will want to have a signed letter of engagement that sets out in some detail what the lawyer is going to do for you.

Keep in mind that most lawyers concentrate their practices in specific areas. For example, tax attorneys concentrate their practices on complicated tax matters. They can assist with the preparation of tax returns and give advice on how to avoid unnecessary taxes. Enrolled agents, who must pass a comprehensive exam, are able to represent you before the Internal Revenue Service. CPAs and lawyers can also represent you before the IRS.

My Team Action Checklists

The following Action Checklists are included in Chapter 4:

- ❏ Employer Retirement Coordination
- ❏ Personal and Home Services Contacts
- ❏ Health Contacts
- ❏ Financial Contacts
- ❏ Insurance Contacts
- ❏ Legal Contacts

Employer Retirement Coordination

Name of employer: _____

Contact for human relations department:

Name: _____

Phone: _____ Fax: _____

E-mail: _____

Website: _____

Contact for retirement plan manager:

Name: _____

Phone: _____ Fax: _____

E-mail: _____

Website: _____

Contact for retiree health plan:

Name: _____

Phone: _____ Fax: _____

E-mail: _____

Website: _____

My age on my target retirement date:

Years: _____ Months: _____

I have received the following information about retirement policies from my employer:

- ❑ Advance notice of retirement date
- ❑ Pension vesting and eligibility
- ❑ Pension benefit calculation
- ❑ Pension payout options
- ❑ Pension beneficiary election
- ❑ Length of time to process pension election
- ❑ 401(k) benefit calculation
- ❑ 401(k) payout options
- ❑ 401(k) beneficiary election
- ❑ Length of time to process 401(k) benefit election

❑ Eligibility requirements for retiree health benefits
❑ Retiree health benefit coverage
❑ Dependent health coverage
❑ Prescription drug coverage
❑ Medicare coordination of benefits
❑ Length of time to process retiree health benefit election
❑ COBRA options
❑ Continuation of life insurance coverage
❑ Vision benefit
❑ Dental benefit
❑ Unused leave payout
❑ Return of keys, badge
❑ Document retention policy

Personal and Home Services Contacts

Home

Household chores: _____

Phone: _____ E-mail: _____

Website: _____

Address: _____

_____

House cleaning: _____

Phone: _____ E-mail: _____

Website: _____

Address: _____

_____

Home maintenance: _____

Phone: _____ E-mail: _____

Website: _____

Address: _____

_____

Property manager: _____

Phone: _____ E-mail: _____

Website: _____

Address: _____

_____

Plumber: _____

Phone: _____ E-mail: _____

Website: _____

Address: _____

_____

Electrician: _____

Phone: _____ E-mail: _____

Website: _____

Address: _____

_____

Computer technician: _____

Phone: _____ E-mail: _____

Website: _____

Address: _____

_____

Neighbors: _____

Phone: _____ E-mail: _____

Address: _____

_____

Neighbors: _____

Phone: _____ E-mail: _____

Address: _____

_____

Neighbors: _____

Phone: _____ E-mail: _____

Address: _____

_____

Lawn service/Gardener: _____

Phone: _____ E-mail: _____

Website: _____

Address: _____

_____

Snow removal: _____

Phone: _____ E-mail: _____

Website: _____

Address: _____

_____

Security system maintenance:_____

Phone: _____ E-mail: _____

Website: _____

Address: _____

_____

Food:

Grocery delivery: _____

Phone: _____ E-mail: _____

Website: _____

Address: _____

_____

Favorite nearby restaurant: _____

Phone: _____ E-mail: _____

Website: _____

Address: _____

_____

Favorite nearby restaurant: _____

Phone: _____ E-mail: _____

Website: _____

Address: _____

_____

Meal delivery:_____

Phone: _____ E-mail: _____

Website: _____

Address: _____

_____

Meals on Wheels: _____

Phone: _____ E-mail: _____

Website: _____

Address: _____

_____

Transportation and Travel

Car maintenance: _____

Phone: _____ E-mail: _____

Website: _____

Address: _____

_____

Transportation services: _____

Phone: _____ E-mail: _____

Website: _____

Address: _____

_____

Taxi company: _____

Phone: _____ E-mail: _____

Website: _____

Address: _____

_____

Paratransit: _____

Phone: _____ E-mail: _____

Website: _____

Address: _____

_____

Travel agent: _____

Phone: _____ E-mail: _____

Website: _____

Address: _____

_____

Social Services

Area agency on aging: _____

Phone: _____ E-mail: _____

Website: _____

Address: _____

_____

Senior center: _____

Phone: _____ E-mail: _____

Website: _____

Address: _____

_____

Day care center: _____

Phone: _____ E-mail: _____

Website: _____

Address: _____

_____

Volunteer services: _____

Phone: _____ E-mail: _____

Website: _____

Address: _____

_____

Friendly visitor: _____

Phone: _____ E-mail: _____

Website: _____

Address: _____

_____

Spiritual leader/Pastor/Priest:_____

Phone: _____ E-mail: _____

Website: _____

Address: _____

_____

Faith-based pastoral care: _____

Phone: _____ E-mail: _____

Website: _____

Address: _____

_____

Other

Hair care: _____

Phone: _____ E-mail: _____

Website: _____

Address: _____

_____

Veterinarian: _____

Phone: _____ E-mail: _____

Website: _____

Address: _____

_____

Emergency response service (Medical Alert): _____

Phone: _____ E-mail: _____

Website: _____

Address: _____

_____

Health Contacts

Acupuncturist:_____

Condition: _____

Phone: _____ E-mail: _____

Website: _____

Address: _____

_____

Round-trip mileage: _____

Audiologist: _____

Condition: _____

Phone: _____ E-mail: _____

Website: _____

Address: _____

_____

Round-trip mileage: _____

Cardiologist: _____

Condition: _____

Phone: _____ E-mail: _____

Website: _____

Address: _____

_____

Round-trip mileage: _____

Dentist: _____

Condition: _____

Phone: _____ E-mail: _____

Website: _____

Address: _____

_____

Round-trip mileage: _____

Ear, nose, and throat (ENT): _____

Condition: _____

Phone: _____ E-mail: _____

Website: _____

Address: _____

_____

Round-trip mileage: _____

Gastroenterologist: _____

Condition: _____

Phone: _____ E-mail: _____

Website: _____

Address: _____

_____

Round-trip mileage: _____

Laboratory: _____

Condition: _____

Phone: _____ E-mail: _____

Website: _____

Address: _____

_____

Round-trip mileage: _____

Massage therapist: _____

Condition: _____

Phone: _____ E-mail: _____

Website: _____

Address: _____

_____

Round-trip mileage: _____

Music therapist: _____

Condition: _____

Phone: _____ E-mail: _____

Website: _____

Address: _____

_____

Round-trip mileage: _____

Neurologist: _____

Condition: _____

Phone: _____ E-mail: _____

Website: _____

Address: _____

_____

Round-trip mileage: _____

Nutritionist: _____

Condition: _____

Phone: _____ E-mail: _____

Website: _____

Address: _____

_____

Round-trip mileage: _____

Optometrist: _____

Condition: _____

Phone: _____ E-mail: _____

Website: _____

Address: _____

_____

Round-trip mileage: _____

Ophthalmologist: _____

Condition: _____

Phone: _____ E-mail: _____

Website: _____

Address: _____

_____

Round-trip mileage: _____

Pharmacist (local): _____

Phone: _____ E-mail: _____

Website: _____

Address: _____

_____

Round-trip mileage: _____

Pharmacist (mail order): _____

Phone: _____ E-mail: _____

Website: _____

Address:

_____

Physical therapist: _____

Condition: _____

Phone: _____ E-mail: _____

Website: _____

Address: _____

_____

Round-trip mileage: _____

Physical trainer: _____

Condition: _____

Phone: _____ E-mail: _____

Website: _____

Address: _____

_____

Round-trip mileage: _____

Podiatrist: _____

Condition: _____

Phone: _____ E-mail: _____

Website: _____

Address: _____

_____

Round-trip mileage: _____

Primary care physician: _____

Condition: _____

Phone: _____ E-mail: _____

Website: _____

Address: _____

_____

Round-trip mileage: _____

Specialty physician: _____

Condition: _____

Phone: _____ E-mail: _____

Website: _____

Address: _____

_____

Round-trip mileage: _____

Specialty physician: _____

Condition: _____

Phone: _____ E-mail: _____

Website: _____

Address: _____

_____

Round-trip mileage: _____

Specialty physician: _____

Condition: _____

Phone: _____ E-mail: _____

Website: _____

Address: _____

_____

Round-trip mileage: _____

Specialty physician: _____

Condition: _____

Phone: _____ E-mail: _____

Website: _____

Address: _____

_____

Round-trip mileage: _____

Speech therapist: _____

Condition: _____

Phone: _____ E-mail: _____

Website: _____

Address: _____

_____

Round-trip mileage: _____

Other: _____

Phone: _____ E-mail: _____

Website: _____

Address: _____

_____

Round-trip mileage: _____

Other: _____

Phone: _____ E-mail: _____

Website: _____

Address: _____

_____

Round-trip mileage: _____

Other: _____

Phone: _____ E-mail: _____

Website: _____

Address: _____

_____

Round-trip mileage: _____

Financial Contacts

Financial professionals I rely on:

Accountant: _____

Firm: _____

Phone: _____ Fax: _____

Address: _____

_____

E-mail: _____ Website: _____

Account #: _____

    ❑ I have verified the credentials and complaint history.

    ❑ I understand how the financial professional will be paid.

    ❑ I have a letter of engagement.

Financial adviser: _____

Firm: _____

Phone: _____ Fax: _____

Address: _____

_____

E-mail: _____ Website: _____

Account #: _____

    ❑ I have verified the credentials and complaint history.

    ❑ I understand how the financial professional will be paid.

    ❑ I have a letter of engagement.

Stockbroker: _____

Firm: _____

Phone: _____ Fax: _____

Address: _____

_____

E-mail: _____ Website: _____

Account #: _____

    ❑ I have verified the credentials and complaint history.

    ❑ I understand how the financial professional will be paid.

    ❑ I have a letter of engagement.

Tax adviser: _____

Firm: _____

Phone: _____ Fax: _____

Address: _____

_____

E-mail: _____ Website: _____

Account #: _____

    ❑ I have verified the credentials and complaint history.

    ❑ I understand how the financial professional will be paid.

    ❑ I have a letter of engagement.

Tax preparer: _____

Firm: _____

Phone: _____ Fax: _____

Address: _____

_____

E-mail: _____ Website: _____

Account #: _____

    ❑ I have verified the credentials and complaint history.

    ❑ I understand how the financial professional will be paid.

    ❑ I have a letter of engagement.

I need to engage a financial professional.

Recommendations received:

Name: _____

Firm: _____

Phone: _____ Fax: _____

Address: _____

_____

E-mail: _____ Website: _____

    ❑ I have verified the credentials and complaint history.

    ❑ I understand how the financial professional will be paid.

    ❑ I have a letter of engagement.

Name: _____

Firm: _____

Phone: _____ Fax: _____

Address: _____

_____

E-mail: _____ Website: _____

    ❑ I have verified the credentials and complaint history.

    ❑ I understand how the financial professional will be paid.

    ❑ I have a letter of engagement.

Name: _____

Firm: _____

Phone: _____ Fax: _____

Address: _____

_____

E-mail: _____ Website: _____

    ❑ I have verified the credentials and complaint history.

    ❑ I understand how the financial professional will be paid.

    ❑ I have a letter of engagement.

I have identified the following services that I need to receive from the financial professionals:

_____

_____

_____

_____

_____

I want to ask the following questions of the financial professionals:

_____

_____

_____

_____

_____

Insurance Contacts

Insurance agents I rely on:

Name: _____

Firm: _____

Phone: _____ Fax: _____

Address: _____

_____

E-mail: _____ Website: _____

❑ I have verified the complaint history with my state insurance regulator.

Name: _____

Firm: _____

Phone: _____ Fax: _____

Address: _____

_____

E-mail: _____ Website: _____

❑ I have verified the complaint history with my state insurance regulator.

Name: _____

Firm: _____

Phone: _____ Fax: _____

Address: _____

_____

E-mail: _____ Website: _____

❑ I have verified the complaint history with my state insurance regulator.

I need to engage an insurance agent.

Recommendations received:

Name: _____

Firm: _____

Phone: _____ Fax: _____

Address: _____

_____

E-mail: _____ Website: _____

❑ I have verified the complaint history with my state insurance regulator.

Recommended by: _____

Name: _____

Firm: _____

Phone: _____ Fax: _____

Address: _____

_____

E-mail: _____ Website: _____

❑ I have verified the complaint history with my state insurance regulator.

Recommended by: _____

I have identified the following services that I need to receive from the agent:

_____

_____

_____

_____

_____

I want to ask the agent the following questions:

_____

_____

_____

_____

_____

Legal Contacts

Lawyers I rely on:

Name: _____

Firm: _____

Phone: _____ Fax: _____

Address: _____

_____

E-mail: _____ Website: _____

❑ I have verified the complaint history with the bar association.

❑ I understand how the lawyer will be paid.

❑ I have a letter of engagement.

Name: _____

Firm: _____

Phone: _____ Fax: _____

Address: _____

_____

E-mail: _____ Website: _____

❑ I have verified the complaint history with the bar association.

❑ I understand how the lawyer will be paid.

❑ I have a letter of engagement.

I need to engage a legal professional.

Recommendations received:

Name: _____

Firm: _____

Phone: _____ Fax: _____

Address: _____

_____

E-mail: _____ Website: _____

❑ I have verified the complaint history with the bar association.

❑ I understand how the lawyer will be paid.

❑ I have a letter of engagement.

Recommended by: _____

Name: _____

Firm: _____

Phone: _____ Fax: _____

Address: _____

_____

E-mail: _____ Website: _____

    ❑ I have verified the complaint history with the bar association.

    ❑ I understand how the lawyer will be paid.

    ❑ I have a letter of engagement.

Recommended by: _____

I have identified the following services that I need to receive from the lawyer:

_____

_____

_____

_____

_____

_____

I want to ask the lawyer the following questions:

_____

_____

_____

_____

_____

_____

CHAPTER 5

WELCOME YOUR NEW ADVENTURE

You've retired! Now what are you going to do? You no longer have that steady grind—pleasing the boss, getting to work on time, and being tied to a set schedule of how you spend your day. That's what most people look forward to in retirement. I've thoroughly enjoyed being able to do what I want to do, when I want to do it. You have your days to fill as you please. To some people, that's pure pleasure. Others may feel some trepidation.

You may be among those who, like me, were reluctant to retire because they wrapped their life and their personal image around what they do at work. For many years I swore I would never retire. My work was fulfilling and enjoyable. The closer I got to a possible retirement age, though, the more I thought about what I could do after I quit my job that would be equally satisfying and fill my time.

Now that I'm retired, I'm happy and busy doing most of the things I had planned, such as writing this book, plus new things I hadn't counted on, like kayaking with my daughter on the Shenandoah River. Of course, as with any plans, I've had to be flexible to make some modifications as I've settled in to a new lifestyle. Caregiving for my spouse and grandkids has cut into some of my travel plans, but I'm just delaying—not cancelling—my next trip to Europe, and I'm taking shorter excursions closer to home.

This chapter helps you start thinking about filling your days now so you don't find yourself bored and watching TV all day in your lounge chair—unless that is exactly what you want to do. Take time to brainstorm what brings you joy and satisfaction.

Volunteering, taking classes, traveling, singing in a choir, going to the gym, learning a new language, and continuing to work (albeit in a different capacity) may be among the things that you want to include in your new schedule. AARP research of people 50+ found that travel is the number one aspiration. This chapter helps you identify your priorities and work through some of the options that await your retirement adventure. This is your chance to embrace new opportunities and challenges.

My To-Do Checklist

Done   **Need to Do**

❑   ❑   Find or expand volunteer opportunities

❑   ❑   Learn something new

❑   ❑   Make a travel bucket list

❑   ❑   Work your way into a new job

❑   ❑   Start your own business

✓ Find or expand volunteer opportunities

During all the years you've worked, you've acquired skills, knowledge, and a social network. Through volunteer work, you can share your expertise and have a meaningful impact. There are lots of options.

You may already be involved with volunteering at your place of worship, with a professional organization, or with a civic group. Now you have time to step up your involvement. I've long been involved with a national association and one of the schools I attended, but now that I'm retired, I have the time to take on more active leadership roles by serving on the board of directors. My husband had been semi-involved with his military school alumni association, frequently going to reunions. He now has time to research the war service records of his classmates, contribute articles to the newsletter, and be a docent at the school's museum. This is his way of giving back and staying in touch with his classmates.

Think about what you have to offer. If you have a financial background, find a nonprofit you believe in that needs someone to be a treasurer, read the financials, or help fill out IRS forms correctly. Been in marketing? Most nonprofits would love to have someone help develop a marketing plan or lead or participate in fundraising efforts. Skills from your work in customer service, sales, or editing could be put to use in helping an organization with getting the word out about its projects. If you are good with social media or the Web, put those skills to work to help a charity raise its Twitter profile or redesign its website.

Your volunteer work can also be less structured. A friend is pleased that her new flexible schedule means she can visit church members in nursing homes on weekdays, because before retirement, she could only visit on weekends. Other people I know of organize community drives to collect clothes and toys for refugees, make meals for the homeless, organize charity walks, and volunteer at local schools.

Need ideas? For opportunities in the United States, research possibilities at sites such as CreateTheGood.org. For opportunities abroad, search online for volunteer vacations and longer-term opportunities.

✓ Learn something new

Retirement is a good time to acquire new skills, pursue a new hobby, or learn something you've always been interested in. Cynthia Hutchins, the Director of Financial Gerontology for Bank of America Merrill Lynch, says it well: "You are never too old to learn new things, explore your passions or pursue new opportunities." Opportunities, some free, abound to learn just about anything you want to learn.

Nearly 60 percent of U.S. colleges and universities offer retirees free or deeply discounted tuition. The requirements vary depending on the state and institution. The age range may start at 50, 60, or 65; some schools have income, residential, or prior education restrictions; and you may not have your administrative fees, books, or labs covered. Some institutions may allow you to audit courses but don't award college credit. At other schools, you can take the class only if space is available or the instructor agrees. For example, in my state of Virginia, residents age 60 or older may audit courses in any state school for free. Tuition is also free for Virginians whose federal taxable income is below $15,000 who want to enroll full- or part-time to take classes for credit. In California, the Senior Citizen Education Program enables eligible California residents 60 or older to enroll as regular students for $3 per semester.

A place to start looking for college tuition discounts in your state is aseniorcitizen guideforcollege.com. Also search the websites of the community colleges, colleges, and universities near you for terms like "lifelong learning," "tuition waivers," or "continuing education" to learn the available course offerings, enrollment requirements, and deadlines to apply. I've got my eye on a class in geology or astronomy, new subjects I've always wanted to explore. A woman named Connie posted on a blog that two years ago she enrolled at Tennessee Tech University using the senior citizen tuition waiver. She's now happily pursuing her Bachelor of Fine Arts degree, a lifelong dream, and expects to be able to create art for at least the next couple of decades.

In addition to colleges and universities, check out offerings at local libraries, recreation departments, community and senior centers, county extension services, area agencies on aging, and AARP. Also look into the Osher Lifelong Learning Institutes, which provide non-credit courses and activities specifically developed for adults aged 50 or older.

Don't want to leave the comfort of your home? Look into the plethora of online opportunities. Sign up for a free or mostly free MOOC, or massive open online course, through portals such as Coursera, EdX, and Lynda. Often offered by elite universities such as Duke and Stanford, MOOCs offer bargains on courses. I'm tempted to dip into some of the history courses offered by TheGreatCourses.com. Or search for help learning a new instrument, language, or yoga posture.

Not only will you enrich your life and fill your time. Research shows that learning new things may keep your brain sharp and help you maintain a strong sense of purpose. Why not do what it takes to keep yourself mentally alive and challenged?

✓ Make a travel bucket list

While you were working, your wanderlust probably had to be squeezed into weekends and limited vacation days. You may have had to negotiate with your boss or co-workers for when and how long you could be gone. Now, depending on your resources, you have the time and the freedom to do that travel you've been putting off. Your flexible schedule allows you to travel during off-peak times when hotels and airfares are more affordable. You can stay as long as you like and not have to rush back to work on Monday.

According to an HSBC survey, the top goal for those anticipating retirement is to travel extensively. You may know of friends who have made an RV their roving home. Some couples volunteer for a summer at a national park up north, living in their RV, and then take their home with them to a different park in the south for the winter months. Others take a long road trip visiting family members scattered across the country. Still others see the world, taking round-the-world trips or visiting different countries every year.

What's on your bucket list for travel? Are there places close to home you've not gotten around to visiting? Although I've lived in the Washington, D.C. metro area for decades, I've got a list of museums I've yet to visit. Now I can play tourist in my own home town in the off season when other tourists aren't swarming around. On a recent day trip, I took in a country music jam session at the Floyd Country Store in Floyd, Virginia. Each year I like to see the fall foliage along the Blue Ridge Parkway. In past years I had to do it on the weekend with scores of other leaf-peepers. Midweek, I now have the road to myself.

Samantha Brown, AARP's travel ambassador, believes that travel is a necessity, and that no matter our age, we are all on a journey to understand ourselves, our world, and who we are in it. Nothing gives us that opportunity like travel. I cherish special memories of getting to know my husband's Finnish relatives in their homes in Helsinki, visiting the tiny but exquisitely ornate Russian Orthodox church in Hamina where a relative serves as priest, and finding the birthplace of my father-in-law in Vassa. The week I spent hiking alone in the Italian mountains taught me that I thoroughly enjoy being all by myself. Through my travels I've also meet wonderful people like Anna, who was my translator during a trip to Moldova. Anna teaches English to young children, but age-appropriate books are in short supply. I've taken pleasure in sending her boxes of my children's favorite books.

Interested in volunteering while experiencing another culture? Want to help renovate a school in Asia, work in a health clinic in Tanzania, or teach English in Latin America? You should explore "voluntouring." Companies like Cross Cultural Solutions, Globe Aware, and Global Volunteers can help you find short-term opportunities that put your skills to work for a good cause, while you make new friends and gain a new outlook on your life and the world around us. Some of your expenses, although not airfare, may be tax deductible.

As enriching as travel can be, the logistics can sometimes be daunting. Want to learn to make bread from a French baker, brush up on Greek mythology while sailing the Greek islands, volunteer with school children in Peru, hike with burros in the Grand Canyon, ride the train coast to coast, or bike along the Rhine? With many retirees having travel in their plans, you can bet a travel tour group can help you make the trip. On the Internet you'll find a plethora of newsletters, discounts, and tips for the senior adventurer. Any bookstore has shelves of travel guides for places nearby to exotic. Websites like AARP's travel. aarp.org help you select a destination based on your interests, plan your trip, and locate discounts.

For those like me who want to plan their own itinerary to go at their own pace, the Internet makes it simple, although it can be time-consuming. I made all the arrangements online for a ten-day stay in Croatia. By surfing the Internet I booked hotels, made ferry reservations, learned about home-stays in "sobes," verified the hours at my favorite museums, checked on the weather, and calculated the exchange rate. From landing in Dubrovnik to takeoff in Zagreb, everything was in place. The time I spent in anticipation of the trip figuring out the arrangements and selecting the options was just as fun as taking the trip.

For those who have European travel plans, avoid the crowds and heat of summer by aiming for the "shoulder seasons": April through mid-June, or September and October. Pack light to lighten your load and save your back. My recommendation is to lay out everything you think you want to take and then eliminate half, keeping only clothing that you can easily wash and hang to dry overnight. Plan on clothes that easily mix and match that you can layer. I almost always take along a trusty black trench coat with a removable liner that serves me well in just about any climate and in chilly airplanes. What shoes to take is a hard choice because they take up so much space. But they do need to be comfortable, easily removed for going through security lines, and appropriate for your planned activities, whether it's hiking, beachcombing, or dancing. Whoever thought of putting suitcases on wheels was thinking of me. My one small roll-aboard bag served me well during four weeks in Italy getting on trains and navigating cobblestone paths. And I never get on a plane without my e-reader, which is much more convenient to slip in my purse than a book. But don't leave it on the plane, like I did once. Never got it back!

Keep in mind airline restrictions for number, size, and weight of suitcases, especially when traveling abroad. Before you start packing, check with the airline for the most recent restrictions. As we all know, overhead luggage space is shrinking and the cost for extra bags is increasing. By now, frequent flyers are all too familiar with the TSA restrictions on liquids and any hazardous items. I pack trial-sized toiletries and hotel shampoo samples in a small, clear plastic, zipper bag that's easy to remove when I go through security.

To avoid security hassles and waits in line, apply for TSA PreCheck (Pre✓®) at tsa.gov/tsa-precheck/apply, which costs $85 for five years. You can pre-enroll online, but you will need to schedule a face-to-face interview at an enrollment center where you'll be finger-printed. Most airports have an enrollment center, but you can find the full list of locations on the TSA website. You'll need to bring your passport or driver's license and birth certificate. Now that I have it, I love not having to take off my shoes and drag my computer out of my bag.

Here are some points to consider when evaluating whether to purchase travel insurance before taking a trip outside the United States, and if you do, what to buy. Different policies cover different risks, so be sure you know what you need and what coverage you are getting.

Medicare does not cover medical expenses if you get sick or injured when outside of the United States. Check to see what, if any, coverage you have with any Medicare supplemental policy, as some Medigap policies do cover some emergency medical expenses outside the States. Compare medical travel insurance policies for any age restrictions or exclusions for pre-existing conditions. And be sure to read the fine print about what is or is not covered. Evacuation coverage pays for the costs of getting you to medical care in case of any emergency when you are unable to fly home commercially, but possibly only to the nearest care, rather than your preferred hospital.

Trip cancellation insurance might be worth the cost if you are booking a major trip well in advance of your departure date and you are concerned that in the meantime you might become ill, a relative will get sick or die, or political unrest will develop at your destination. But be sure you understand what reasons are acceptable to entitle you to a refund—just changing your mind or coming down with a cold may not be sufficient reasons. Before purchasing a policy through a tour operator, travel agent, or cruise line, get a sample of the policy and carefully go over the fine print to make sure your specific concerns are covered. I suggest using an online travel insurance broker such as InsureMyTrip.com or Travel-Guard.com, which offer coverage from many different insurance carriers, so you can better compare coverage and prices. A travel agent may be selling the policy that pays the highest sales commission rather than the best one for you. Also check out what other coverage you might have if your bag is lost or an item is stolen. Your homeowners insurance or credit card company may cover some losses. Better yet, don't pack any valuables. (I wear a simple wedding band on trips abroad and leave my wedding ring at home.)

Whether you are taking a day trip close by or roaming far from home, take precautions. Travel scams abound. From time to time I get mail, e-mail, and phone calls that announce I've won a "free" vacation. Some solicitations even enclose what looks like an airplane ticket. Those come-ons go straight into the trash. There's nothing free behind those offers; rather, you can count on hidden costs, pressure to upgrade, a hefty deposit to get your "free" reservation, or any number of sand traps that ruin your vacation and cost you.

✓ Work your way into a new job

Just because you retired from your current job doesn't mean you've stopped working. According to a 2013 Merrill Lynch retirement study, 71 percent of pre-retirees expect to work during their retirement years and hope to find jobs that offer flexible hours. Even if you've been forced to retire, you have skills you can continue to use in many other ways. You may need to find new employment to pay the bills or to avoid prematurely drawing from your retirement savings or taking Social Security. Perhaps you want to pursue a new interest or a long-term dream, or just keep active.

Part-time employment, freelancing, or consulting work may meet your needs. I scanned a website that lists local part-time job opportunities and found dozens of positions for bookkeepers, receptionists, library assistants, chain store seasonal associates, and after school counselors, but my favorite is a wine hospitality specialist at a local vineyard. Most listings gave me an idea of what the work would involve regarding hours, wages, and any education, experience, or training requirements. The key to finding work you'll love is to seek out a fit between your gifts and interests and the world of opportunities out in the work place.

AARP has developed a range of resources for 50+ job seekers at AARP.org/work. For ideas about how to get a job that's the right fit for you, read through *Great Jobs for Everyone 50+*, by job expert and award-winning author Kerry Hannon (aarp.org/GreatJobs). For a comprehensive how-to on landing the job, including how to use online jobs services safely, see *Getting the Job You Want After 50 for Dummies*, also by Hannon (aarp.org/JobsFor Dummies). More AARP books to help you get a job can be found at AARP.org/bookstore.

A word of caution: You'll probably want to pass by any promise of making a lot of money in a hurry with no experience required. In this category are most of the "work-at-home" jobs, such as stuffing envelopes, doing data entry, or selling products. Never get involved with a job opportunity that requires you to send money to get started, provide your bank account information, or buy equipment. Some business opportunities are risky business. A legitimate business opportunity must follow the Business Opportunity Rule and give you a week before you sign anything or pay any money as well as a disclosure statement that, among other things:

- Identifies the seller.
- Tells you about certain legal actions involving the seller or its key personnel.
- Tells you if the seller has a cancellation or refund policy and if so, the terms of that policy.
- Provides a list of references.

You can also insist on getting proof in writing of any earnings potential. Check out the company with the Better Business Bureau, state attorney general, or local consumer protection office. Have a lawyer, accountant, or business adviser review the contract with you. Interview the references or other owners of the business, but remember that scammers can use fake testimonials.

✓ Start your own business

Want to strike out on your own and go into business for yourself? Entrepreneurism among our age group is definitely on the rise. People in their 50s and 60s start nearly twice the number of companies as those launched by those in their 20s, according to the Kauffman Foundation. Start ups by this age group grew to 25 percent of all new entrepreneurs in 2015, compared to 14 percent in 1997. In terms of business survival rates, enterprises founded by seniors tend to have more staying power. According to a study by British charity The Prince's Initiative for Mature Enterprise (PRIME), 70 percent of businesses started by Brits in their 50s survived for at least five years, compared to only 28 percent of businesses started by those aged under 50. Important reasons account for the growth and success of older entrepreneurs: They have their own source of capital in retirement savings, wide professional networks to build upon, and a wealth of industry experience.

In the enthusiasm of considering self-employment and making money on your own terms, don't neglect the legal details. Let's say you have a business plan and marketing plan to become a consultant in web design, open a boutique where you will sell crafts, or start a dog-walking service. Whatever your service or product, you'll need to comply with local business laws. Check with zoning ordinances to make sure you can conduct that type of business from your home or other location. If you plan on working out of your home, does your homeowners association have any restrictions, such as visitor parking for your customers? You will also need a business license. The town or county clerk will be able to help you determine the type of license or other permits you need.

You should talk with a lawyer about whether it's advisable to create a business entity. When I started working for myself, I set up a single member limited liability corporation

(LLC) in my own name. To do so, I had to create articles of incorporation, which were filed with the state corporation commission, develop an operating agreement that described how the LLC will be operated, obtain a federal tax identification number (EIN), set up an accounting system to separate my business expenses and income from my personal funds, and open a separate business bank account. When I opened mine, the bank required a copy of my state certificate of organization, local business license, and EIN. In a few states, you also have to inform the public through a newspaper notice that you've created an LLC. I also spoke with my tax accountant to make sure I was complying with federal and state tax laws. She explained that I would need to report any profits or losses as income on my individual federal and state tax returns and pay both income and self-employment taxes for Medicare and Social Security.

In addition to creating a limited liability corporation, you could also do business as a sole proprietor, partnership, corporation, or S corporation. Each has important features depending on your business needs. Your lawyer can explain the pros and cons of each type of business structure, but here are the basics.

- As a sole proprietor, you are the company and are responsible for all of its assets and liabilities.

- With an LLC, the member owner or owners have some of the personal liability protections of a corporation with some tax advantages over sole proprietorships and lower start-up costs than a corporation.

- In a partnership, two or more people share skills, money, or property and each shares in the profits or losses. The partners can agree on the percentage of contributions and distributions, how partnership decisions are made, and how new partners are brought in or bought out. The partnership must file with the IRS an information return, but the profits or losses are paid in the individual tax returns of the partners.

- A corporation is an independent legal entity owned by shareholders. Unlike LLCs or partnerships, a corporation is solely responsible for any company liabilities and must pay taxes on its profits. Because of the additional management and reporting requirements, the corporate structure is used for larger businesses with multiple employees.

- An S corporation is a separate kind of corporation or LLC that has applied to the IRS for this tax status. Instead of the S corporation paying taxes, the profit or loss is reported on the individual tax returns of the owners. Shareholders who work for the S corporation must be paid reasonable compensation.

As you can see, setting up the right type of business entity has many ramifications and details such as required owner or shareholder meetings, minutes, bylaws, stock transfers, and records maintenance. In Chapter 2 I talk about some of the things you need to do if retirement means closing down your business.

Where you are going to conduct your business is another decision to make. If the only business tools you need are your computer and mobile phone, the kitchen table or spare bedroom is all the space you need. For my sanity, I had to have an office out of the house. I found a location that catered to small businesses by offering services a la carte. In addition to a small office with a desk and a chair, I could purchase, as needed, copying, faxing, phone answering, notary, mail drop, conference room, and computer technical assistance. This arrangement fit my needs and my budget. If you are renting space, pay attention to the lease terms, especially how long you are locked in to paying for the space. As your needs for space change as you add employees, if the location doesn't draw the business traffic you need, or your business plan doesn't work out, you want to be able to get out of the lease without penalty. To be on the safe side when I started out, I took a month-to-month lease, then signed a half-year lease. I've notified my landlord that I'm ready for an annual lease when it comes time to renew.

If your business plan involves catering or any food preparation, check with your county health department for any sanitation requirements. You may want to rent space in a commercial kitchen or food incubator that is already set up to code requirements.

I don't have any employees of my LLC, but if I did I would need to obtain workers compensation insurance in case any employee was injured on the job, pay state unemployment taxes, and set up withholding for Medicare and Social Security. Other business insurance options would cover physical injury or property damage claims related to my business.

If you work from home, you can deduct some of the operating expenses, such as part of the mortgage and utilities, and if you use your car, you can deduct the actual mileage you use for business purposes. Get good tax advice about home office deductions as the rules are detailed and tricky. Rely on an experienced tax adviser or certified public accountant to make sure you have a good accounting system for your income and expenses and for help in preparing state and federal tax returns. As your business grows, the legal details grow, too. Check in frequently with your lawyer. The Small Business Administration has useful information about starting a business at sba.gov/content/follow-these-steps-starting-business, with links to state requirements, business plans, and funding options.

New Adventure Action Checklists

The following Action Checklists are in Chapter 5:

- ❑ Volunteer Opportunities
- ❑ Things I'd Like to Learn
- ❑ Education Opportunities
- ❑ Travel Bucket List
- ❑ Back to Work Inventory
- ❑ Business Start Up

Volunteer Opportunities

I have the following skills and talents to volunteer:

- ❑ Accounting
- ❑ Animal care
- ❑ Caregiving
- ❑ Cooking
- ❑ Driving
- ❑ English as a foreign language
- ❑ Fund-raising
- ❑ Home repairs
- ❑ Landscaping
- ❑ Leadership
- ❑ Lobbying
- ❑ Marketing

- ❑ Mentoring
- ❑ Nursing
- ❑ Playing a musical instrument
- ❑ Singing
- ❑ Social media
- ❑ Spiritual counseling
- ❑ Teaching
- ❑ Tutoring
- ❑ Web design
- ❑ Writing
- ❑ Other: _____

I am interested in volunteering for organizations that offer the following types of services:

- ❑ Advance a cause I care about. Specify: _____
- ❑ Build or repair homes
- ❑ Care for animals
- ❑ Monitor nursing home care
- ❑ Promote legislation
- ❑ Provide meals for those in need
- ❑ Provide medical or nursing care
- ❑ Provide services for sick or elderly people
- ❑ Support crime victims
- ❑ Support disabled veterans
- ❑ Support refugees
- ❑ Tutor adults
- ❑ Work with children (mentoring, teaching)
- ❑ Other: _____

Things I'd Like to Learn

These are the things I want to learn:

Courses

❑ Astronomy	❑ Journalism
❑ Art history	❑ Mathematics
❑ Brain fitness	❑ Philosophy
❑ Business	❑ Politics
❑ Computers	❑ Psychology
❑ Geology	❑ Religions
❑ Great books	❑ Other: _____

Languages

❑ Arabic	❑ Hebrew
❑ Chinese	❑ Japanese
❑ French	❑ Spanish
❑ German	❑ Other: _____

Skills

❑ Accounting	❑ Painting
❑ Acting	❑ Photography
❑ Cooking	❑ Quilting
❑ Dancing	❑ Scuba diving
❑ Golf	❑ Swimming
❑ Fly fishing	❑ Tennis
❑ Flying	❑ Woodworking
❑ Horseback riding	❑ Writing
❑ Marksmanship	❑ Yoga
❑ Playing musical instrument	❑ Other: _____

Education Opportunities

I have investigated educational opportunities at the following colleges near me:

Name: _____

Website: _____

Address: _____

Phone: _____

Age for tuition waiver: _____

Tuition: Free $ _____

Discount: $ _____   ❑ By course ❑ By semester

Admission requirements:

    Resident of state or county: ❑ Yes   ❑ No

    High school diploma or GED: ❑ Yes   ❑ No

    Bachelor's degree: ❑ Yes   ❑ No

Admission fee: $_____

Book fee: $_____

Lab fee: $_____

Student activity fee: $_____

Application deadline: _____

Audit: ❑ Yes   ❑ No

Instructor approval: ❑ Yes   ❑ No

Space available: ❑ Yes   ❑ No

College credit: ❑ Yes   ❑ No

Name: _____

Website: _____

Address: _____

Phone: _____

Age for tuition waiver: _____

Tuition: Free $ _____

Discount: $ _____   ❑ By course ❑ By semester

Admission requirements:

      Resident of state or county: ❑ Yes   ❑ No

      High school diploma or GED: ❑ Yes   ❑ No

      Bachelor's degree: ❑ Yes   ❑ No

Admission fee: $_____

Book fee: $_____

Lab fee: $_____

Student activity fee: $_____

Application deadline: _____

Audit: ❑ Yes   ❑ No

Instructor approval: ❑ Yes   ❑ No

Space available: ❑ Yes   ❑ No

College credit: ❑ Yes   ❑ No

I have investigated the following online educational opportunities:

Website: _____

Cost: _____

Prerequisites: _____

Website: _____

Cost: _____

Prerequisites: _____

Website: _____

Cost: _____

Prerequisites: _____

Website: _____

Cost: _____

Prerequisites: _____

I have investigated other educational opportunities at the following locations:

- ❏ AARP
- ❏ Area agency on aging
- ❏ Community college
- ❏ Computer center
- ❏ County extension service
- ❏ Library
- ❏ Recreation center
- ❏ Senior center
- ❏ Other: _____

Classes I want to take:

_____

_____

_____

_____

_____

_____

Travel Bucket List

Close to home:

_____

_____

_____

_____

_____

_____

Day trips:

_____

_____

_____

_____

_____

_____

Family/friends to visit:

_____

_____

_____

_____

_____

_____

Special events:

_____

_____

_____

_____

_____

_____

_____

Recreational or sporting events:

_____

_____

_____

_____

_____

Cities/states:

_____

_____

_____

_____

_____

U.S. regions:

_____

_____

_____

_____

_____

National parks:

_____

_____

_____

_____

_____

Islands:

_____

_____

_____

_____

_____

_____

Countries:

_____

_____

_____

_____

_____

_____

Cruises:

_____

_____

_____

_____

_____

_____

Volunteering combined with travel:

_____

_____

_____

_____

_____

_____

Back to Work Inventory

I want to work for the following reasons:

- ❑ I want to pursue a passion I was never able to pursue.
- ❑ I want to give back.
- ❑ I need the money.
- ❑ I want to do something useful with my time.
- ❑ I'm bored.
- ❑ My spouse is still working.
- ❑ I have skills to share.
- ❑ Other: _____

I want my next job to include the following:

- ❑ Full-time hours (35–40 hours a week)
- ❑ Part-time hours
- ❑ Flexible hours
- ❑ Weekends only
- ❑ Health insurance
- ❑ Sick and vacation leave
- ❑ Work from home
- ❑ Near where I'm living now
- ❑ Near _____
- ❑ Similar to what I was doing before retirement
- ❑ Different than what I was doing before retirement
- ❑ Uses these skills: _____
- ❑ Other: _____

Business Start Up

I have made the following preparations to start my own business:

- ❏ Consulted with financial adviser (refer to Chapter 3)
- ❏ Consulted with lawyer (refer to Chapter 3)
- ❏ Developed business plan
- ❏ Developed marketing plan
- ❏ Determined how I'm going to finance my business
    - ❏ Bank loan
    - ❏ Family loan
    - ❏ Personal loan
    - ❏ Loan
    - ❏ Small Business Administration loan
    - ❏ Retirement savings
- ❏ Determined how I'm going to organize my business
    - ❏ Sole proprietorship
    - ❏ Limited liability company (LLC)
    - ❏ Partnership
    - ❏ Limited liability partnership (LLP)
    - ❏ S corporation
    - ❏ Corporation
- ❏ Determined where I'm going to conduct my business
    - ❏ Home office
    - ❏ Office share
    - ❏ Purchase space
    - ❏ Rental space
    - ❏ Telework
    - ❏ Other: _____
- ❏ Registered business name with state
- ❏ Checked any zoning ordinances
- ❏ Obtained business licenses or permits
- ❏ Obtained occupational license
- ❏ Obtained employer identification number (EIN)
- ❏ Ordered phone, Internet, utilities in business name
- ❏ Created accounting system
- ❏ Obtained business insurance
- ❏ Set up employee withholdings (workers comp, unemployment, Social Security, Medicare)

CHAPTER 6
DECIDE WHERE TO LIVE

Retirement—like having a baby or getting a job in a new location—is another of those big forks in the road that causes many folks to take a good look at where they are going to live. Some find retirement to be a perfect opportunity to select a new place to live. Others may want to stay just where they are. In fact, AARP research consistently finds that the vast majority of people 50 and older want to stay in their homes and communities for as long as possible.

For those who plan to stay put, look around and make sure you have the home of your dreams—as much as possible within your budget, that is. Think about how you live in the space you have now and what you might want in the future.

If you're thinking of moving, check out the "livability" of the community you live in and those you're considering. Does it have convenient transportation? Retail stores? Are there sidewalks and parks to walk in? I'll explain how to find out.

Beyond the right community, what type of housing will best fit your needs now and into the future? My first choice for a retirement home seemed perfect when we bought it 15 years ago, long before we retired: a little farmhouse about two hours from our city home. It's been great having a nearby getaway. But now the realities of retirement have settled in—along with the realities of getting older! What looked perfect then has a few flaws we didn't take into account: The bedroom and bath are on the second floor up narrow steep stairs, the very long driveway takes hours to clear of snow, and the grandkids are too far away.

Another housing option that works for many retirees is to divide time between two places. Snowbirds have the opportunity to enjoy the best weather of two locations, while avoiding the extremes of northern winters and southern summers. How much time you spend in each location has legal and tax consequences you should consider before migrating with the birds.

Another option I'm trying out is shared housing with my daughter's family. So far it's working out great, but it does take some cooperation and lots of communication for three generations to get along. In this chapter I share some tips on how to make it work for everyone.

My To-Do Checklist

Done	Need to Do	
❏	❏	If you're staying put, make your home the home of your dreams
❏	❏	Compare the livability of the communities you are considering
❏	❏	Determine what's important about where you live
❏	❏	Consider dividing your time between two locations
❏	❏	Think about living with family
❏	❏	Investigate "villages" in your community
❏	❏	Explore whether an active living community is right for you
❏	❏	See if a continuing care retirement community (CCRC) is what you want
❏	❏	Understand what is and isn't provided in an assisted living facility
❏	❏	Look into skilled nursing facilities
❏	❏	Understand the differences in how property can be titled
❏	❏	Prepare for emergencies

✓ If you're staying put, make your home the home of your dreams

Just about everyone wants to stay in their home for as long as they can. Now is the time to do an assessment. What do you like? Dislike? What do you need that you don't have now? Will you need to make room for a home office or more visitors and entertaining? Should you consider simple adjustments or more drastic renovations to make your home more livable for now and into your later years? What can you afford to change?

Also assess the safety and comfort of your home, for yourself and your family and for visitors, from children in strollers to people who use wheelchairs or walkers. Some simple changes can make a home safer and more comfortable: handrails, grab bars, night lights, and adjustable shower seats, to name a few. Use the Home Safety Checklist as you walk through rooms to spot safety hazards and reduce the chance for falls. For more detailed home safety checklists, tips on do-it-yourself fixes, and resources for improvements that may take a trained professional, use the AARP Home Fit Guide at aarp.org/homefit. While you're there, take a few minutes to test your knowledge with the Home Fit Quiz.

You don't have to do this yourself. One of the first clues that my husband was developing mobility issues happened in the bathroom. It was getting hard for him to safely climb in and out of our bathtub. We contacted a Certified Aging in Place Specialist (CAPS) contractor to walk through our home to point out what we could do make our home safer. He recommended we put in some grab bars: suction-held handholds on the bathroom wall and toilet safety bars. I did it myself for less than $100. I also removed throw rugs and installed motion sensor night-lights. CAPS is a designation for home remodelers and builders who have been trained on how to make homes more livable. You can find a CAPS contractor in your area on the National Association of Home Builders website at nahb.org.

✓ Compare the livability of the communities you are considering

Are you on the fence about whether you should move? Do some research to see how your community rates as being age-friendly and compare it to other communities you might be interested in. A great tool to use is the AARP Livability Index (AARP.org/livabilityindex). You can search the index by address, zip code, or community name to find the overall livability score for hundreds of locations. It looks at factors such as affordability and variety of housing, safe and convenient transportation, clean air and water, access to quality health care, civil and social engagement, and equal opportunity and inclusion. You can customize the index to place higher or lower emphasis on the features most important to you. I compared my suburban home and my country place: both came up with the same overall score.

✓ Determine what's important about where you live

There's great variety in places that people want to live: in the city or in the country, where it is always warm or where seasons change, in the mountains or at the beach. How close do you want to be to family or others you care about? Do you want to move to a smaller home to save money so you can travel more? Do you want someone else to do the maintenance and mow the lawn? You also need to consider affordability now and over time. Be sure to check out the property taxes, as well as state income and sales taxes. Use the What's Important About Where I Live Checklist to see what is most important to you and to your spouse or others who live with you in selecting a new place to live. If you don't agree, talk together about your priorities to come to an agreement.

✓ Consider dividing your time between two locations

When there are important reasons for staying where you are as well as moving somewhere else, consider taking advantage of the best of both by splitting your time between locations. Don't want to permanently pull up roots where you've been living for decades but would enjoy a change of pace, scenery, or weather? You could try the new location for a month or two to see how it works for you. To ease into the transition, stay with friends who are living in the area you are considering or get a one- to three-month rental. Seasonal rent will be more expensive than annual rent, but trying it out in stages can be worth it in the long run.

Once you've picked the location where you want to spend more time each year than just a vacation, you need to determine how long you'll stay. There could be complicating legal and tax consequences. It's a basic legal concept that you can only have one legal residence or domicile, even if you are living in more than one place. What makes a place a domicile depends on a number of mostly subjective factors that indicate you intend to make a place your permanent home: where you spend most of your time, where you vote, what driver's license you have, where you register your car, where you bank, and how you are involved or connected with the new community.

The state where you have your legal residence is going to expect you to pay taxes, and you may have to pay taxes in more than one state. One reason Florida is so popular for snowbirds is that it doesn't have income tax for residents. You can become a Florida resident by filing a declaration of domicile with the clerk of court with "proof" of your intent of making Florida your predominant and principal home, such as having a job, a Florida driver's license or Florida tags for your car, or registering to vote. California, on the other hand, does tax the income of nonresidents who stay for more than six months, earn any income, or make mortgage payments. Check with a tax adviser or lawyer in both states about state taxes you might have to pay if you are living in more than one state.

Another factor to consider is your medical coverage. You'll need to make sure that your health insurance plan will cover you in both locations. If you have coverage through a health maintenance organization (HMO) or Medicare Advantage plan, find out if there are doctors in the network in both locales. With today's electronic medical records, it's a lot easier to transfer medical files among health care providers, but you'll probably want to have a primary care doctor in both locations. Renewing prescriptions is easy with electronic records. I can refill my prescriptions on record at a national chain anywhere there's a local store or have my mail order service send them to whichever address I prefer.

I know from experience that having two residences has other practical complications. To a degree, it means I have two of everything: pots and pans, sheets, stapler, and hammer. Typically, whatever I need is in the other place and I have to buy a duplicate. I used to have separate phone lines in both places, but now I just rely on my cell phone, with a provider that has good coverage in both locations.

✓ Live with family

Multigenerational families are becoming more popular, although families living under one roof is as old as human history. According to the US Census, in 2000 there were 3.9 million multigenerational households; in 2010 that number had grown to 5.1 million. Among the many reasons for sharing a home: caregiving for the oldest or youngest members of the family, divorce or widowhood, unemployment or home foreclosure, and recent immigration. But for others, it's a preference that just makes good sense, particularly with today's high cost of living. Whether you move in with your adult children, or they move in with you, living together provides a safety network among the generations. Other arrangements could include siblings, friends, or extended family members who want to come together to share a household.

Two or three generations living together does take some work, lots of communication, and much respect. If you're planning on moving in with your grown kids, or they're coming under your roof, you need to talk in advance about how this is going to work out for all. Everyone in the family is going to need space for independence and privacy, as well as a place to keep personal items. Some families may be able to remodel to create a separate suite or entrance for each generation. When we moved in with our daughter, we expanded a half bath on the first floor to add a walk-in shower. Now not only does the oldest generation have a fully accessible full bathroom, but, as it turns out, it comes in handy when both grandkids are getting ready for school at the same time, and it's a super place to wash the dogs and muddy boots.

We've found it essential to have some mutual rules about who does the laundry, dishes, housecleaning, cooking, and shopping. How much TV time at what volume? When are bedtimes, naptimes, or other quiet times for everyone in the house? How much childcare or elder care is expected? Be sure you work out how you are going to resolve issues when you disagree. Frequent, face-to-face communication is essential, so little annoyances don't fester. Toys in the hallway, shoes under the table, and lights left on in empty rooms are some of the little things we've worked on in our three-generation home.

The biggest issue is going to be the household finances, just as money can cause problems any time two or more people live together. While a formal agreement may not be necessary, getting the details in writing will help avoid problems down the road. You need to agree on how all living expenses are shared. If you have a family plan for your mobile phone, work out how you are going to divide the data and who pays for the overage. When you go out to eat as a family, does one person always pick up the check? You may be willing to be the family chauffeur, but others may want some help paying for the gas or getting the oil changed in return. Otherwise, you run the risk of someone feeling put upon or being taken advantage of. The Living Together Checklist sets out some of the expenses that could be shared among household members.

Discuss if one member of the family is going to provide services instead of financial contributions to the household. One way is to calculate, for instance, how much Carol's services in providing after-school child care five days a week saves the family in out-of-pocket expense and use that amount as her contribution toward the week's groceries. A more formal financial arrangement may be appropriate if a family member provides substantial caregiving. A family caregiver agreement can be a way to pay a family caregiver for the time spent taking care of a loved one. This is especially important if the caregiver has to stop working or reduce hours worked to free up time to be a caregiver. Often, caring for a loved one can be a long-term commitment and a full-time job. For some families, if there are funds available, it's important to compensate family members for the significant amount of time, effort, and money they spend providing care to a loved one. Many families would prefer to keep the money in the family rather than pay a home health care agency for aides or attendants to perform similar services. Paying a family member for caregiving services might help someone who needs care but cannot qualify for Medicaid until the estate is reduced. Some long-term care insurance policies also allow family caregivers to be compensated, but only if there is a formal, reasonable contract. You'll find more about this in Chapter 10.

✓ Investigate "villages" in your community

How would you like to be able to stay in your own home and community, delay or eliminate the need for institutional care, and have easy access to services and supports to make your life easier? To fulfill these common desires, some communities have organized aging-in-place "villages," where neighbors help and support each other. The village concept began in 2001 when a group of seniors in the Beacon Hill area of Boston got together to help each other, provide mutual support, and negotiate some discounts on services. Now over 200 villages have been organized or are in development. While each village is unique to the needs of the community it serves, in general they help coordinate and deliver services and support to village members and build a sense of community.

A village is typically a nonprofit organization with a volunteer board of directors that uses a mix of paid staff and volunteers. The village doesn't provide services directly but uses volunteers (who could be village members, other volunteer organizations, students providing community service, etc.) for some services and pre-screened providers who have agreed to charge negotiated or discounted prices to village members. The range of available services could include information referrals, home health care, access to transportation, or assistance with household tasks, home maintenance, meal preparation, or computer problems, along with social and educational activities, such as book clubs or outings to the theater or concerts. Most village members can just call one number to arrange for a volunteer to drive them to a doctor's appointment, get the names of reliable or member-recommended plumbers, have a Boy Scout shovel the sidewalk, or enlist a neighbor to fix the Internet connection.

Village members pay an annual membership fee in the range of $150 to $500 for an individual or $600 to $800 for a household. Some are able to provide reduced fees for those with lower incomes. The fee covers some of the volunteer services and administrative costs. Services by providers would be an additional cost. Villages also rely on grants and contributions to cover the overhead costs of running the village, as well as relying on donated volunteer time and skills.

Village residents have found the benefits of belonging to a village include being able to remain in one's own home and community, delaying or eliminating the need for institutional care, having a voice in the types of services provided, and encouraging volunteerism, neighborliness, and a sense of community.

Your local area agency on aging is one place you can contact to learn about any villages that are in your area.

✓ Explore whether an active living community is right for you

They go by many different names, but an "active living" or 50+ community is one option available for those who want to move to a new location. Each of these communities or developments has unique characteristics, but in general, they may have a mix of single-family residences, duplexes, garden units, or multi-storied units on a single campus. Many of these developments feel like a resort, include a golf course or other leisure activities, and focus those who can live independently. Typically they provide no assistance with daily activities, such as meals or personal care. Rather, the campus may include cafes, craft activities, social events, health clubs, swimming pools, and party rooms. They may offer a schedule of cultural events, classes at a local college, or bridge tournaments. Also included would be maintenance of the common areas, landscaping, and security.

After my father died, my mom moved into a lovely senior community in Denver. Her condo was in a high-rise building with fabulous views from her balcony of the Rocky Mountains. She was thrilled not to have any more yard work, home maintenance, and snow shoveling, and my sister lived nearby. Mom's choice kept her very busy with a full schedule of activities, concerts, trips, volunteering with her new friends, and being with family.

You may have the option to own the residence, hold a share in a condominium, or rent the unit. Some may be age-restricted, requiring that at least one of the residents be above a certain age. If you think this is the type of lifestyle you would enjoy, look into the activities offered and the people who live there; the annual fees, including homeowner association dues; and the resale potential if you later decide to move.

✓ See if a continuing care retirement community (CCRC) is what you want

You could also contract with a continuing care retirement community (CCRC), where you move from independent living to higher levels of services and care as your medical needs change, while staying within the same campus or residential community. These communities give older adults the option to live in one location for the duration of their lives, with much of their future care already figured out. Most CCRCs have at least three levels of housing: independent living for those who don't need any personal care assistance; assisted living for those who need some help with activities of daily living; and skilled care for those who need ongoing medical care. Upon entering, healthy adults can reside independently in single-family homes, apartments, or condominiums. When assistance with everyday activities becomes necessary, they can move into an assisted living unit or nursing care facilities.

If you and your spouse are considering a CCRC as a couple, be sure you understand what will happen if one of you needs a higher level of care or dies, or if your circumstances dramatically change. Investigate whether you can get a refund or leave any of your entrance fee to your estate should a change be necessary.

Before making a decision, spend ample time visiting each part of the facility. Most CCRCs invite prospective residents to stay in a guest suite for several days so you can get acquainted with how the community works. The Continuing Care Retirement Community Checklist has questions you should ask when visiting.

A colleague who recently moved into a CCRC raves about how easy it is to make friends. She wrote me, "Our neighbors are super nice and meeting people has been very relaxed and fun. I actually think we already know more people here than we did in the 11 years in our old neighborhood. With 1,300 residents, it's hard to not find the ones you want to hang out with. There's no pressure to socialize and privacy is respected; it's just easier to get to know people. We are 40 minutes from [my son] Dave and his family. It's really nice to be so close. Moving to be near to grandkids is very usual motivation here."

The most expensive of all long-term care options, CCRCs require a hefty entrance fee as well as monthly charges. Entrance fees can range from $100,000 to $1 million—an up-front sum to prepay for care as well as to provide the facility money to operate. Monthly charges can range from $3,000 to $5,000, but may increase as needs change. These fees depend on a variety of factors including your and your spouse's health, the type of housing you choose, whether you rent or buy, the number of residents living in the facility, and the type of service contract. Other options, including housekeeping, meal service, transportation, and social activities, may incur additional fees.

The three basic types of contracts for CCRCs are:

- **Life care or extended contract**: This is the most expensive option, but offers unlimited assisted living, medical treatment, and skilled nursing care without additional charges.

- **Modified contract**: This contract offers a set of services provided for a set length of time. When that time is expired, other services can be obtained, but for higher monthly fees.
- **Fee-for-service contract**: The initial enrollment fee may be lower, but assisted living and skilled nursing will be paid for at their market rates, when or if they become needed.

It is very important to review each option as well as your long-term financial plan. Often, charges above and beyond the entrance cost and monthly fees arise. Make sure you understand just how much money you'll need to support this housing option.

Also, make sure the facility you are considering will be financially viable over the long term. Carefully review all financial reports, licensing and inspection reports, and any complaint investigations. Get assurance that 10 to 15 years down the road the CCRC will still be operating and able to provide you with the care you've already paid for. Also be sure you understand how you can get out of the contract and what money will be returned, if any, if you change your mind.

The contracts for CCRCs can be very complicated and the fee structures are intricate. Be certain that you talk with a lawyer or a financial adviser before you sign a CCRC contract.

✓ Understand what is and isn't provided in an assisted living facility

Assisted living facilities are for those who can't or don't want to live on their own but don't need nursing care. Most offer a combination of housing, meals, personal care, social activities, and 24-hour supervision. Services typically include prepared meals in a common dining area, basic housekeeping, and assistance with activities of daily living, such as bathing, dressing, and grooming. Depending on state regulations, the facility may be able to provide some assistance with medication and basic nursing care, but cannot provide more involved skilled medical care. As needs change, they typically offer different levels of care and services at different price levels. The facility size may range from small homes with just a few people to a high-rise apartment-style building for hundreds of residents. Each resident might have a single room or a suite of rooms with a kitchenette.

My mom's assisted living unit was a suite with a living area, kitchenette where she made her own breakfast, bedroom, and private bath. She tried out living in this facility after she broke her hip and liked the care and attention she received there so much that she decided to move in permanently, ultimately selling her condo in the retirement community. During her four-year stay in assisted living, she moved through different levels of care as her health changed. At first, she needed a higher level of care while she recuperated from her broken hip. When she improved, she dropped to a lower level of care. A couple of years later as her overall health declined, she needed more assistance at a higher level of care. When she needed special medical care, we hired a private duty nurse who came a few hours each day because the staff aides were not allowed by state regulation to provide that type of medical care.

Keep in mind that assisted living residences are not regulated by the federal government. Each state decides how they're licensed. Be sure to find out from your area agency on aging or state health department how the state where you are searching handles this.

Make sure any residence you are considering is appropriately licensed. Check, too, with the state licensing agency and long-term care ombudsman's office to see if any complaints have been filed against the facilities on your list of possibilities. Don't assume that a state license ensures quality care. You can find the local ombudsman at eldercare.gov.

If you are considering an assisted living facility, you'll want to understand all the provisions in the contract—even the fine print. Have a lawyer review the contract before it is signed. Because not all assisted living facilities are the same, not all admissions contracts are the same. It's a good idea to read and compare the contract terms for several facilities before making a choice. You may have to ask for a copy of the contract because it is usually not part of the shiny marketing packet.

Ask questions and get an explanation from the facility for any terms in the contract you don't understand. Then be sure to ask the lawyer those same questions, just to verify the facility's explanation. Be wary of facilities that say the contract is standard, it's what everyone signs, or it can't be changed. Watch for contract terms that require you to submit any disputes to arbitration, cutting off your legal right to litigate any serious issues.

Know before the search begins the types or level of services that you need now and will need in the foreseeable future. You won't want to move in only to find that the facility can't provide what is needed, or have to start the search process all over again for a different facility when needs change.

Make sure that the types of services or level of care you need and will receive are spelled out as part of the contract. State regulations may determine the levels of medical care the facility can provide. Just because something is mentioned in the promotional brochure does not mean it will show up in the contract. Compare what is advertised or promised to what is actually mentioned in the contract.

The contract should also explain what medical services are available, such as doctors or nurses onsite or on call, assistance with medication, or a preferred pharmacy. Be sure to find out if residents are able to use their choice of health care providers, care aides, and pharmacies, if they wish.

You'll want to know if you will have a private bedroom or share with others. What is the maximum number of roommates, and what is the procedure if the roommates are not compatible? Residents should have the opportunity to request a room or roommate change. You will want to have personal items within your living space. Be sure you know what personal items you can bring with you and what the facility will furnish, such as lounge chairs, special mattresses, sleep sofas or futons for overnight guests, a television, a night stand, or even family pictures. Can your family members stay overnight, share meals with the residents, visit at any time, or take you out for trips?

Be sure you have clarity about costs. Most assisted living facilities have tiers of services, with higher costs as more services are needed. Care services may have a separate price tag than the costs of room and board. Other facilities may charge for specific services in addition to basic care. Compare the rate schedule for extras such as transportation to medical appointments or events, beauty care, guest meals, parking space, exercise room, laundry, medication delivery, and more. You may also want a list of services the facility is not going to provide.

Other important contract provisions include how long the contract lasts and how to get out of the contract if the choice is not a good fit. Under what circumstances can you get out of the contract and what refunds or adjustment of any prepaid fees will be made? Is it a month-to-month contract, or is it renewed annually? Will the price increase with each renewal? How frequently will the schedule of fees change, and how much notice is given about a change in rates? Under what circumstances can residents be asked to leave? It could be a change in health status, a lengthy hospital stay, disruptive or unsafe behavior, or failure to pay the monthly charges. Note what the contract says about how the decision is made to change the level of care and what happens if the level of care needed is more than the facility is licensed to provide. Good contracts will also explain residents' rights and the process for filing complaints or grievances.

Who signs the resident agreement has significant legal and financial consequences. Ordinarily, the resident signs, agreeing to the terms of the contract and to be the person responsible for payment of the fees. There may be circumstances when someone else is going to be the "responsible party." The "responsible party" is personally liable for all payments. If you are an agent with powers of attorney or a guardian for the resident, you must make clear to the facility that you are signing on behalf of the resident. You would sign as "(your name), as agent for (resident)." In that way, you would not be personally responsible for the costs.

Before signing any contract, have it reviewed by a lawyer experienced with residential facility issues.

✓ Look into skilled nursing facilities

The need for skilled nursing care may arise suddenly, with little time available for comparison shopping. In some areas, available beds are limited and choices may be limited. However emotional the decision to move to a skilled care facility, take the time to carefully review the contract before signing it and have a lawyer go over it with you. Admissions contracts are complex, so ask the facility about any language that's confusing.

As the prospective resident, you are the only person who should sign the skilled nursing facility contract, unless you have a guardian or have given authority to an agent with powers of attorney to sign contracts on your behalf. Guardians, agents, or any others who have legal access to your money and who sign on your behalf will not be personally liable for the costs of care. Family members should only sign the contract as the "responsible party" or "guarantor" if they understand they are personally responsible to pay the nursing facility expenses. Nursing facilities cannot require family members to guarantee payment.

Look at what is included in the facility's basic daily or monthly rate. It will usually cover room and meals, housekeeping, linens, general nursing care, medical records services, recreation, personal care, and similar services. Extra charges in most nursing facilities include:

- Physician's services, including the work of specialists like dentists, ophthalmologists, or podiatrists
- Medications
- Physical therapy

- Diagnostic services, such as laboratory work, x-rays, and electrocardiograms
- Personal services, such as telephone calls, personal laundry, beauticians, and barbers. Medicare and Medicaid may cover some of these extra charges. Private pay residents may be billed for personal services either once for the length of the resident's stay, as a flat charge each month, or each time a service or material is provided

Some other contract provisions to watch out for and avoid include restrictions on applying for Medicaid, limits on visiting hours, and requirements for a family member to guarantee payment. Other troublesome provisions sometimes buried in the fine print require residents to make a deposit if they are eligible for Medicaid, to have an advance directive or do not resuscitate order on file, or to consent in advance to all medical care. Under new federal rules, facilities receiving Medicaid funds can no longer require residents to resolve disputes through arbitration, rather than the courts. Also, make sure you understand the "bed hold" policy, which explains what happens if you have an extended hospital stay and want to return to the nursing facility. These contract provisions, and more, are regulated by federal and state laws. Use the Skilled Nursing Facility Contracts Checklist to note provisions that should be reviewed with a lawyer.

✓ Understand the differences in how property can be titled

Retirement is a good time to look at how your current property is titled and, if you're moving, how you want your new property titled. There are many different ways to own, or hold title to, your residence:

- You can own it in your own name.
- You can own it jointly with others.
- You can put your home into your trust, which would then own it.
- You can own the space where you live but not the building.
- You can own the right to have access to a unit for a limited time.
- You can keep the right to live in your home for as long as you live, even after giving or selling ownership to someone else.

Here are explanations of the different ways you can own what you call home. The differences are important to what rights you have now and what happens to the property when you die.

Individual Ownership

You can own real property *individually* in your own name. This means that you alone have the right to sell it, rent it, transfer it by will, and use it in any legal way. You need to state in your will who you want to inherit this property. If you do not have a will, your state's law of *intestacy* will determine who gets it. Intestacy law sets up a priority scheme of inheritance. To a degree, it tries to anticipate who the typical person would want to inherit his or her property if the property owner had gotten around to writing a will. You should check to see what your state's priority scheme is, but typically real estate would first go to a spouse, and if no spouse, then to children; and if no children, then to parents; then to siblings; and so forth out multiple branches of the family tree to the closest living next of kin. Most intestacy laws also include rules of what to do when there are bumps in the family tree such as adopted children, deceased children with living offspring, or multiple marriages. Only if no living next of kin can be located does the state get your property, called *escheat* to the state.

Joint Ownership

There are multiple ways you can own real estate with someone else. Your deed establishes whether you are joint owners or common owners. *Joint owners with right of survivorship* have equal ownership and rights to use and enjoy the property. When one of the joint owners dies, the surviving owner or owners automatically continue to own the property. The last surviving owner ends up as the sole owner of the property. This last owner can then leave that property by will to anyone they want, or it will be distributed through intestacy rules. All joint owners must agree to sell or mortgage the property. For couples who are not married, this type of property ownership ensures that the surviving partner will automatically inherit the property. Joint owners don't have to be spouses. If they are, some states call this type of ownership *tenants by the entireties*.

Common Ownership

Ownership in common (called "tenants in common") is the other primary way to own real estate with someone else. The key difference between ownership in common and joint ownership is what happens to the share of ownership when a common owner dies. Unlike joint ownership with right of survivorship, the surviving owner does not inherit any greater interest or share in the property. The common owner's share passes to his or her estate on death.

Siblings who own property together, such as a beach house, may want to consider ownership in common so that each sibling's interest will pass down to their own children, rather than to the sibling or nieces and nephews. For example, Juanita and Louise as sisters share equal ownership in common of a cabin on a lake where their families frequently spend summers. Each sister has a will that states that when she dies, her property passes to her own children. When Juanita dies, Louise still owns half of the property, along with Juanita's kids, who own the other half.

Community Property

For spouses in nine states (Arizona, California, Idaho, Louisiana, Nevada, New Mexico, Texas, Washington, and Wisconsin), all property acquired during the marriage automatically becomes community property. The laws vary in each of these states, but the basic theory is that each spouse acquires an equal interest in the real estate. When a husband or wife dies, only half of the marital property is inheritable because the surviving spouse already owns his or her own right to half of the marital property. Each spouse has the right to assign by will the ownership of his or her portion of the community property. Property that either spouse brought into the marriage or inherits is considered separate property. The couple can agree in writing to different spousal rights.

Trust Property

Another way to title property is to have it held in trust. The grantor is the person who creates the trust and deeds the property to the trust. Although as grantor you no longer "own" the property (your trust does), you determine who as trustee is to manage that property (it could be yourself, if you wish), how you want the property managed, and when and how the trustee is to transfer that property to the beneficiaries. You name the beneficiaries of the trust, including yourself while you are living, and secondary beneficiaries who you want to receive the property in the trust after you die. The trustee is responsible for the management, upkeep, taxes, and so on of the trust property. (Note that the IRS considers that income from most trust assets belongs to the grantor, so it must be included in the grantor's income tax return.) Because you no longer own the property in the trust, it is not part of your probate estate. The language in the trust document, rather than your will, determines who receives the trust property after your death. There's more information about trusts in Chapter 10.

Rental Property

As a renter you may not own where you call "home" but you still have legal rights while you live there. You could rent an apartment in a retirement living complex, have a suite in an assisted living facility, or stay in a room in a skilled nursing facility. Your rights and obligations are spelled out in the rental contract, including how long you can stay, how much you pay, what services you'll get, and what you do when you want or need to move. It's a good idea to have a lawyer review any rental agreement you don't completely understand. The lease and any rights to the property end at your death.

Condominiums

Typically, a condominium owner individually owns a specific unit as well as jointly owns with all the other unit owners the common areas such as the public hallways, lobby, grounds, and recreational areas. The Master Deed or Declaration describes the space that you own, the common areas, and any restrictions on how you can use or modify your unit or the common areas.

You should also become familiar with any condominium association documents. The condominium association includes all the unit owners who manage the condominium through an elected board of directors. A condominium association may also have a separate set of bylaws and rules that further set out how the condominium is to be managed, pet restrictions, color choices, and how monthly unit fees are assessed, among many details.

Timeshares

A timeshare is a way to own the right to use property, rather than direct ownership of the property. With most timeshares, multiple people have the right to use the same property, with each having a specific period of time when they have exclusive use of the property. You may purchase a specific week in a specific unit, be able to negotiate a rotating time schedule, or trade your share for use of multiple properties. Because there are so many variations on the timeshare concept, the contract is very important. Make sure you understand how you can reserve your share, what you can and cannot do with the share, how to get out of the contract, and what happens to the timeshare on your death. Caution: Some timeshares severely restrict when you can access the property; others are very hard to sell or terminate. Take your time to crunch some numbers away from the charm of the property or pressure from the salesperson.

Life Estate

By creating a life estate, you can transfer the ownership of your home to another person but reserve the right to continue to live in the home until you die. Upon your death, the other person automatically gets the right to take possession. Example: George and Mildred together own their home and want to remain there until the last of them dies. They can create a joint life estate with their children who in legalese are called the "remaindermen." This means that George and Mildred can live at home until the last spouse dies; then the kids automatically own the whole property. As a life tenant, George and Mildred continue to be responsible for the taxes, insurance, and maintenance of the property. Their kids own the property, but they can't force their parents to move. Talk with a lawyer and your tax adviser about the estate and tax ramifications of this way to hold real estate.

✓ Prepare for emergencies

No matter where you are living, you want to make sure you and your family are prepared for natural disasters such as hurricanes, flooding, or fires. Many people who have experienced a devastating flood, earthquake, wildfire, hurricane, ice storm, or an extended power outage never thought it would happen to them. According to The Hartford, 75 percent of all U.S. households are at risk for one or more natural disasters. It's important to know what types of disasters are likely where you live so that you can better prepare for them. And if you're new to the area, you may not know which disasters are likely to occur, how severe an event could be, or what you should do to prepare. Any planning—however much or little—will help to make such situations easier to deal with.

It's essential that you have an emergency evacuation plan and an emergency preparedness kit. Use the Emergency Preparedness Checklist, which is based on guidance from the Federal Emergency Management Agency (FEMA), to do both. Go over the plan with your family to make sure you can stay calm in any emergency and know what to do to be safe. Your plan should pay particular attention to any special needs, including an escape chair that can be used to get down the stairs if someone in your family uses a wheelchair or walker, extra hearing aid batteries, food for a service dog, back-up power for oxygen units, and a list of all drug prescriptions for everyone in the family.

Where to Live Action Checklists

The following Action Checklists are in Chapter 6:

- ❑ Home Safety
- ❑ What's Important About Where I Live
- ❑ Living Together
- ❑ Continuing Care Retirement Communities (CCRCs)
- ❑ Assisted Living Facility Contracts
- ❑ Skilled Nursing Facility Contracts
- ❑ Emergency Preparedness

Home Safety

Steps/Stairways/Walkways

Yes   No

Yes	No	
❑	❑	Are they in good shape?
❑	❑	Do they have a smooth, safe surface?
❑	❑	Are there handrails on both sides of the stairway?
❑	❑	Are there light switches at the top and bottom of the stairs?
❑	❑	Is there grasping space for both knuckles and fingers on railings?
❑	❑	Are the stair treads deep enough for your whole foot?
❑	❑	Would a ramp be feasible in any of these areas if it became necessary?

Floor Surfaces

Yes	No	
❑	❑	Is the surface safe?
❑	❑	Is the surface nonslip?
❑	❑	Are there any throw rugs or doormats that might slip underfoot?
❑	❑	Is carpeting loose or torn?
❑	❑	Are there changes in floor levels?
❑	❑	If so, are they obvious or well-marked?
❑	❑	Do you have to step over any electric, telephone, or extension cords?

Driveway and Garage

Yes	No	
❑	❑	Is there always space to park?
❑	❑	Is it convenient to the entrance?
❑	❑	Does the garage door open automatically?

Windows and Doors

Yes	No	
❏	❏	Are windows and doors easy to open and close?
❏	❏	Are locks sturdy and easy to operate?
❏	❏	Do doorways accommodate a walker or wheelchair?
❏	❏	Can you walk through the doorways easily?
❏	❏	Is there space to maneuver while opening and closing doors?
❏	❏	Does the front door have a view panel or peephole at the right height?

Appliances/Kitchen/Bath

Yes	No	
❏	❏	Is the room arranged safely and conveniently?
❏	❏	Do the oven and fridge open easily?
❏	❏	Are stove controls clearly marked and easy to use?
❏	❏	Is the counter the right height and depth?
❏	❏	Can you work sitting down?
❏	❏	Are cabinet doorknobs easy to use?
❏	❏	Are faucets easy to use?
❏	❏	Do you have a handheld shower head?
❏	❏	Are the items you use often within reach?
❏	❏	Do you have a step stool with handles?
❏	❏	Can you easily get in and out of the tub or shower?
❏	❏	Do you have a bath or shower seat?
❏	❏	Are there grab bars where needed?
❏	❏	Is the hot water heater regulated to prevent scalding or burning?

Lighting/Ventilation

Yes   No

❑   ❑   Are there enough lights, and are they bright enough?

❑   ❑   Do you have night lights where needed?

❑   ❑   Are areas well ventilated?

Electrical Outlets/Switches/Alarms

Yes   No

❑   ❑   Can you turn switches easily on and off?

❑   ❑   Are outlets properly grounded to prevent a shock?

❑   ❑   Are extension cords in good shape?

❑   ❑   Do you have smoke detectors in all key areas?

❑   ❑   Do you have an alarm system?

❑   ❑   Do you use a personal emergency response system?

❑   ❑   Is the telephone readily available for emergencies?

❑   ❑   Does the telephone have volume control?

❑   ❑   Can you hear the doorbell ring all throughout the house?

What's Important About Where I Live

This checklist prepared by The Hartford helps you clarify your priorities for where you want to live. As you think through each item, be realistic about your future desires and current resources. You may like a variety of the options, but to give you the clearest picture of your priorities, mark "most prefer" for your highest priorities. Your spouse or others who live with you should also fill out this worksheet. Then compare and negotiate any differences.

	Most Prefer	Neutral	Least Prefer
Relationships			
Close to children			
Close to grandchildren			
Close to parents			
Close to other family			
Close to friends			
A place where you know your neighbors			
A place to make new friends			
Other:			
Region			
Close to current location			
Four seasons of weather			
Warm weather			
Cold weather			
Near the beach			
Near the mountains			
Near a lake			
Near the desert			
Other:			
Resources			
Affordable			
Lots of entertainment			
Close to shopping			
Close to outdoor recreation			
Lots of dining out			
Nearby place of worship			
Close to hospital			
Close to health care			

	Most Prefer	Neutral	Least Prefer
Close to college			
Easy access to airport			
Close to public transportation			
Close to interstate highways			
Neighborhood where I can walk to shops and services			
Close to work			
Close to volunteer opportunities			
Golf community			
Active adult community			
Gated community			
Other:			

Living Together

The people I am living with agree to share household expenses as follows:

Item	Amount	Person #1	Person #2	Person #3
Rent				
Mortgage				
Property taxes				
Homeowners insurance				
Electricity				
Water/sewer				
Cable service				
Internet service				
Telephone				
Lawn service				
Fuel				
Minor maintenance				
Major repairs				
Groceries				
Meals out				
Gasoline				
Car loan				
Car repair				

Continuing Care Retirement Community (CCRC)

I have answers to the following questions about the CCRC I'm considering:

General Community Questions

- ❑ How many homes/units are there?
- ❑ How many homes/units are available at this time and can I see specific spaces?
- ❑ Is there a waiting list? If so, how long may it take to be accepted and admitted?

Grounds and Facility Location

- ❑ Are the facility's grounds well maintained, manicured, and easy to navigate?
- ❑ Is the facility located in a desirable area?
- ❑ Are there ample conveniences in and around the community (grocery stores, cleaners, shopping)?
- ❑ Are my doctors within close proximity?
- ❑ Is a hospital nearby?
- ❑ Is bus or mass transit available nearby?
- ❑ Is this a smoke-free facility? Are there designated spots for smokers?
- ❑ Is there adequate security?

Initial Impressions of Staff and Community

- ❑ Was I greeted upon entering?
- ❑ Is the main office easy to find?
- ❑ Is the staff professional and happy to help?
- ❑ Do residents seem happy and well cared for?
- ❑ Are residents social and interacting with one another?

Staff

- ❑ What credentials do staff members hold?
- ❑ What is the hiring procedure for staff, doctors, and nurses?
- ❑ Are staff, doctors, and nurses required to take continuing education classes?
- ❑ What hours do facility administrators work and are they usually available for questions throughout the day?

Residents

Arrange to talk to current residents. Consider asking:

- ❏ How long have you lived here?
- ❏ How do you like living here?
- ❏ How are the services?
- ❏ How is the care?
- ❏ Is the staff attentive without being intrusive?
- ❏ Are the doctors and nurses helpful and accommodating?
- ❏ Is there anything missing?
- ❏ Is it worth the cost?

Housing

- ❏ Do the housing options meet your needs?
- ❏ Are there different floor plans available and options to choose from?
- ❏ Are both single- and double-occupancy homes available?
- ❏ Are residences equipped with modern conveniences (laundry, dishwasher, etc.), full kitchens, and individual thermostats?
- ❏ Are common areas properly cooled/warmed, furnished, and clean?
- ❏ Do homes/units have outdoor living space for residents to enjoy?
- ❏ Is there ample light and are rooms/homes equipped with sprinkler systems and emergency exits?
- ❏ Are the assisted living and nursing facilities clean and modern?
- ❏ Are layouts in all types of housing wheelchair and walker friendly?
- ❏ Are floor plans efficient and pleasing?
- ❏ Is each residence equipped with handicap bars, nonslip floors, and other safety features?
- ❏ Do multi-level residences have elevators?
- ❏ Are furnished residences available?
- ❏ Can rooms/homes be painted? Are there decorating rules?
- ❏ Are rooms in the assisted and nursing facilities private? Does each room have a bath in the suite?
- ❏ Are units/houses set up for cable and telephone service? Are these utilities included in monthly fees or paid separately per unit/house?
- ❏ Is parking available to residents? And is additional parking easy to find for visitors?
- ❏ Are pets allowed?

Meals and Meal Programs

- ❑ Do the assisted living facilities offer group meals or in-room meal programs?
- ❑ What meal programs are offered?
- ❑ Are special diets catered to?
- ❑ Can residents make special requests?
- ❑ How many entrée choices are offered daily?
- ❑ What is the meal schedule and can meal times be flexible?
- ❑ Are snacks included in any of the meal plans?
- ❑ Can guests dine in with their loved ones? If so, is there a fee?
- ❑ Ask to see a sample of a month's worth of menus to see how meals are varied.
- ❑ Ask to sit in on a meal to see if the choices are to your liking.

Assisted Living Facility Contracts

Contract was reviewed by a lawyer on: _____

Contract was signed by the resident on: _____

Contract was signed on behalf of the resident by: _____

in the legal role of: _____

(agent with power of attorney, guardian)

"Responsible party" for payment of fees is: _____

Term (length) of the contract is: _____

Contract can be reviewed/renewed on: _____

Contract can be terminated by the resident if: _____

Contract can be terminated by the facility if:_____

Intent to terminate requires _____ days notice.

Levels of care the facility is licensed to provide are:

_____with _____ services

_____with _____ services

_____with _____ services

Procedure for change in level of care: _____

Fee schedule for each level of care provided: ❏ Yes   ❏ No

Price list for extra services provided: ❏ Yes   ❏ No

Initial or application fee is: _____

Refundable: ❏ Yes   ❏ No

Renters' insurance required: ❏ Yes   ❏ No

Private room: ❏ Yes   ❏ No

Maximum number to share a room is: _____

Procedure for selecting or changing rooms or roommates:

_____

_____

Furnishings provided by facility:

_____

_____

Furnishings provided by resident:

_____

_____

Responsibility for lost or damaged personal property:

_____

_____

Overnight guest policy:

_____

_____

Guest meal policy:

_____

_____

Visitation restrictions:

_____

_____

Grievance procedure:

_____

_____

Statement of residents' rights provided: ❑ Yes   ❑ No

Medication assistance provided: ❑ Yes   ❑ No

Skilled Nursing Facility Contracts

Contract was reviewed by a lawyer on: _____

Contract was signed by the resident on: _____

Contract was signed on behalf of the resident by: _____

in the legal role of: _____

(agent with power of attorney, guardian)

"Responsible party" for payment of fees is: _____

Term (length) of the contract is: _____

Contract can be reviewed/renewed on: _____

Contract can be terminated by the resident if: _____

Contract can be terminated by the facility if:_____

Intent to terminate requires _____ days notice.

Contract can be terminated by facility under these conditions:

- ❑ Necessary for the resident's welfare
- ❑ Skilled care is no longer required
- ❑ Health and safety of others is endangered
- ❑ Failure to pay for services
- ❑ Facility ceases to operate

Levels of care the facility is licensed to provide:

_____with _____ services

_____with _____ services

_____with _____ services

Procedure for selecting or changing rooms or roommates:

_____

_____

Facility is Medicare/Medicaid certified: ❑ Yes   ❑ No

Fee schedule for each level of care provided: ❑ Yes   ❑ No

Basic daily rate includes:

- ❑ Room
- ❑ Meals
- ❑ Housekeeping
- ❑ Linens

- ❏ General nursing care
- ❏ Medical records services
- ❏ Recreation
- ❏ Personal care
- ❏ Other:_____

Price list for extra services not included in the basic rate provided: ❏ Yes   ❏ No

Procedure for change in price lists:

_____

Application fee: $ _____

Refundable: ❏ Yes   ❏ No

Procedure for change in ownership or management of the facility:

_____

Private room: ❏ Yes   ❏ No

Maximum number to share a room: _____

Procedure for selecting or changing rooms or roommates:

_____

_____

Furnishings provided by facility:

_____

_____

Furnishings provided by resident:

_____

_____

Responsibility for lost or damaged personal property:

_____

_____

Overnight guest policy:

_____

_____

Guest meal policy:

_____

_____

Visitation restrictions:

_____

_____

Grievance procedure:

_____

_____

Private room:	❑ Yes	❑ No
Statement of residents' rights provided:	❑ Yes	❑ No
Requirement of private pay:	❑ Yes	❑ No
Right to apply for Medicare and/or Medicaid:	❑ Yes	❑ No
Bed hold policy consistent with Medicare/Medicaid requirements:	❑ Yes	❑ No
Limits on liability for resident's injury:	❑ Yes	❑ No
Requirement to have advance directive, DNR:	❑ Yes	❑ No
Arbitration requirements:	❑ Yes	❑ No

Emergency Preparedness

Preparation Steps

- ❑ Check insurance policies for wind, flooding, fire, or other storm damage coverage
- ❑ Determine an evacuation plan
- ❑ Designate a primary contact person, preferably outside of the area
- ❑ Know evacuation routes
- ❑ Know locations of emergency shelters
- ❑ Plan for special assistance if mobility is an issue
- ❑ Register with utility company if using electrical medical equipment
- ❑ Store cold packs for medication that needs refrigeration
- ❑ Prepare food for special dietary needs
- ❑ Have supply of food for service dogs
- ❑ Maintain a supply of water
- ❑ Prepare an emergency kit

Emergency Kit Items

- ❑ Blankets and pillows
- ❑ Books, games, puzzles
- ❑ Cash and coins
- ❑ Cell phone and charger
- ❑ Change of clothing and sturdy shoes
- ❑ Contact lens solution
- ❑ Credit/debit/ATM cards
- ❑ Directions to shelter or evacuation route
- ❑ Extra pair of glasses
- ❑ Flashlight and extra batteries
- ❑ First aid kit and manual
- ❑ Hearing aid batteries
- ❑ Incontinent supplies, if necessary
- ❑ Map of area
- ❑ Matches in waterproof container
- ❑ Moist towelettes
- ❑ Medications (5–7 day supply)
- ❑ Personal medication record
- ❑ Portable battery-powered TV or radio
- ❑ Toilet paper

- ❑ Copies of important papers in waterproof/fireproof box
- ❑ Birth certificate
- ❑ Blank checks
- ❑ Copies of prescriptions
- ❑ Driver's license
- ❑ Health insurance and Medicare cards
- ❑ Insurance policies (cover page)
- ❑ List of allergies or special needs
- ❑ List of bank accounts
- ❑ List of credit/debit/ATM card numbers
- ❑ List of type and model numbers of medical equipment
- ❑ List of health care providers (names and phone numbers)
- ❑ List of family members and emergency contacts
- ❑ Marriage certificate
- ❑ Medical directives
- ❑ Medical records
- ❑ Passport
- ❑ Personal property inventory
- ❑ Print-out of the checklists in this book
- ❑ Power of attorney
- ❑ Social Security card
- ❑ Telephone tree of emergency contacts
- ❑ Plan for care of pets

CHAPTER 7
RETIRING ABROAD

More and more retirees are opting to pull stakes and live in another country. An estimated 6.8 million Americans live abroad, according to the U.S. State Department. And as of 2011, the Social Security Administration was sending monthly benefits to 346,000 retirees living outside the United States.

Retiring abroad can be a fresh start, full of adventure and travel, and, in many countries, the cost of living is lower. If you're planning to retire abroad, or thinking of it, this chapter is for you.

Embracing a new culture, and perhaps learning a new language, is a big move. It takes a lot of time, energy, and effort to do all the research and planning involved in making the decision and, eventually, the move. It also takes a serious dose of self-reflection to decide whether this is right for you. You need to weigh the pros and cons and make some wise decisions about where you'll go and what you'll do once you get there. This chapter helps you sort through some of things you need to consider and, if you do decide to make the move, how to prepare to leave.

My To-Do Checklist

Done	Need to Do	
❏	❏	Set your priorities
❏	❏	Narrow down ideal retirement destinations
❏	❏	Ask the embassy about residency requirements
❏	❏	Figure out how you'll manage your finances
❏	❏	Consider how to handle your legal affairs
❏	❏	Check access to and coverage for health care
❏	❏	Prepare to leave

✓ Set your priorities

Here are some factors to look at when considering a move abroad and choosing your overseas retirement destination. Only you can determine how much weight to give each one. See the Choosing My Destination Checklist to help with your decision-making process. Be sure to talk it through with your partner or any person who'll be making the move with you.

- **Accessibility:** How close do you want to be to family and friends back home? How frequently do you plan on returning to the states or having loved ones visit? Where is the closest international airport, and are there nonstop or direct flights?

- **Activities:** Are the things you enjoy doing available? If you like good restaurants or cultural attractions, will there be enough of these to keep you busy six months or a year after the newness has worn off?

- **Affordability:** How does the cost of living stack up with your income and budget? Are expenses—rent or mortgage, utilities, food, etc.—comparable to what you're now paying or will they take a bigger bite out of your budget? What is the exchange rate? What about taxes—sales tax, property tax, income tax? Take into account, too, the cost of moving as well as visiting family and friends or having them visit you.

- **Climate:** Are you looking for four seasons or year-round warm weather? Have you spent time there during the worst weather season so you'll know what to expect?

- **Cultural differences:** Do you look forward to making new friends among people who may be very different than you? If you need familiar items in the grocery stores and pharmacies, can you locate them? Can you easily find—and afford—restaurants you like and ingredients for your favorite dishes? Do you like the music, the holidays, the traditions, the pace of life? What are you willing to change and what can't you live without?

- **Health care:** Would you have access to adequate and affordable health care? (You'll find a section devoted to it later in this chapter.)

- **Housing:** Are homes for rent or sale at a reasonable price? If you buy a property and later change your mind, will you be able to sell it easily enough? Can you, as a foreigner, legally own property?

- **Language:** Would you need to learn a new language, and, if so, are you ready and able to do so? (Some people are more proficient at learning a new language than others.) Or would you feel more comfortable in a country, or neighborhood, where everyone spoke your language?

- **Safety:** How safe is the country and, specifically, the area you're thinking of? What is the political situation? The crime rate? You can check the U.S. Department of State website for up-to-date travel advisories.

- **Social Security:** If you are thinking about retiring abroad, find out if you can receive your Social Security or other federal agency benefits outside the United States.

- **Transportation:** If you are considering driving in your new location, review the local traffic laws and licensing requirements. What's the traffic like? Or is there public transportation you can access? Are you fit enough to ease into a lifestyle that may include more walking or biking to get around?

- **Visa and residency requirements:** Immigration and residency laws differ greatly from country to country. Determine if you need a visa to enter and reside in the country you're considering by reviewing the Department of State's Country-Specific Information.

✓ Narrow down ideal retirement destinations

Perhaps the most fun and easiest thing to do is to explore all the possible locations in other countries that offer what you are looking for. A quick search online for best places to retire abroad turns up dozens of sites to help you choose where you might enjoy living, including AARP (aarp.org/home-garden/livable-communities/best_places_to_retire_abroad). I tried out the quiz on internationalliving.com (search "quiz"); it picked Panama for me. I'd never thought of moving there, but it has many of the attractions I'd enjoy.

Find out as much about the new destination as you can. You must spend time in a location before you even think about moving there. Go at least once, if not more. And stay for a while. It's a good idea to rent for a season so you can get a better sense of what it's like to live there and what it costs day-to-day. If you're thinking of a tropical climate and air conditioning is essential, you'll find out how much electricity will cost. If you're planning on having a car to travel around the country, you'll learn whether you can deal with the traffic, perhaps signs in another language, and the cost of gasoline. Track down people who live or have lived there to get candid impressions of the pros and cons of living there. Some websites with information from those who are living overseas are internationalliving.com and expatinfodesk.com.

✓ Ask the embassy about residency requirements

Some countries encourage American retirees to settle there, but it is important to check with the country's embassy for any requirements for residency permits or retirement visas. Whatever country you want to move to, be prepared to provide all of the required documentation and know where and when to apply. It might be at the embassy in the United States before you leave or with the local immigration office after you arrive. You can find information on how to contact a foreign embassy at usembassy.gov.

Each country has its own immigration laws and requirements depending on why you want to come to the country (to work, study, or retire), what country you are leaving from, and how long you plan to stay. Some countries may require a health examination or criminal background check. Most will require proof of income and not allow you to work if you are planning on retiring there. You may need a written statement from a financial institution showing that you have a regular source of retirement or investment income. Countries typically require a minimum of $2,000 per person per month, although the amount could be higher or lower, depending on the country. Panama, for example, requires retirees to have an income of $1,000 to receive its Pensionado (Retired) Visa. England requires those over age 60 who want to live there to have £25,000 annually to obtain an Independent Means Visa.

Other countries have different requirements. If you plan to stay more than 90 days in Germany, you should obtain a residence permit before you leave the United States. Germany requires a bank statement covering the last three months plus proof of medical insurance and a copy of the rental agreement where you will be living to obtain a temporary residence permit. This permit must be renewed annually. Later on during your stay you would apply for a settlement permit, Niederlassungserlaubnis, which requires you to demonstrate basic knowledge of the German language, political system, and society, plus other requirements.

One other matter to check on with the embassy is any restrictions on owning property. For example, foreigners in Mexico cannot own property within 62 miles of any border or 31 miles of the coastline. For country-specific information, visit internationalliving.com/global-property-ownershi.

✓ Figure out how you'll manage your finances

With today's ease of online banking, managing your finances while living abroad won't be too difficult, but you need some advance planning. You'll want to set up direct deposits of your income and arrange for automatic payment of your regular bills. As long as you have Internet access—either where you're living or at an Internet café—you can check bank balances from just about anywhere in the world. ATM machines provide ready access to the local currency. You may want to leave a few signed, blank checks with a very trusted friend or relative in case there is a payment that needs to be made that you didn't plan for.

You'll probably want to set up a bank account in your new location. That way you can transfer funds from your U.S. bank account for day-to-day expenses. If on any day in the year you have more than $10,000 on deposit in a foreign bank account, you will need to file the annual Report of Foreign Bank and Financial Accounts with the U.S. Treasury. If you no longer have a state-side address, you may run into bureaucratic difficulties with the foreign bank. In an effort to thwart the financing of terrorist activities, the USA Patriot Act restricts some financial transactions between U.S. and foreign banks.

Don't forget the IRS. In addition to the taxes you'll pay in your new home, you're going to have to pay federal and state income taxes in the United States, even while living abroad. U.S. citizens with income generated in the United States will need to file tax returns. You may get credit for the taxes you pay in the other country, but it is complicated. My high school classmate who has lived in France for many years tells me that that figuring out the taxes she has to pay in the United States and in France is a nightmare. Plan for how you are going to prepare your taxes and how you will receive various tax reporting documents such as W-2s or 1099s that need to be attached to your returns. Be sure to get expert tax advice from a CPA or Enrolled Agent who specializes in international taxation issues.

You can continue to receive your Social Security retirement benefits in most countries, although there are some restrictions depending on the country where you'll be living. Use the tool socialsecurity.gov/international/payments.html to find out if you can get your benefits in your new country. Social Security considers being "outside the U.S." to be away from the United States or its territories for 30 days in a row. If you'll be living in a country where Social Security won't send benefits, you may be able to go to the U.S. embassy to pick up your check or arrange to have your payments held until you get to a country where you can get the back payments. You can use direct deposit to a bank in any country that has an international direct deposit agreement with the United States. Those who are survivors or dependents getting benefits on someone else's account have special rules for payments outside the United States. Read the Social Security publication 05-10137 for all the details or go to your local Social Security office before you depart.

✓ Consider how to handle your legal affairs

Seek legal advice before settling abroad. Determine whether your trust and powers of attorney may be legally enforceable in your country of destination. If you are permanently changing your place of residence, the probate laws of the new country will determine how your property is distributed at your death, so you'll need to draft a new will. If you own property in two countries at the time of your death, the legal issues get complicated. In addition to your lawyer in the United States, you may need a lawyer there as well. The U.S. embassy or consulate can provide you with a list of local English-speaking lawyers willing to assist U.S. citizens. Especially in local real estate matters, it is important to understand any contracts you are asked to sign. Be especially thorough in reviewing documents not in English.

✓ Check access to and coverage for health care

Depending on what country you are going to, health care may be excellent and affordable, or it may be extremely limited. Expect that the health care system will be different than in the United States—for better or worse. Medications may have different names, wait times to schedule appointments may be lengthy, and language barriers may make communicating with medical experts difficult.

On the other hand, in your new country the cost of care may be inexpensive even if you have to pay out of pocket. As a tourist in Finland, I dislocated a finger when I slipped while boarding a train in Helsinki. By the time the train arrived in Kuusamo, I knew I needed to see a doctor before setting out on a week-long backpacking journey. I was seen immediately at the small hospital by a doctor who had interned in the United States, spoke excellent English, and fixed my finger. There was much discussion in the billing office when it came time for me to check out. As I wasn't a citizen of a European Union country and didn't have a European health insurance card, the billing office wasn't sure how much to charge me. They seemed almost apologetic that I would have to pay about 100€ (just under $100 at the time) for the entire visit—X-ray, emergency room fee, doctor fee, splint, and medications. I could not have gotten better care and would have paid much more at home in Virginia.

Check any other health insurance policy you have to determine coverage for emergency, hospital, or general health care while you are abroad. If you receive Medicare or plan to, be aware: Medicare covers no medical costs outside the United States. Medicare supplement (Medigap) plans other than Plans A and B will cover 80 percent of medically necessary emergency care that you need within the first 60 days of your travel, with an annual $250 deductible and a lifetime cap of $50,000. Those Medigap policies won't give you protection after the first 60 days or for general health care.

You may want to investigate special travel health insurance that would cover you during an extended stay out of the country. When considering medical evacuation coverage, be sure you understand the coverage scope. Some policies will pay for transport only to the closest hospital, not to your choice of hospitals, in the United States. Some major health insurance companies also offer international or "expat" health insurance. As when purchasing any type of insurance, compare terms and prices among all available plans to get the coverage you need and can afford.

Depending on where you locate, if you become a legal resident you may be able to join the public health system or any private health system. Find out the options and requirements at the embassy before you leave.

✓ Prepare to leave

Before you get set to leave, you have a long list of details to take care of. The decisions you make may depend on how long you intend to stay abroad. Whether your plan is to stay for a year, permanently, or as long as it works out, you'll need to think about what happens to your home and stuff, how you will stay in touch, and what important documents to take with you.

Your House

If you are currently renting, you should check to see when the lease term is up, how far in advance you need to give notice that you are vacating, and whether you'd pay an early termination penalty. If you own your current residence, will you rent or sell it? Property management companies can help you find and screen tenants, collect rents, and do repairs or maintenance. They typically charge 7 to 10 percent of the monthly rent.

The sale of your home involves getting the house ready to sell, determining the sale price, working with a real estate agent or selling it yourself, negotiating the sale terms, and all of the other legal details that accompany a real estate transaction. If you sell your home for more than you originally paid for it (plus the amount of any major improvements), you may have to pay capital gains tax. If you have owned your home and used it as your main residence for two of the five years prior to the sale date, you can exclude $250,000 of any capital gains ($500,000 if you file a joint return with your spouse). If you decide first to rent your home while you are living abroad and then later decide to sell it, don't get tripped up by the two out of five years' requirement that you've used the home as your principal residence. For more information on the tax consequences, refer to IRS publication 523, Selling Your Home.

Personal Possessions

You'll need to decide what to do with all your possessions, from furniture to pots and pans, out-of-season clothing to sports equipment. Some options are to have a humongous yard sale, do a whole house auction, rent a storage locker, use a friend's garage, arrange for door-to-door moving and storage, and ship items to your new location. Shipping is the most expensive option so you'll want to carefully plan what you absolutely have to have in the new place. Refer to Chapter 3 for tips on how to downsize, sell, recycle, and dispose of personal items and documents. Make sure you have a place to keep each item listed on the Where I Put It Checklist in that chapter. It's a comprehensive list of things you need to do something with or get rid of. Be sure to note the new location of what's here and what's there!

Vehicles

Check with your state's department of motor vehicles about what you need to do if you are going to store your car for a long time. Do you need to renew registration or safety inspections before you leave? Is the place you are storing your car secure, and will someone periodically start it to keep the battery charged and drive it at least once a month to avoid flat spots on your tires? For long-term protection, keep your car under cover in a garage or enclosed storage unit.

Here are some additional long-term storage tips from Edmunds and Geeks on Cars:

- Wash and wax the car to protect the finish and make it less attractive to rodents.
- Change the oil and oil filter and flush and change the transmission, radiator, and brake fluids to avoid settling of grime.
- Top off the gas tank to prevent moisture from accumulating.
- Inflate tires to recommended pressure or ten pounds more, or use jack stands to avoid flat spots or dry-rot.
- Disconnect the negative battery cable to keep the battery from depleting or remove the battery and connect it to a trickle charger.
- Put steel wool in the exhaust pipe or cover it tightly with a plastic bag to prevent moisture accumulation.
- Put moth balls or dryer sheets inside the trunk, engine, and passenger compartments to deter rodents.
- Check with your insurance company about available options. You may be able to maintain some coverage but at a reduced rate. If someone else is going to be driving your car while you are gone, be sure to add that person to your insurance policy as an authorized driver.

Preventive Health Care

Get any recommended immunizations that may be required in your new location. You can check on any health issues you need to be aware of by going to the Centers for Disease Control Travelers' Health Center at wwwnc.cdc.gov/travel/destinations/list. Make copies of any prescriptions for medications. If you use a mail-order service, find out if your meds can be mailed to your new address. Also get prescriptions for your eyeglasses or contacts. You may want to take multiple pairs with you or leave an extra pair with a friend who could mail it to you in an emergency. Carry a list of all medications you take and transport prescription medications in the original containers. Bring along your immunization record and health history. Stock up on vitamins, over-the-counter medications, and medical supplies you rely on in case they are not readily available when you arrive.

Identification

Make several copies of your passport and keep them in different locations. Scan or take a photo of your passport and store it in the cloud or on your smartphone. Leave a copy with someone you trust and can get in touch with in an emergency.

Documentation

Use the checklists in this book to keep track of information you'll need to bring with you. Make copies, scans, or digital photos of your auto, health, and home insurance policies. Fill out the Credit and Debit Card Checklist in Chapter 8 and give a copy to a friend who can contact the companies if you should lose your wallet. Take along contact information for insurance agents, doctors, pharmacies, veterinarians, and any service providers you may need to get in touch with. Record the serial numbers of any cameras, computer equipment, or other electronics you are taking with you. Take the checklists of frequent flyer or other travel reward accounts, as well as all your passwords, PINs, and user IDs.

Staying Connected

E-mail, texts, Skype, and various apps make it easy to stay in touch with friends and family at home. Be sure to find out if your texts will go through and if your e-mail service is going to work where you locate, or get a web-based account and address that you can access wherever there's Internet service. And don't forget your regular mail. You can file a change of address with the U.S. Post Office. If you get a lot of junk mail and catalogs that you don't care to have follow you, you could have your mail forwarded to a friend, who would discard what you don't want and send on any important mail to you. Once you are settled, you then can selectively notify those businesses or people you want to hear from of your new mailing address. You can try using the Direct Marketing Association's "do not mail" service at dmachoice.org to cut down on junk mail, but it can take a very long time to get off some lists! Cancel or forward any magazine subscriptions.

Retiring Abroad Action Checklists

The following Action Checklists are in Chapter 7:

- ❏ Choosing My Destination
- ❏ Residency Requirements
- ❏ Pre-departure Preparation

Choosing My Destination

Clarify your priorities for where you want to live outside of the United States. As you think through each item, be realistic about your desires and your resources. Select your level of preference for these items. You may like a variety of the options, but to give you the clearest picture of your priorities, mark "most prefer" for those items that are your highest priorities. Your spouse or others who would move with you should also fill out this worksheet. Then compare and negotiate any differences.

	Most Prefer	Neutral	Least Prefer
Relationships			
Near people I know			
Where I can make new friends			
With those who speak English			
With those who speak a language other than English			
Other:			
Location			
Close to current location			
Accessible to current location			
Four seasons of weather			
Warm weather			
Cold weather			
Urban			
Rural			
Mountains			
Ocean			
Lake, river, or pond			
Africa			
Asia			
Australia/New Zealand			
Canada			
Europe			
Middle America			
Middle East			
South America			
United Kingdom			
Other:			

	Most Prefer	Neutral	Least Prefer
Community and Culture			
Walk or easily get to shops and services			
Slower pace of life			
Secure community			
Food I like			
Outdoor activities			
Cultural activities			
Other activities I enjoy			
Resources			
Cost of living is lower than now			
Cost of living is higher than now			
Cost of living is same as now			
Access to hospital			
Access to health care			
Access to public transportation			
Access to international airport			

Residency Requirements

The country I want to retire to has the following residency requirements:

Embassy: _____

Contact person: _____

Address: _____

_____

Telephone: _____ E-mail: _____

Website: _____

Residency permit: ❑ Yes   ❑ No

Requirements:_____

_____

_____

_____

Location to apply: _____

Deadline to apply: _____

Apply before departure: ❑ Yes   ❑ No

Retirement visa: ❑ Yes   ❑ No

Requirements: _____

_____

_____

_____

Location to apply:

_____

Deadline to apply:

_____

Apply before departure: ❑ Yes   ❑ No

Required immunizations:

_____

Health examination:	❏ Yes	❏ No
Criminal background check:	❏ Yes	❏ No
Proof of income:	❏ Yes	❏ No
Income documentation:	❏ Yes	❏ No
Property ownership restrictions:	❏ Yes	❏ No

Pre-departure Preparation

I have made the following preparations for my departure:

Rental Property

Lease term: _____

Notice to vacate	❑ Yes	❑ No
Security deposit received	❑ Yes	❑ No

Home Ownership

Engage property management company	❑ Yes	❑ No
Engage real estate agent	❑ Yes	❑ No
Sale by owner	❑ Yes	❑ No
Hire lawyer	❑ Yes	❑ No
Consult tax professional	❑ Yes	❑ No

Personal Possessions

Yard sale	❑ Yes	❑ No
Auction	❑ Yes	❑ No
Give to family/friends	❑ Yes	❑ No
Donate to charity	❑ Yes	❑ No
Store with family/friends	❑ Yes	❑ No
Sclf-storage unit	❑ Yes	❑ No
Warehouse storage	❑ Yes	❑ No
Ship to new location	❑ Yes	❑ No
Insurance for items in storage	❑ Yes	❑ No

Vehicles

Sell	❑ Yes	❑ No
Loan to family/friends	❑ Yes	❑ No
Store	❑ Yes	❑ No
Registration/inspection	❑ Yes	❑ No
Insurance	❑ Yes	❑ No

Health

Prescriptions for medications	❑ Yes	❑ No
Prescriptions for glasses/contacts	❑ Yes	❑ No
Personal medication record	❑ Yes	❑ No
Health history	❑ Yes	❑ No
Immunization record	❑ Yes	❑ No
Health insurance	❑ Yes	❑ No

Financial

Social Security	❑ Yes	❑ No
Direct deposit of income	❑ Yes	❑ No
Auto-payment of bills	❑ Yes	❑ No
U.S. bank account	❑ Yes	❑ No
Foreign bank account	❑ Yes	❑ No
U.S. income taxes	❑ Yes	❑ No

Passport

Expiration date: _____

Extra copies	❑ Yes	❑ No

Documents

Vehicle insurance	❑ Yes	❑ No
Home insurance	❑ Yes	❑ No
Personal property insurance	❑ Yes	❑ No
Important contacts	❑ Yes	❑ No
International driver's license	❑ Yes	❑ No
Credit card list	❑ Yes	❑ No
Bank account information	❑ Yes	❑ No
Digital assets	❑ Yes	❑ No
Equipment serial numbers	❑ Yes	❑ No
Internet access	❑ Yes	❑ No
Income tax return	❑ Yes	❑ No

CHAPTER 8

TAKE CONTROL OF FINANCIAL MATTERS

Finances are, of course, a critical component to getting the most of your retirement, so you'll want to pay plenty of attention to your nest egg, income, and budget. Whether you actively follow the stock market, use online trading, rely on a financial adviser, or keep your nest egg in bank savings accounts, mutual funds, or certificates of deposit, you most likely have two basic goals: to have enough money throughout retirement to cover your expenses comfortably, and to have enough left over to take care of your loved ones.

Entering this new financial phase of your life, consider simplifying your financial life. I entered retirement with five separate bank accounts in three different banks. At the time I opened each, it made sense to have different accounts for different purposes. But no longer! Consolidating into fewer accounts made things so much easier to manage and avoided potential fees.

However and wherever you bank and have investments, you'll want to record in one place all your account numbers, PINs, and so on, both for you and for your family, should something happen to you. It's also essential that you understand the different ways you can own your bank accounts, so I've included a primer on that.

You can use the checklists as a convenient place to record information about the bank accounts you have, securities you own, where you have investment accounts, and how you can contact your bank, credit union, and credit card companies. This chapter also briefly covers some of the ways you can invest your money, including stocks, bonds, and mutual funds. Be sure to do your own homework on your financial strategy and consult with your financial professional before making any decisions. Don't have a financial professional? Check out chapter 4 on building your financial team.

One checklist I've found crucial to getting my financial life in order: Credit and Debit Cards. For each credit card, list the account information as well as whether you have signed up to have the monthly payment automatically deducted from a bank account (and which bank account, if you have more than one).

Three billion dollars is taken from Americans over age 65 every year through financial exploitation. Whether it is the scamming telemarketer or a scheming relative, you could be at risk of having your hard-earned retirement savings taken from you. In this chapter, you'll find the signs of scams, investment fraud, and possible financial exploitation to help you keep safe.

My To-Do Checklist

Done   **Need to Do**

❏   ❏   Organize information about how you bank

❏   ❏   Review how financial accounts are titled

❏   ❏   Check to make sure your savings bonds are still a sound investment

❏   ❏   Keep original documents that are valuable or irreplaceable in a safe deposit box

❏   ❏   Make sure your investments match your investment objectives

❏   ❏   Pay attention to investment fees

❏   ❏   Document the terms of any personal loans

❏   ❏   List credit and debit cards

❏   ❏   Recognize the signs of scams and financial exploitation

✓   Organize information about how you bank

Banks used to be pretty plain vanilla. They offered checking and savings accounts, lent money to buy homes and cars, and maybe gave you a toaster when you opened a new account. Now you probably take advantage of a proliferation of services and have multiple types of accounts. In addition to a checking account and a savings account, you might have a certificate of deposit or money market account; carry a credit card or debit card with a PIN (personal identification number); use a financial adviser housed in the bank; rely on the automatic teller machine (ATM) to get cash and transfer funds between accounts; and pay your bills online. You may do your banking completely online, never stepping into a brick-and-mortar location.

Banks offer a wide range of services. They handle savings and checking accounts and make short- and long-term loans for personal and business use. Many also provide estate and investment services. To help you figure out how best to choose your bank—or banks—and manage your accounts, here's a quick primer.

Checking accounts are considered *demand deposits*. In other words, as the depositor, you have the right to demand, or to withdraw, any or all of your funds at any time during regular banking hours. Many financial institutions now offer interest-bearing checking accounts, along with traditional fee-based checking plans. Most banks charge stiff fees for each overdrawn check. They may offer overdraft protection by linking your checking account to your savings account, although some institutions will charge a fee for overdraft protection. Be sure you understand what fees your bank will collect for overdraft protection or overdrawn checks.

Savings accounts are another type of demand deposit. Savings accounts pay you interest, which is noted, along with deposits and withdrawals, on a statement that is mailed periodically (generally monthly or quarterly) or is available online. Some savings accounts require that you keep a minimum amount on deposit to earn interest. Monthly service fees that some banks charge if you don't keep that minimum balance may eat up the small amount of interest earned, so pay close attention to the fees that show up on your statement. Shop around for another bank with lower fees and let the bank know that you switched because of the fees charged.

Money market savings accounts pay a higher rate of interest than a standard savings account but may require you to maintain a certain minimum balance in your account.

Certificates of deposit (CDs) are *time deposits*. Customers who use certificates of deposit agree to leave their money in the bank for a certain period, for example, two years. During that time, you may not withdraw those funds without incurring significant interest penalties. In return for having this long-term use of your money, banks generally pay a higher rate of interest than they do for savings accounts.

Factors that affect the interest you can earn on your deposit accounts include your bank's method of compounding interest and of crediting the funds you put in the account and debiting the money you withdraw. Banks can compound interest in a variety of ways, so it pays to compare the details before opening a savings account or buying a CD. Interest can be compounded daily, monthly, quarterly, semi-annually, or annually. The more often it's compounded, the more your savings earn. For that reason, interest compounded daily can grow your savings faster than interest that is compounded monthly or annually. Whether you've invested in a certificate of deposit or a regular savings account, ask your bank how often it compounds interest. Banks are required to disclose the frequency with which interest is compounded and credited, according to the Federal Reserve Board. (The reverse of this is that with debts, the more frequently the bank compounds interest on your loan, the more you will pay on your debt.)

Most banks insure their deposits through the Federal Deposit Insurance Corporation (FDIC). This governmental agency was established to protect people from losing their deposited assets if a bank fails. Up to $250,000 in most types of accounts is insured. Be sure that your bank is insured by the FDIC and check the coverage limits on your accounts. Use the FDIC's EDIE (Electronic Deposit Insurance Estimator) calculator at fdic.gov/edie/index.html.

The FDIC insurance covers deposit accounts, including checking and savings accounts, money market deposit accounts, certificates of deposit, and IRA accounts. It does not insure any other type of investment product you might purchase through your bank, such as mutual funds. If the total amount of your deposits exceeds the maximum amount of deposit insurance, you can establish accounts in several name combinations (for example, husband alone, husband and wife, wife alone, or husband and child) or, if necessary, in several banks.

Credit unions operate very much like banks, although they are organized differently from banking institutions. Typically you need to be a member of some identified group to have an account, but in turn, you become a part owner of the credit union, along with all the other depositors. Credit unions offer services that encourage you to save and often provide their members loans at lower rates than banks. They offer checking and savings accounts (although they may be called share or draft accounts), credit cards, and online banking.

Federally chartered credit unions are regulated by the National Credit Union Administration. Check to make sure your credit union account is insured by the National Credit Union Share Insurance Fund (NCUSIF). Like the FDIC, the NCUSIF insures credit union accounts up to $250,000. You can find or check out a credit union at ncua.gov/DataApps /ResearchCU/Pages/default.aspx.

With today's multiple ways to do banking, we can accumulate a sometimes bewildering collection of banking cards, personal identification numbers (PIN), passwords, and user names. These are the keys that you use to do your banking without ever entering a bank: getting cash from an ATM, transferring funds, and paying bills via online banking.

But beware: They are also the very valuable keys that others can use to raid your accounts. You need to be extraordinarily careful about lending your ATM card, keeping your PIN private, and creating your passwords. For example, don't record your PIN on a piece of paper that you carry next to your debit card. Make sure that no one is looking over your shoulder when you enter your PIN at an ATM. Change your passwords frequently and avoid something that would be obvious to a hacker, such as your birth date, mother's maiden name, or child's name. Identity thieves can easily find this information about you on online social network, school alumni, or genealogical sites. Using numbers, symbols, and a mix of uppercase and lowercase letters can help you build stronger passwords. For tips on creating safe passwords and more, see AARP's *Protecting Yourself Online for Dummies* e-book at AARP.org/ProtectingYourselfOnline.

✓ Review how financial accounts are titled

How you own various bank and other financial accounts can make a big difference in who can withdraw money from your accounts and who will be entitled to the money on deposit when you die. Keep in mind these differences if you are planning on opening any new accounts. Among the possible ways you can own financial accounts are these:

- **Individually**: Only you can deposit or withdraw money from this type of account. Money retained in an individual account will be distributed according to the terms of your will, or if you do not have a will, according to state law.

- **Agency or convenience account**: You and any co-signer can access money in this type of bank account, but the money in the account does not belong to the co-signer on your death. This is the type of account most people should use if they want a family member to have access to a checking account to help pay bills when they are out of town or in the hospital. Money remaining in this account will be distributed according to the terms of your will, or if you do not have a will, according to state law.

- **Joint with right of survivorship**: As soon as you create a joint account with right of survivorship, all money in the account belongs to you and the co-owner and on your death automatically goes to the surviving co-owner. Adding a son, daughter, or any other person to your account as joint owner is the same as making a gift of all money now on deposit and any future deposits. The co-owner can write checks for any purpose and could, in fact, withdraw it to zero and head for Australia. For Medicaid purposes, adding a joint owner (other than your spouse) to an account is considered a transfer for less than fair market value and could delay your eligibility for Medicaid.

- **Pay on death (POD)**: You can spend the money, change the beneficiary, or close the account at any time. The person you name as beneficiary on this type of account automatically receives the balance in the account on your death but has no right or authority to access the account until then. Some people use POD accounts to set aside money to pay funeral expenses.

✓ Check to make sure your savings bonds are still a sound investment

Savings bonds have long been an easy and secure way to save, but you need to pay attention to whether any bonds you may have stashed away are still a good investment. Depending on what type of savings bonds you have purchased and their maturity date, they may still be earning interest or just sitting at maturity and no longer growing in value. There is more than $15 billion in unredeemed bonds. The US Treasury Department does not send out notices when bonds have reached maturity and stopped earning interest, but it is easy to find out. You can use the Treasury Hunt tool on the Web at savingsbonds.gov/indiv/tools/tools_treasuryhunt.htm to find out how much each bond is worth today. The Treasury Hunt tool lists bonds issued after 1974 that have reached final maturity. This site will also tell you how to file claims for lost, stolen, destroyed, or undelivered bonds. While I was shredding some old papers, I stumbled across a $100 saving bond that was 15 years old. It was still earning interest, but I decided to cash it in just so I wouldn't lose it again.

You may want to consider moving your mature savings bonds to a Treasury Direct account where the proceeds will be deposited to a Certificate of Indebtedness. Find out more about how this works at Smart Exchange, treasurydirect.gov/indiv/research/indepth/smartexchangeinfo.htm.

✓ Keep original documents that are valuable or irreplaceable in a safe deposit box

Safe deposit boxes provide a place for storing valuables and documents at a small cost. Safe deposit boxes protect your stocks, bonds, gold, silver, and other valuables from both burglary and fire damage. You may want to store in your safe deposit box important papers such as your marriage license, deeds to your real estate, car titles, and insurance policies. Be sure to record what is in your safe deposit box in the Where I Put It Checklist in chapter 3 and make sure a trusted family member knows where the boxes and keys are located.

Most banks rent safe deposit boxes for a yearly fee or provide them as a free service or at a discounted cost depending on the type of checking or savings accounts you have. Safe deposit boxes come with a key. When you want to store items or access items, you must use both your key and a bank key simultaneously. Neither key alone will open the box for safety precautions. For further protection, you must also provide your signature and identification each time you seek access to the box. Your signature will be compared to the signature that you placed on file when you first rented the box.

To protect you and the property in your box, banks restrict who can get into your box, as well as when and how they can do so. These security protections may hinder your family's need to have easy access, so you won't want to keep your will and advance directives in it.

A safe deposit box, like a bank account, may be owned in your name only or jointly. Joint ownership gives someone else access to your box should you need to get something out of the box when you can't—say you are sick or out of town. In addition, joint ownership allows the co-owner access to the box after your death.

While joint owners of a safe deposit box have equal access to the box, access does not mean that they own the contents of the box. Putting your diamond ring into a safe deposit box does not change the ring's owner or make a gift of the ring to the joint owner of the box. If you have any questions about the rights of a co-owner to your box, check with your bank or your lawyer.

✓ Make sure your investments match your investment objectives

Now that you have come to that fork in the road called retirement, you should take a good look at your investment portfolio and your objectives. Do they match? I know that my risk tolerance has changed now that I'm not getting a steady paycheck and am relying on my investments for everyday expenses. Many of us saw what happened to our nest eggs when the stock market took a dive in 2008. I've been able to recover somewhat, but I realize that I've got to invest more conservatively because I have fewer years to recover from any future market plunges. As soon as I had a target retirement date, the first person I contacted was my financial adviser to go over any necessary changes in my investment strategy. I'm still thinking long term because I could have two or three decades to invest.

Here's some basic information about investment options. Your financial adviser can give you much more detail about your options and whether you are adequately diversified.

Stocks

When you own a stock, you own part of a company. Companies sell these pieces of ownership, known as shares, to raise money to finance their business. When you buy a stock, you are basically betting that the company will grow. As the company does well, your stock generally increases in value. You can earn money on your investment when either the price of the stock rises or the company shares profits by paying a dividend. If the company does poorly, you can lose some or all of the money you paid for the share.

More than 3,000 companies that you can invest in are listed on the New York Stock Exchange. Stocks are categorized in multiple ways: by industry (auto, biotechnology); market sector (utilities, health care); or geography (United States, Asia). They can also be categorized by size, as in large-capitalization, or large-cap (generally companies worth more than $5 billion), mid-cap ($1 to $5 billion), or small-cap ($250 million to $1 billion). Another way to group stocks is based on financial experts' perception of the company's basic financial health and historical performance. These categories include growth stocks, value stocks, or income stocks. Knowing how a particular company's stocks are categorized helps you diversify your investments in different types of companies. Diversification reduces your risk of losing money.

Bonds

When you buy a bond, you loan money to a company or government entity. The entity commits to paying you interest at a fixed rate for the life of the loan and to return to you the value of the loan by a certain date, called the maturity date. When you invest in a bond, you are taking the risk that the company or entity may not be able to pay the interest or the principal. You also run the risk that if interest rates rise and you need to sell the bond, your bond may lose value. This is because other investors can buy higher rate bonds, so you have to sell yours at a lower price to attract a buyer. If you buy a *callable* bond, the company has the right to pay you back before the maturity date. This is normally done when the company can borrow at a cheaper rate.

Bonds issued by the federal government are the safest. Treasury bills, notes, and bonds are available with maturities ranging from one to thirty years. They can be easily sold, but like all bonds their values rise and fall as interest rates change. You pay no federal income tax on the interest you earn.

State and local governments also issue municipal bonds to pay for things like roads, schools, and public safety. You pay no federal income tax on the interest, and you may not have to pay state taxes if you live in the area where the bond is issued. Because of this tax advantage, the interest rates on governmental or municipal bonds are lower than on other types of bonds.

Mutual Funds

When you buy shares of a mutual fund, you own a bit of various stocks, bonds, or other types of investments in the fund. Buying shares of a mutual fund helps you diversify because you are spreading the risk of losing your money among many different investments. Investments within a mutual fund are chosen by a professional manager based on the fund's investment objectives. The fund's objectives, set out in a public document called a prospectus, might be to own growth stock or government bonds, or invest in a particular industry, such as pharmaceuticals.

More than 15,000 mutual funds are available, so sorting out what each invests in is challenging. These are some of the common types of mutual funds:

- Stock funds that invest in the stocks of many companies
- Bond funds that are a collection of bonds purchased with pooled money from many investors
- Money market funds that include short-term, low-risk loans

- Balanced funds that include a mix of stocks and bonds
- Life cycle funds, or target retirement date funds, that are designed to increase the percentage of bonds in relation to stocks as the investor gets closer to retirement age

Money market accounts and money market funds have similar names but significant differences. A *money market account* is a type of savings account you have at a financial institution. Typically the financial institution will pay a higher rate of interest than it pays on regular savings accounts. You are able to make withdrawals at any time and can access the funds by withdrawing them at an ATM or by writing a check. As with other accounts in FDIC-insured banks, your money would be insured up to $250,000. You may have to maintain a minimum amount to avoid fees and be restricted on how many withdrawals you can make in a month. A *money market fund*, on the other hand, is a type of mutual fund that is required by law to invest in low-risk, short-term debt. These funds are not insured.

Index funds or exchange traded funds (ETF) are similar investment funds to mutual funds. They try to replicate the performance of an index, such as the Standard & Poor's 500 index, by investing in all the securities in that index. This is called passive management, which results in lower management fees than mutual funds.

What All This Means

If you are fortunate enough to have different types of investments, whether you hold them separately or they are included within retirement accounts, you need to strategically think about which funds you are going to tap into first. Most financial advisers recommend that retirees leave their tax-exempt assets until other accounts have been used. By leaving tax-exempt assets until the end, those funds can continue to grow without the added burden of paying taxes on the withdrawals. Expert advice for good tax planning is essential, whatever your personal circumstances.

While much investing can be done online, keeping track of your investments still involves lots of paper. You can accumulate a small mountain of paper associated with prospectuses, proxy notices, annual reports, and monthly, quarterly, and annual statements. I keep a big three-inch binder for my brokerage statements. To save on space I shred the monthly statements when I get my quarterly statement, and then shred the quarterly statements when the annual summary comes in. Another way to save on paper is to request electronic statements and notices and save them to a digital folder. By organizing your investment information, you'll make your retirement life run more smoothly, simplify preparing tax returns, and lessen the work that your family will have to do if they need to help you manage your investments.

✓ Pay attention to investment fees

With any type of investment, you need to not only carefully match the fund's objectives with your own investment objectives, but you also need to pay attention to the fund's fees. High fees or expense ratios can reduce your earnings. Even a small percentage difference in the fees among funds can add up to a big difference in the dollars you can make. Here's how it works.

Even seemingly small differences in expenses—say, half a percentage point a year—can make a big difference in how much wealth you accumulate over time. Here's an example from the Investor Protection Trust: Suppose you have $10,000 to invest for retirement, which is 30 years away. You can buy Mutual Fund ABC, which invests in stocks of big US companies, or Mutual Fund XYZ, which does the same. The only difference is that fund ABC charges annual expenses of 1.5 percent per year, and fund XYZ charges 0.5 percent per year. Before expenses, the stocks in both funds return, on average, 10 percent per year. The impact of fees, though, can be dramatic. After ten years, ABC is worth $22,600, while XYZ is worth $24,700. At the end of 20 years, the difference is even more dramatic: ABC is worth $51,100, and XYZ has grown to $61,400. At retirement in 30 years, ABC has grown to $115,500, and XYZ has grown to $152,203—a $37,000 difference! Over 30 years, that 1 percent more in expenses resulted in 24 percent less value.

Most investors don't know or understand how much they are paying in fees that are associated with all the different investment options. It's even hard for employers setting up 401(k) plan options to decipher the costs. The US Labor Department has been working since 2012 to make 401(k) fee disclosures more transparent, but more work needs to be done. According to Forbes, even when investors can find the fees buried in the fine print, they don't know if they are paying too much. How much should you reasonably expect to pay in fees? In 2014, Forbes noted that the average stock fund in a 401(k) took 0.72 percent annually, while bond funds took 0.52 percent. Index funds have lower costs and typically charge less than 0.30 percent.

Here are some of the fees typically associated with common investments. Some fees are based on actions you take; others are charged on an ongoing basis.

- Mutual funds charge their operating expenses as an **expense ratio** that is deducted from the investment return. For example, if a fund has a 0.90 percent expense ratio, for every $1,000 invested, $9 goes toward expenses. If the $1,000 has a 1 percent return, 9 cents goes toward expenses, and the investor gets 91 cents, rather than $1.

- **Investment advisory fees** are typically a percentage of the amount of money being managed. If the investment adviser charges 1 percent for every $100,000 invested, the investor pays $1,000 year in fees. The fees are debited from the account monthly or quarterly. Most advisers charge more than 1 percent, with smaller accounts being charged a higher percent, perhaps as high as 1.75 percent.

- Brokerage firms typically charge **transaction fees** of $10 to $50 per trade each time an investor places an order to buy or sell mutual funds or stocks. A $50 fee on a $5,000 trade results in a 1 percent fee while that same fee on a $50,000 trade is only 0.10 percent.

- **Sales charges**, also called **purchase fees** or a **front end load**, are commissions charged at the time an investor buys mutual fund shares. For example, if you have a 5 percent sales charge when you buy a $10 share, your share is worth $9.50 because 50 cents is charged up front. Another way to calculate the sales charge is when you buy a $10 share, the purchase price is $10.50. Sales charges range from 3 to 5 percent.

- **Redemption fee** or **back end load** is the fee you pay when you sell certain mutual funds. To discourage trading, the percentage of this surrender fee typically decreases the longer you hold on to the fund. Funds with back lend loads may be 5 percent if you sell within the first year, 3 percent if you sell in the second year, and phase out over five to six years. Mutual fund redemption fees of usually 2 percent typically disappear if you hold for a certain period—generally 60 days to a year.

- An **annual account fee** of $25 to $50 is charged on some brokerage accounts or mutual funds to cover accounting and reporting fees, or just to maintain your account, especially if your account falls below some stated amount. IRAs may charge a custodian fee of $10 to $50 a year to cover the cost of reporting to the Internal Revenue Service.

- Some financial advisers or financial services companies are paid a **12b-1 fee**, capped at 1 percent of the amount you've invested, for marketing expenses of mutual funds. Even so-called no-load funds (those with no front end or back end loads) can levy 12b-1 fees to cover marketing costs up to 0.25 percent a year.

- **Management fees** are taken from the amount invested to pay the mutual fund's portfolio manager. In total, these fees typically run from 0.5 percent to 2 percent a year. (The 12b-1 fees are part of the overall management fees.)

The list could go on, but this is just a sampling of some of the fees that erode your retirement savings. Take the time to investigate the fees you are paying now, wherever your money is invested. You can find a mutual fund's expense ratio, or total annual fund operating expenses, in the fund's prospectus or on the fund's website. This will tell you the percentage of the fund's total assets that goes toward paying its recurring fees every year.

All 401(k) plans carry fees and expenses that have a direct impact on your investment return. It can be hard to calculate what fees are costing you because you don't pay them directly. Rather, they are subtracted before your return is reported. Check your account statement documents to find the amount of money you actually paid for investment expenses. In addition, most 401(k) fees are explained in your summary plan document (SPD). You can also ask your human resources or personnel department for an explanation.

Calculators to help you determine how fees impact your savings can be found at 40lkfee.com, http://apps.finra.org/fundanalyzer/1/fa.aspx, and bankrate.com/calculators /retirement/mutual-funds-fees-calculator.aspx. The US Department of Labor has an online publication, *A Look at 401(k) Plan Fees for Employees*, at dol.gov/ebsa/publications/401k _employee.html.

One brighter note: You may be able to deduct some fees for financial planning and investment management on your income taxes. You can get an itemized deduction if these fees exceed 2 percent of your adjusted gross income (AGI). For example, if your AGI is $100,000, you can deduct the amount you pay for investment management fees over $2,000. Sorry, you cannot deduct mutual fund expense rations.

✓ Document the terms of any personal debts or loans

Have you borrowed money from a relative, friend, or associate? Does someone owe you money? If so, write it down on the Personal Debts and Loans Checklist.

All personal loans should be in writing so both you and your borrower know the terms for paying back the money. If you intend to forgive any debts at your death, be sure to put your intentions in writing in your will. Forgiving a loan becomes a gift, which can have consequences in settling your estate, determining your taxes, and being eligible for Medicaid.

✓ List credit and debit cards

It's important that you have a list of all your credit and debit card accounts. You need to have this list readily available now in case you need to report that a card has been lost or stolen. Later, your family needs this information so they will know what companies to contact after your death to close your accounts. The credit card companies, as well as the credit reporting bureaus, need to be told to flag the account with a note that the owner is deceased. Sad as it may sound, identity thieves are known to read obituaries to seek potential victims. Scammers will try to use any still-open credit card accounts of a dead person as long as they can get away with their thievery.

Credit card debt is an enormous drag on your retirement security. You should be working hard to pay off your credit cards, targeting first the one with the highest interest rate.

✓ Recognize the signs of scams and financial exploitation

Every day, hundreds of people—folks just like you and me, no matter how smart, savvy, and accomplished—fall for scams. I know this all too well. My husband got a call one day from someone pretending to be our daughter, claiming to need $3,000 to get out of jail. With a well-rehearsed script and fancy acting, she convinced my husband to wire the money. Needless to say, our daughter was just fine and the money was forever gone.

Scammers have dozens of tricks they use to con people out of their money. Most pitches have been around for decades, such as "Congratulations, you have won . . ." promising a fantastic sum of money if you'll just pay a fee to claim your winnings. Realistic-looking websites for fake charities raising money for disaster relief, starving children, and homeless dogs tug at heartstrings as they steal money. It's well known that consumers who fall for a scam or give to a fake website are bound to be contacted again and again.

You can be sure that my husband now is super alert and cautious about any questionable telephone call or e-mail because I've made sure he knows about scammers' tactics. Unfortunately, too many people don't know that they've been scammed—otherwise the tricks wouldn't be so successful time and time again. You need to watch for the signs of scams, such as many calls from telemarketers, sweepstakes mail, or boxes of trinkets, greeting cards, or small prizes that can be part of a money-stealing gimmick. Learn more about avoiding scams and fraud at aarp.org/fraudwatchnetwork.

If you or someone you know has been victimized by a scammer, you can report it to one of several options: your local law enforcement, your state attorney general's office (at naag.org, click on the Attorneys General tab and then the photograph of your state's attorney general to get information on how to report), the Federal Trade Commission (ftc.gov/complaint), or the Consumer Financial Protection Bureau (cfpb.gov/complaint). To report suspected elder abuse or financial exploitation, contact your local Adult Protective Services (APS). The elder care locator at eldercare.gov or 1-800-677-1116 can give you the local APS number to call. If a possible scam victim is in a skilled nursing facility, contact the long-term care ombudsman. You can find the number to call at ltcombudsman.org.

Scammers' favorite weapons are the telephone, e-mail, social media, or mail, pretending to be their prey's best friend. On the other hand, people who exploit others most likely actually are the victim's friend or even a family member. These exploiters isolate their potential victims by cutting them off from their usual social network, frequently by saying they can be trusted more or love them more than others. To be successful, exploiters need to do two things: create a false sense of trust and do it in secret. By cultivating trust, they are able to convince their victim that they should be given access to the victim's money or property, use his or her ATM card, or be added to bank accounts, be deeded property, or be named in a will. They have to try to hide what they are doing from others—including the victim—or set up smoke screens of deception so what they are doing won't be discovered. Use the Signs of Scams and Financial Exploitation Checklist to watch for these red flags.

In addition to scams, older people are particularly targeted for investment schemes. They have retirement money to invest and the schemers know that. A shockingly large number of older Americans are already victims of financial swindles and millions more are in danger of being exploited. The Securities and Exchange Commission warns that the Internet is a common tool used by fraudsters. They can easily and cheaply reach millions of people with messages that look real and credible. A website, online message, or "spam" e-mails can reach large numbers with minimum effort. Many online investment newsletters are credible, but some newsletter writers claim to be independent but stand to profit from convincing you to buy the investments they promote. Others use online messages to drum up interest in a stock with false or misleading statements about the value of the shares. Once the price is pumped up, they dump their shares, the price falls, and you lose. Think twice and do extra research before you invest in any opportunity you find online.

The Financial Industry Regulator Authority (FINRA) offers the following red flags so you can stay on guard and avoid becoming drawn into an investment scam.

- **Guarantees**: Be suspect of anyone who guarantees that an investment will perform a certain way. All investments carry some degree of risk.
- **Unregistered offerings**: Many investment scams involve unlicensed individuals selling investment products that have not been registered with the Securities and

Exchange Commission. These so-called private placements could include common stocks, limited partnerships, bonds, notes, hedge funds, oil or gas deals, or fictitious instruments, such as prime bank investments. Private placements can be very risky because they are not subject to some of the laws and regulations that are designed to protect investors and may be difficult, if not virtually impossible to sell. Because unregistered investments are less regulated, fraudsters may use them to conduct investment scams.

- **Overly consistent returns**: Any investment that consistently goes up month after month—or that provides remarkably steady returns regardless of market conditions—should raise suspicions, especially during turbulent times. Even the most stable investments can experience hiccups once in a while.

- **Complex strategies**: Avoid anyone who credits a highly complex investing technique for unusual success. If you don't understand how the investment is supported to make money, don't just chalk it up to your naivety or stupidity. Legitimate professionals should be able to explain clearly what they are doing. It is critical that you fully understand any investment you're seriously considering—including what it is, what the risks are, and how the investment makes money.

- **Missing documentation**: If someone tries to sell you a security with no documentation—that is, no prospectus in the case of a stock or mutual fund, and no offering circular in the case of a bond—he or she may be selling unregistered securities. The same is true of stocks without stock symbols.

- **Account discrepancies**: Unauthorized trades, missing funds, or other problems with your account statements could be the result of a genuine error—or they could indicate churning or fraud. Keep an eye on your account statements to make sure account activity is consistent with your instructions, and be sure you know who holds your assets. For instance, is the investment adviser also the custodian of your assets? Or is there an independent third-party custodian? It can be easier for fraud to occur if an adviser is also the custodian of the assets and keeper of the accounts.

- **Pushy salesperson**: No reputable investment professional should push you to make an immediate decision about an investment or tell you that you've got to "act now." If someone pressures you to decide on a stock sale or purchase, steer clear. This type of pressuring is always inappropriate.

Your state securities regulator should be the first place you call before you turn over money to any broker or investment adviser. Go to nasaa.org to get the website for your state's regulator. There you can access extensive employment, disciplinary, and registration information about advisers who are appropriately licensed to sell investments. All securities that have been registered with the Securities and Exchange Commission are searchable on EDGAR at sec.gov/edgar/searchedgar/webusers.htm. (Trivia answer: EDGAR stands for Electronic Data Gathering and Retrieval!)

Financial Action Checklists

The following Action Checklists are in this chapter:

- ❏ Checking Accounts
- ❏ Savings Accounts
- ❏ Certificates of Deposit
- ❏ Credit Unions
- ❏ Savings Bonds
- ❏ Safe Deposit Boxes
- ❏ Stocks and Bonds
- ❏ Treasury Bills and Notes
- ❏ Municipal Bonds
- ❏ Mutual Funds
- ❏ Money Market Funds
- ❏ Personal Debts and Loans
- ❏ Credit and Debit Cards
- ❏ Signs of Scams and Financial Exploitation

Checking Accounts

I have the following checking accounts:

Name of institution: _____

Phone: _____ Fax: _____

Address: _____

_____

Website: _____

Account #: _____

ATM PIN #: _____

Online banking user ID: _____

Online banking password: _____

Name of institution: _____

Phone: _____ Fax: _____

Address: _____

_____

Website: _____

Account #: _____

ATM PIN #: _____

Online banking user ID: _____

Online banking password: _____

Name of institution: _____

Phone: _____ Fax: _____

Address: _____

_____

Website: _____

Account #: _____

ATM PIN #: _____

Online banking user ID: _____

Online banking password: _____

Name of institution: _____

Phone: _____ Fax: _____

Address: _____

_____

Website: _____

Account #: _____

ATM PIN #: _____

Online banking user ID: _____

Online banking password: _____

Name of institution: _____

Phone: _____ Fax: _____

Address: _____

_____

Website: _____

Account #: _____

ATM PIN #: _____

Online banking user ID: _____

Online banking password: _____

Savings Accounts

I have the following savings accounts:

Name of institution: _____

Account #: _____

Phone: _____ Fax: _____

Address: _____

_____

Website: _____

Online banking user ID: _____

Online banking password: _____

Name of institution: _____

Account #: _____

Phone: _____ Fax: _____

Address: _____

_____

Website: _____

Online banking user ID: _____

Online banking password: _____

Name of institution: _____

Account #: _____

Phone: _____ Fax: _____

Address: _____

_____

Website: _____

Online banking user ID: _____

Online banking password: _____

Certificates of Deposit

I have the following certificates of deposit (CDs):

Name of institution: _____

Account #: _____

Maturity date: _____

Phone: _____ Fax: _____

Address: _____

_____

E-mail: _____ Website: _____

Online banking user ID: _____

Online banking password: _____

Name of institution: _____

Account #: _____

Maturity date: _____

Phone: _____ Fax: _____

Address: _____

_____

E-mail: _____ Website: _____

Online banking user ID: _____

Online banking password: _____

Name of institution: _____

Account #: _____

Maturity date: _____

Phone: _____ Fax: _____

Address: _____

_____

E-mail: _____ Website: _____

Online banking user ID: _____

Online banking password: _____

Name of institution: _____

Account #: _____

Maturity date: _____

Phone: _____ Fax: _____

Address: _____

_____

E-mail: _____ Website: _____

Online banking user ID: _____

Online banking password: _____

Credit Unions

I have the following credit union accounts:

Name of institution: _____

Phone: _____ Fax: _____

Address: _____

_____

E-mail: _____ Website: _____

Account #: _____

ATM PIN #: _____

Online account user ID: _____

Online account password: _____

Name of institution: _____

Phone: _____ Fax: _____

Address: _____

_____

E-mail: _____ Website: _____

Account #: _____

ATM PIN #: _____

Online account user ID: _____

Online account password: _____

Savings Bonds

My savings bonds are located _____.

I have the following savings bonds:

Series	Denomination	Serial Number	Issue Date

Safe Deposit Boxes

I have the following safe deposit boxes:

Name of institution: _____

Phone: _____ Fax: _____

Address: _____

_____

E-mail: _____ Website: _____

Box #: _____

Key location: _____

Box rent: _____

Names of those with authorized access: _____

Items stored in this box: _____

_____

_____

_____

_____

_____

_____

Name of institution: _____

Phone: _____ Fax: _____

Address: _____

_____

E-mail: _____ Website: _____

Box #: _____

Key location: _____

Box rent: _____

Names of those with authorized access: _____

Items stored in this box: _____

_____

_____

_____

_____

_____

_____

Name of institution: _____

Phone: _____ Fax: _____

Address:_____

_____

E-mail: _____ Website: _____

Box #: _____

Key location: _____

Box rent: _____

Names of those with authorized access: _____

Items stored in this box: _____

_____

_____

_____

_____

_____

_____

Also record what you have in your safe deposit boxes on the Where I Put It Checklist in chapter 3.

Stocks and Bonds

I have the following stocks, bonds, stock funds, or bond funds:

Name of institution/Brokerage firm: _____

Account #: _____

Phone: _____ Fax: _____

Address: _____

_____

E-mail: _____ Website: _____

Online account user ID: _____

Online account password: _____

Name of institution/Brokerage firm: _____

Account #: _____

Phone: _____ Fax: _____

Address: _____

_____

E-mail: _____ Website: _____

Online account user ID: _____

Online account password: _____

Name of institution/Brokerage firm: _____

Account #: _____

Phone: _____ Fax: _____

Address: _____

_____

E-mail: _____ Website: _____

Online account user ID: _____

Online account password: _____

Treasury Bills, Notes, and Bonds

I have the following Treasury Direct account:

Account name: _____

Password: _____

Account #: _____

I have the following treasury bills, notes, or bonds:

Name of institution/Brokerage firm: _____

Account #: _____

Phone: _____ Fax: _____

Address: _____

_____

E-mail: _____ Website: _____

Online account user ID: _____

Online account password: _____

Name of institution/Brokerage firm: _____

Account #: _____

Phone: _____ Fax: _____

Address: _____

_____

E-mail: _____ Website: _____

Online account user ID: _____

Online account password: _____

Municipal Bonds

I have the following municipal bonds:

Name of institution/Brokerage firm: _____

Account #: _____

Phone: _____ Fax: _____

Address: _____

_____

E-mail: _____ Website: _____

Online account user ID: _____

Online account password: _____

Name of institution/Brokerage firm: _____

Account #: _____

Phone: _____ Fax: _____

Address: _____

_____

E-mail: _____ Website: _____

Online account user ID: _____

Online account password: _____

Name of institution/Brokerage firm: _____

Account #: _____

Phone: _____ Fax: _____

Address: _____

_____

E-mail: _____ Website: _____

Online account user ID: _____

Online account password: _____

Mutual Funds

I have the following mutual funds:

Name of institution/Brokerage firm: _____

Account #: _____

Phone: _____ Fax: _____

Address: _____

_____

E-mail: _____ Website: _____

Online account user ID: _____

Online account password: _____

Name of institution/Brokerage firm: _____

Account #: _____

Phone: _____ Fax: _____

Address: _____

_____

E-mail: _____ Website: _____

Online account user ID: _____

Online account password: _____

Name of institution/Brokerage firm: _____

Account #: _____

Phone: _____ Fax: _____

Address: _____

_____

E-mail: _____ Website: _____

Online account user ID: _____

Online account password: _____

Money Market Funds

I have the following money market funds:

Name of institution/Brokerage firm: _____

Account #: _____

Phone: _____ Fax: _____

Address: _____

_____

E-mail: _____ Website: _____

Online account user ID: _____

Online account password: _____

Name of institution/Brokerage firm: _____

Account #: _____

Phone: _____ Fax: _____

Address: _____

_____

E-mail: _____ Website: _____

Online account user ID: _____

Online account password: _____

Personal Debts and Loans

I owe the following people or entities money:

Internal Revenue Service: _____

Contact phone: _____

Address: _____

_____

Amount due. _____

State Department of Taxation: _____

Contact phone: _____

Address: _____

_____

Amount due: _____

Name of lender: _____

Contact phone: _____

Address: _____

_____

Amount due: _____

Name of lender: _____

Contact phone: _____

Address: _____

_____

Amount due: _____

The following people owe me money:

Name of borrower: _____

Contact phone: _____

Address: _____

_____

Amount due: _____

Name of borrower: _____

Contact phone: _____

Address: _____

_____

Amount due: _____

Name of borrower: _____

Contact phone: _____

Address: _____

_____

Amount due: _____

Credit and Debit Cards

I have the following credit or debit cards:

Name of credit/debit card: _____

Customer service phone: _____

Address: _____

_____

Account #: _____

PIN: _____

Name(s) on account: _____

On auto-pay: Yes   No

To bank account: _____ Date of payment: _____

Name of credit/debit card: _____

Customer service phone: _____

Address: _____

_____

Account #: _____

PIN: _____

Name(s) on account: _____

On auto-pay: Yes   No

To bank account: _____ Date of payment: _____

Name of credit/debit card: _____

Customer service phone: _____

Address: _____

_____

Account #: _____

PIN: _____

Name(s) on account: _____

On auto-pay:　　　　　Yes　　　　　No

To bank account: _____ Date of payment: _____

Name of credit/debit card: _____

Customer service phone: _____

Address: _____

_____

Account #: _____

PIN: _____

Name(s) on account: _____

On auto-pay:　　　　　Yes　　　　　No

To bank account: _____ Date of payment: _____

Name of credit/debit card: _____

Contact phone: _____

Address: _____

_____

Account #: _____

PIN: _____

Name(s) on account: _____

On auto-pay:　　　　　Yes　　　　　No

To bank account: _____ Date of payment: _____

My user names and passwords for online access are located _____

Signs of Scams and Financial Exploitation

- ❑ Excessive telemarketing callers
- ❑ Multiple payments to charities
- ❑ Receipt of trinkets and prizes
- ❑ Sweepstakes mail
- ❑ Significant change in spending pattern
- ❑ Unusual activity in bank accounts
- ❑ Financial transactions that can't be explained
- ❑ Use of credit card or ATM card by others
- ❑ Bank statements no longer being received
- ❑ Checks made out to cash
- ❑ Wire transfers to nonfamily members
- ❑ New "best friend"
- ❑ Exclusion from usual circle of friends or social activities
- ❑ Someone new making financial transactions or decisions
- ❑ Missing money or property
- ❑ Change in names on bank accounts, deeds
- ❑ Change in power of attorney or will
- ❑ Change in beneficiaries on life insurance, retirement accounts
- ❑ Suspicious signatures on checks or documents

CHAPTER 9

MANAGE RETIREMENT PLANS AND BENEFITS

If you are like many people, one of the hardest things to do upon entering retirement is to move from a savings mode to a spending mode. It can be scary to stop getting a regular paycheck and start having to withdraw from those hard-earned savings.

The money you have been setting aside is now probably going to be a primary source of funds to pay your expenses during retirement. Throughout your working years, you've been contributing to Social Security; now may be the time to start receiving your benefits. You also (hopefully) have been setting aside a portion of your wages into some type of retirement account, such as a 401(k) or IRA (individual retirement account). You may have pension income you earned while working, if you were lucky enough to have worked for a company or organization that still has pension plans.

Knowing about the money held in your retirement plans, as well as Social Security and veterans' benefits, will help you sort out how much money you have to live on. Some retirement plans have special rules about when and how you can withdraw money, with significant tax penalties for not doing it the right way.

This chapter briefly covers some of the most common retirement savings options and their unique characteristics. Rely on the advice of financial professionals for the specifics. Use the checklists as a convenient place to record information about your retirement plans, as well as Social Security and veterans' benefits. Chapter 4 has tips on how to select financial professionals as well as checklists with contact information for your brokers or financial advisers when you need answers to your questions. Take care to hire the right people. You've worked hard to save the money you need to retire. Now you will want your nest egg to work for you so you can enjoy the retirement dreams of your lifetime.

My To-Do Checklist

Done   **Need to Do**

❏   ❏   Document all retirement plans and accounts to understand the withdrawal rules

❏   ❏   Track down all pension benefits

❏   ❏   Understand Social Security benefits and how to navigate the system

❏   ❏   Take advantage of benefits available to veterans and their caregivers

✓ Document all retirement plans and accounts to understand the withdrawal rules

Most of your working life you have been saving for retirement. Now that you have retired, you are going to tap into those savings. You need to gather all pertinent information about 401(k)s, IRAs, and any other retirement plans. You'll want to understand the rules for withdrawal for each plan.

Many employers offer *401(k) retirement plans* that put off the need to pay taxes on both the contributions the employee and employer make and the plan's earnings until the employee withdraws funds from the plan, usually at retirement. These 401(k) plans are called *defined contribution* plans. The employee makes a specific dollar contribution with each paycheck to a personal plan account. The plan invests the contributions (and the employer's, if any) in mutual funds or other investments that the employee selects from the plan's menu of investment choices. The plan account is credited with any returns on the investment. Unlike fixed pension payments, the amount received depends on investment performance (which may be positive or negative).

401(k)s

You may have several options for how you receive withdrawals from your 401(k). You'll need to check with your plan manager or human relations department for your choices with your specific plan. Also check with your financial adviser for any tax consequences for the option you choose. Any money you take out of your 401(k) becomes taxable as ordinary income unless you roll over the amount into an IRA or other eligible employer plan. Some typical options include the following:

- **Total distribution**: You get a single payment of all funds, which can be paid directly to you or rolled over into an IRA. If you don't reinvest in an IRA or other qualified plan, you'll pay taxes on the full amount, which could be a big bite out of your nest egg.

- **Installment or periodic distribution**: You receive monthly payments from the plan in an amount you select for a specific time period, which may be limited to under ten years. The payments could be made to you or to an IRA. If to you, disbursements are taxable as income. Your spouse or domestic partner will need to consent to this option. Your beneficiary would receive any remaining balance.

- **Life annuity**: By purchasing a qualified annuity, you receive guaranteed monthly payments as long as you live. If you are married or have a domestic partner, you'll need his or her written consent to select this option. When you die, the insurance company keeps any remaining funds.

- **Joint with 50 percent surviving spouse annuity**: You get a reduced amount for your lifetime. If your spouse or domestic partner outlives you, he or she will get 50 percent of the amount you were receiving, for life. Some plans may offer other percentages for the surviving spouse annuity.

What to do with your 401(k) account depends on your circumstances, other sources of retirement income, lifestyle plans, investment goals, estate plans, and tax situation. Explore all the options and crunch some numbers with a financial adviser. For example, you could invest in an annuity. Compare the terms of the annuity offered by your 401(k) plan with other annuities: Which payout is higher? A rollover from your 401(k) to an annuity is tax-free, but annuity payouts are taxable.

Be careful how you make the rollover to avoid tax surprises. Have your 401(k) plan transfer the money directly to your IRA custodian. If, instead, the check comes directly to you, you have 60 days to make the transfer to an IRA, and 20 percent will be withheld for taxes. If you fail to make the transfer of the full amount (including the 20 percent withheld) within 60 days, you'll have to pay taxes on the entire amount.

Traditional and Roth IRAs

You will also want to review any existing IRAs. As of 2015, the law allows a person who is under age 50 and has earned income to deposit up to $5,500 in an IRA account each year; people over 50 can deposit up to $6,500. Contributions to a *traditional* IRA may be wholly or partially tax deductible or nondeductible depending on whether the individual is also covered by a qualified pension plan or a 401(k), as well as the individual's tax filing status and income level. Traditional IRAs delay having to pay taxes on earnings from contributions until you start to withdraw funds, usually when you retire. If you withdraw money from your IRA before age 59 1/2 you'll have to pay a 10 percent penalty in addition to any income taxes. *Roth* IRA contributions, on the other hand, are not deductible, but withdrawals are tax-free.

Other Tax-Deferred Plans

You should also record if you have other tax-deferred plans. These plans help defer taxes until you have reached an age where most likely your earnings have begun to decline because you are in a lower income tax bracket. For example, if you were self-employed, you may have established a *Keogh* plan, which allows for larger, tax-deferred yearly contributions and greater benefits than does an IRA. A *SIMPLE* IRA is a simplified plan, similar to a 401(k) plan, but with lower contribution limits and less costly administration. Another tax-deferred retirement for self-employed people is a simplified employee pension plan, or *SEP*, which is a type of IRA. Just to add to the alphabet soup, there's also a *SARSEP*, which is a SEP set up before 1997 that includes a salary reduction arrangement.

Because savings in retirement plans allow money to grow without paying any taxes, the tax laws require all those with retirement plans to start making withdrawals—and paying taxes—when they reach age 70 1/2—or pay a penalty. These withdrawals are called *required minimum distributions* (RMDs). The RMD rules apply to all employer-sponsored retirement plans, including profit-sharing plans, 401(k) plans, 403(b) plans, and 457(b) plans. The RMD rules also apply to traditional IRAs and IRA-based plans such as SEPs, SIMPLE IRAs, and SARSEPs. The Internal Revenue Service (IRS) provides life expectancy tables and worksheets to help you calculate the amount of any RMDs; see IRS Publication 590 at www.irs.gov/pub/irs-pub/p590a.pdf. The tax penalties for failing to take the correct RMD by December 31 of each year are a stiff 50 percent of the distribution that should have been taken. The Roth IRA rules are different because you have paid taxes on the money you contributed.

You can start taking withdrawals from all your retirement accounts without penalty at any time after age 59 1/2, and you can withdraw more than the required minimum amount.

✓ Track down all pension benefits

While many employers no longer offer pensions, if you worked for any company or organization that offered you a pension, be sure you take advantage of that benefit. You should check with all past employers—public and private—to determine if any payments are available to you.

Pensions are a way to accumulate tax-advantaged savings that can be tapped for a steady stream of income when you are no longer working for wages. Some pensions are financed entirely by the employer; others are co-financed by the employer and the employee. Pensions are considered to be *defined benefit plans* because upon retirement, employees receive a specific amount of money that is defined in the terms of the pension. To calculate how much an employee will receive, the plan uses a formula that includes the salary history and number of years the employee was eligible to receive pension benefits; this is called being vested in the pension. When you start receiving the pension, you have the option to elect if your surviving spouse or domestic partner will continue to receive a portion of the pension after you die.

Talk with the pension fund manager where you work (or worked) if you have questions about the details of any pension. You'll need to confirm that you are vested in the pension, how your pension benefit amount is calculated, how old you must be before you can start receiving benefits, if you can work and get pension payments, and if you can delay taking payments after you stop working. My pension amount increases every year that I don't start receiving this benefit, but I have to start when I reach 70 1/2. I'm holding off tapping into my pension as long as possible.

Most pension plans have a variety of options for payouts. Some pension plans may allow you to take a lump sum distribution or select among several payment plan options. Be sure you understand the differences between a life annuity (payments only to you that end at your death), a survivor annuity (payments to you and then to your spouse or domestic partner if he or she outlives you), and a death benefit (payments to you and then to a surviving beneficiary if you die before a set time period). If you take a lump sum distribution, your employer is required to withhold 20 percent and you will need to pay taxes as ordinary income on any money you don't roll over into a qualified retirement account. Once you have elected a payment option, you will not be able to make a change. You can't change your mind once you have set the annuity; the decision is irrevocable. The Consumer Financial Protection Bureau has a list of questions you should ask when deciding whether to take a lump sum distribution or lifetime distribution plan at files.consumerfinance.gov/f/201601_cfpb_pension-lump-sum-payouts-and-your-retirement-security.pdf.

✓ Understand Social Security benefits and how to navigate the system

Because you have been paying into the Social Security system all your working life, you need to understand how Social Security works to take full advantage of the benefits available to you. The rules can be complicated and often change.

Before you can receive monthly cash benefits, you must be credited for a certain amount of work under Social Security. For most benefits, you must have at least 10 years of Social Security-covered employment. Just how many credits you must establish depends on your age and the type of benefit you or your family is applying for retirement, survivor, or disability benefits. You can find details on specific requirements at ssa.gov or at any Social Security Administration (SSA) office located throughout the country. You can find those addresses at the SSA website.

How much Social Security retirement benefit you'll receive depends on the age at which you (and your spouse, if you are married) begin receiving benefits, whether the payments are based on your work record or your spouse's, whether you change from receiving benefits based on your spouse's record to benefits based on your earnings record, and whether your marital status changed over the years. Each year near your birthday Social Security sends a paper statement of your Social Security benefit, or you can go to ssa.gov/myaccount to find out how much you will receive.

Be sure you understand the best time to begin receiving retirement benefits. You can start receiving retirement checks as early as age 62 and disability checks at any age. Be aware, however, that you'll get up to 30 percent less in the monthly benefit if you begin benefits before full retirement age. If you were born between 1943 and 1954, your full retirement age is 66. If you were born after 1960, your full retirement age is 67. For those born between 1954 and 1960, the table at ssa.gov/planners/retire/agereduction.html shows how to determine your full retirement age. If you wait until age 70 to take Social Security retirement benefits, you get an additional amount—up to 30 percent more, depending on how many months after your full retirement age you start receiving benefits. Check out the chart at ssa.gov/pubs/ageincrease.htm for more details on how your benefit amount changes based on when you start your benefits. AARP has an online tool to help you decide the best time to take Social Security at aarp.org/SocialSecurityBenefits. The Consumer Financial Protection Bureau has a similar tool at consumerfinance.gov/retirement.

If you are married, you and your spouse need to know how to get the highest benefits for both of you during retirement and after one of you dies. Spousal benefits can be confusing, but here are some basics. How much a spouse receives depends on both spouses' work history, age benefits start, and full retirement age. A married person can receive either *spousal benefits* based on the other spouse's earnings record (if that spouse is already receiving Social Security) or *retirement benefits* based on his or her own work record, whichever offers the higher benefit. A surviving spouse can receive *survivor benefits* based on the earnings record of the deceased spouse.

There's an important difference between the spousal benefit and the survivor benefit. The spousal benefit amount is half of the benefit the higher-earning spouse would receive at full retirement age, regardless of when the higher-earning spouse decided to begin benefits. It doesn't matter whether the higher-earning spouse begins benefits at 62, 67, or 70, as long as that spouse is getting retirement benefits. But after the higher-earning spouse dies, the surviving spouse's benefit is equal to the amount the higher-earning spouse was receiving. If the higher-earning spouse began taking retirement benefits before full retirement age, the surviving spouse will receive a significant reduction in the amount of benefits.

If the lower-earning spouse retires first, he or she can only get benefits based on his or her own earnings history. Once the higher-earning spouse retires, the lower-earning spouse can shift to the spousal benefit, if it results in a higher amount. The age at which the lower-earning spouse begins benefits will determine the amount of the spousal benefit. After April 2016, the higher-earning spouse cannot file for retirement benefits and then suspend that benefit. This strategy formerly allowed the lower-earning spouse to begin to receive spousal benefits while the higher-earning spouse's account was continuing to grow.

If you're married, you file a joint tax return, and as of 2015 your combined income falls below $32,000, your Social Security benefit is not taxed at the federal level. Half is taxed if your combined income is between $32,000 and $44,000, and 85 percent of your benefit is taxed if your income exceeds $44,000. Most states do not levy income tax on Social Security benefits, including retirement havens like Arizona, the Carolinas, and Florida. But about a dozen states do tax your Social Security benefits, including Connecticut, Kansas, Utah, and Vermont.

Social Security may also be an important source of continuing income for your family members if you are receiving or are eligible to receive retirement or disability benefits. They are eligible for benefits under the following circumstances:

- Unmarried children under 18 (or 19 if a full-time elementary or secondary school student)
- Unmarried children 18 or over who were severely disabled before age 22 and who continue to be disabled
- A wife or husband 62 or older who has been married to the worker for at least one year
- A wife or husband under 62 if she or he is caring for a child who is under 16 (or disabled) and who is receiving a benefit under the worker's earnings

A divorced spouse who has been divorced at least two years can receive benefits at age 62, regardless of whether the former spouse receives them. The marriage must have lasted ten years or more; the former spouse must be at least 62 and eligible for Social Security benefits, regardless of whether he or she has retired; and the divorced spouse must not be eligible for an equal or higher benefit on his or her own—or anyone else's—Social Security record.

You can review your Social Security statement at any time by creating a MySocialSecurity account at ssa.gov/myaccount. For comprehensive information concerning Social Security benefits, see AARP's *Social Security for Dummies* by Jonathan Peterson (AARP. org/SS4Dummies). For answers to frequently asked questions, see AARP's Social Security Q&A Tool at aarp.org/SSQA. Note: Because the Social Security Act is amended from time to time, contact the nearest Social Security office for a full explanation of your rights and those of your family.

✓ Take advantage of benefits available to veterans and their caregivers

If you served in the US military, the Department of Veterans Affairs (VA) offers many benefits and support services that could help you in your retirement years. You've earned it!

The available benefits depend upon the length of your service, when the service was performed, whether you are disabled, whether the disability was caused by active service, and many other criteria. The National Resource Directory is your go-to resource for specific information about services and resources for veterans at the national, state, and local level. This online resource is at www.nrd.gov.

If you are a veteran, you'll want to access all available benefits. Under certain circumstances, the following benefits (and many more) *may* be available to you:

- Alcohol and drug dependence treatment
- Automobile allowance for service-connected loss or permanent loss of the use of one or both hands or feet
- Dental care
- Federal civil service preference
- Help paying for the assistance of another in your home
- Hospitalization benefits
- Insurance
- Loan guaranty benefits
- Nursing home care
- Outpatient medical treatment
- Pension for disability caused by service-connected injury or disease
- Pension for certain non-service-connected disabilities
- Prosthetic appliances
- Vocational rehabilitation and counseling

Even more benefits may be available to disabled veterans and their caregivers. Here are some of the more common services that assist wounded veterans and their caregivers:

Aid and Attendance. Aid and attendance (A&A) is a way to receive an increased VA pension amount if the veteran meets one of the following conditions:

- The veteran requires the aid of another person to perform personal functions required in everyday living, such as bathing, feeding, dressing, toileting, or adjusting prosthetic devices.

- The veteran is bedridden, in that the disability requires that the veteran remain in bed apart from any prescribed course of convalescence or treatment.

- The veteran is a patient in a nursing home due to mental or physical incapacity.

- The veteran's eyesight is limited to a corrected 5/200 visual acuity or less in both eyes; or concentric contraction of the visual field to 5 degrees or less.

Education or training. In-person or online classes, webinars, manuals, or workbooks that provide education related to caregiving activities.

Financial stipend. Compensation for a caregiver's time devoted to caregiving activities, or for loss of wages due to caregiving commitments.

Geriatric Evaluation and Management (GEM). This is inpatient or outpatient short-term comprehensive geriatric evaluation and management.

Helping Hand. Direct support such as loans, donations, legal guidance, housing support, or transportation assistance.

Home and community based services. These are supports and services offered to the veteran either directly by the VA or by local providers who contract with the VA. Services, provided in the community or in the veteran's home, could include skilled home health care, homemaker/home health aide services, community adult day health care, hospice and palliative care, and veteran directed care.

Nursing home care. The VA provides nursing home level care in VA-owned and -operated community living centers, state-owned and -operated veterans' homes, and privately owned facilities that contract with the VA to provide care. Each program has separate admission and eligibility criteria, but the VA pays the full cost for eligible veterans.

Patient advocate or case manager. An individual who is a liaison between the veteran, care providers, and the caregiver to coordinate care.

Patient Aligned Care Teams (PACT). These teams provide primary care in the home.

Post-9/11 Caregiver Program. A program specially created to assist caregivers of veterans who were seriously injured in the line of duty on or after September 11, 2001. Eligible caregivers can receive these benefits:

- A monthly stipend based on the veteran's personal care needs
- Travel expenses, including lodging and per diem, while accompanying veterans undergoing care
- Access to health care insurance through CHAMPVA

- Mental health services and counseling
- Comprehensive caregiver training specializing in caring for those with multiple severe traumas
- Respite care

Religious support. Spiritual-based guidance or counseling.

Respite care. Help to give the caregiver a short-term, temporary break. This could be in-home care, a short stay in an institution, or adult day care for the veteran.

Social support. Online or in-person caregivers' support groups to assist with caregiving-specific stresses or challenges.

Wellness activities. Family leisure and recreational activities, fitness classes, or stress-relief lessons that focus on improving the caregivers' mental or physical well-being.

You will need to have documentation of your military service to apply for any benefits available to you or your family. You can get a copy of a service record (DD-214) at archives.gov/veterans/military-service-records. You can also request your own military records, including medical records, by going online at eVetRecs. You need to include your complete name you used while in the service, service number, Social Security number, branch of service, dates of service, and date and place of birth. You must sign and date the request and fax it to the National Personnel Record Center (NPRC) at 314-801-9195 or mail it to the NPRC, Military Personnel Records, 1 Archives Drive, St. Louis, MO 63138. Your next of kin may also request military records using eVetRecs or by written application using Standard Form 180 and providing proof of death (death certificate and letter from a funeral home or published obituary). You may also need a copy of your marriage license, birth certificate, and children's birth certificates or adoption papers to apply for certain benefits.

Retirement Plans and Benefits Action Checklists

The following Action Checklists are in Chapter 9:

- ❑ Retirement Plans
- ❑ Pensions
- ❑ Social Security Benefits
- ❑ Veterans' Benefits

Retirement Plans

I have the following individual retirement accounts (IRAs):

Financial institution holding the IRA: _____

IRA account #: _____

Phone: _____ Fax: _____

Address: _____

_____

E-mail: _____ Website: _____

Plan amount: _____ as of: _____

User ID: _____ Password: _____

Financial institution holding the IRA: _____

IRA account #: _____

Phone: _____ Fax: _____

Address: _____

_____

E-mail: _____ Website: _____

Plan amount: _____ as of: _____

User ID: _____ Password: _____

I have the following 401(k) plans:

Financial institution/Plan administrator: _____

Account #: _____

Phone: _____ Fax: _____

Address: _____

_____

E-mail: _____ Website: _____

Plan amount: _____ as of: _____

User ID: _____ Password: _____

I have the following 403(b) plans:

Financial institution/Plan administrator: _____

Account #: _____

Phone: _____ Fax: _____

Address: _____

_____

E-mail: _____ Website: _____

Plan amount: _____ as of: _____

User ID: _____ Password: _____

I have the following Keogh plan:

Financial institution/Plan administrator: _____

Account #: _____

Phone: _____ Fax: _____

Address: _____

_____

E-mail: _____ Website: _____

Plan amount: _____ as of: _____

User ID: _____ Password: _____

I have the following SEP plan:

Financial institution/Plan administrator: _____

Account #: _____

Phone: _____ Fax: _____

Address: _____

_____

E-mail: _____ Website: _____

Plan amount: _____ as of: _____

User ID: _____ Password: _____

I have the following Roth IRA:

Financial institution/Plan administrator: _____

Account #: _____

Phone: _____ Fax: _____

Address: _____

_____

E-mail: _____ Website: _____

Plan amount: _____ as of: _____

User ID: _____ Password: _____

Pensions

I have the following pensions:

Employer: _____

Pension ID #: _____

Plan administrator: _____

Phone: _____ Fax: _____

Address: _____

_____

E-mail: _____ Website: _____

Age vested: _____ Age begin withdrawal: _____

Pension amount: _____

Employer: _____

Pension ID #: _____

Plan administrator: _____

Phone: _____ Fax: _____

Address: _____

_____

E-mail: _____ Website: _____

Age vested: _____ Age begin withdrawal: _____

Pension amount: _____

Employer: _____

Pension ID #: _____

Plan administrator: _____

Phone: _____ Fax: _____

Address: _____

_____

E-mail: _____ Website: _____

Age vested: _____ Age begin withdrawal: _____

Pension amount: _____

Social Security Benefits

Name on Social Security card: _____

Social Security #: _____

Type of Social Security benefit: _____

(disability, retirement, spousal, widow, etc.)

Full retirement age: _____

Age began retirement benefit: _____

Spouse's full retirement age: _____

Monthly Social Security benefit amount: _____

Social Security benefit is deposited at _____

Veterans' Benefits

Military service # (DD-214): _____

Entered active service on _____.

Separated from active service on _____.

Service post-9/11:　　❏ Yes　　❏ No

Type of discharge: _____

Branch: _____

Grade or rank: _____

National Guard: _____

Reserves: _____

VA Medical Center: _____

Address: _____

Contact person: _____

Phone: _____

E-mail: _____

As a veteran, I am eligible (or I will investigate eligibility) for the following VA benefits:

Now Receiving	Will Investigate	
❏	❏	Alcohol and drug dependence treatment
❏	❏	Automobile allowance for service-connected loss or permanent loss of the use of one or both hands or feet
❏	❏	Dental care
❏	❏	Federal civil service preference
❏	❏	Help paying for the assistance of another in your home
❏	❏	Hospitalization benefits
❏	❏	Insurance
❏	❏	Loan guaranty benefits
❏	❏	Nursing home care
❏	❏	Outpatient medical treatment
❏	❏	Pension for disability caused by service-connected injury or disease
❏	❏	Pension for certain non-service-connected disabilities
❏	❏	Prosthetic appliances
❏	❏	Vocational rehabilitation and counseling

As a disabled veteran, I and my caregivers are eligible (or I will investigate eligibility) for the following VA benefits:

Now Receiving	Will Investigate	
❏	❏	Caregiver training
❏	❏	Case manager
❏	❏	CHAMPVA health insurance
❏	❏	Financial stipend
❏	❏	Fitness classes
❏	❏	Housing support
❏	❏	Legal guidance
❏	❏	Loans
❏	❏	Mental health services
❏	❏	Patient advocate
❏	❏	Recreational activities
❏	❏	Respite care
❏	❏	Spiritual counseling
❏	❏	Stress-relief sessions
❏	❏	Support groups
❏	❏	Travel expenses

CHAPTER 10

INSURE A SOUND RETIREMENT

As you enter retirement, it's a good idea to review all the various types of insurance you have in place now. You want to make sure under your new circumstances you have the right types of coverage. This chapter gives you an opportunity to understand how your policies protect you and your family, make sure you have the insurance coverage that you need, and see if you want to shed or change any plans. Your circumstances may have changed. Sometime people have life insurance they put in place when the children were young; that need may now be different.

To that end, you'll find overviews of the types of insurance available. The descriptions are not a detailed breakdown of the many types of insurance options available. They should, however, give you some information about the most widely used types of insurance coverage to help you review and organize your own policies.

Documenting all your policies, along with the contact information for each company, has an added benefit: Should something happen to you—an accident, illness, death, or other event that prevents you from continuing to conduct your own financial affairs—your loved ones will have the information they need to file insurance claims, cancel certain policies, or obtain new ones to protect you. An amazing amount of insurance proceeds goes unclaimed because the policyholder's family or heirs were never told about them.

Health insurance is of particular interest to many retirees. Indeed, some people delay retirement to retain their employer's health coverage for themselves and their family. Many wait until age 65, when they can start receiving Medicare coverage. Since Medicare is complex, I help you understand the basics and answer questions about how to apply, what it covers, how it works with other insurance, and what health coverage is available for spouse and other family members.

My To-Do Checklist

Done   **Need to Do**

❑   ❑   Locate all insurance policies

❑   ❑   Go over the terms of all insurance policies

❑   ❑   Update the beneficiaries on your life insurance

❑   ❑   Review your health, disability, and Medicare insurance

❑   ❑   Review insurance coverage for residences

❑   ❑   Keep vehicle insurance current

❑   ❑   Weigh the pros and cons of long-term care insurance

✓ Locate all insurance policies

Once you locate all your insurance policies, be careful to store them in a safe place and tell your family members what policies you have and where they are located. Some companies may require that your heirs hand over your original life insurance policies before they can collect any proceeds. You'll want to have a ready reference with the account numbers and contact information if you need to make any type of claim.

✓ Go over the terms of all insurance policies

Annuity

Annuities are a type of insurance that are typically designed to provide a stream of income. As with other types of insurance, there are many types of annuities. They may be fixed, variable, or indexed, with immediate or deferred payments. A fixed income annuity typically means that the insurance company makes a guaranteed series of specific payments for the duration of the contract. With a variable annuity, the amount you receive can fluctuate depending on the success of the investments the company makes with your money. The return on an indexed annuity is based on a portfolio of investments that mirror one of several stock market indexes, such as the Standard & Poor's 500. With an immediate annuity your payments start immediately; with a deferred annuity, they start at some time in the future.

You can have many options with annuities: how your money is invested within the annuity, at what point your annuity begins to make payments, and for how long and to whom payments will be made. Typically, money invested in the annuity grows tax-deferred, with payouts being taxed when received as the return of principal and ordinary income.

Payouts may be made for a set number of years, or during your lifetime, or for the lifetime of a spouse or other beneficiary. You can also obtain, at additional cost, specific benefits, such as a guaranteed minimum death benefit or a guaranteed minimum withdrawal benefit. A guaranteed minimum death benefit, or GMDB rider, means that your beneficiaries or your estate will receive a set amount as defined in the contract if you die before the annuity begins paying benefits. A guaranteed minimum withdrawal benefit, or GMWB rider, means that while you are alive you will receive a fixed percentage of your investment each year.

Be certain you understand the terms of any annuity you have and periodically review your annuity contract to confirm that it continues to fit your needs. Many annuity contracts let you change some of the options, but before you do be certain you understand the tax consequences to you and to your family. Annuities are very complex investment options, so study any marketing promotions very carefully and do your homework before making any decisions. A good place to start is FINRA's investor alert on equity-indexed annuities at finra.org/investors/protect-your-money.

Life Insurance

Life insurance is primarily intended to ease a beneficiary's financial loss that could result from the policyholder's death. Although death comes to everyone and cannot be considered unexpected in the long run, it can certainly be unexpected when it occurs. Life insurance is a way to make sure that your family has cash to pay for your final expenses, such as for your funeral or the expenses of your final illness. An insurance policy could also provide cash for any estate taxes or unpaid debts as well as financial support to your spouse or dependent children after your death.

Today's life insurance market has multiple options for you to choose from. A short list includes the following: how much coverage to purchase, the amount of the premiums, how the policy is invested, any guarantees on returns, and how and when the policy proceeds are paid out to your beneficiaries. Before purchasing any policy, you need to be certain you understand all the options and the risks involved.

This money may be paid in a lump sum, in a monthly sum for the life of another individual, in monthly sums over a certain length of time, or in some other manner spelled out by the terms of your policy. Regardless of what payment method you select, the amount your beneficiary will receive is set out in the policy. It may even pay double if your death is caused by accident—a so-called *double indemnity* policy. Do your homework to compare your options with multiple insurance companies. Also seek competent advice on any tax consequences to you and your estate that the various options can have.

A widely purchased form of life insurance is *whole life insurance*. This type of insurance pays a sum of money (the "face value") to your beneficiary at the time of your death. You have to pay a premium each year to keep the insurance in force. The amount of the premium is determined by your age at the time you purchased the policy. The younger you are, the smaller the premium on the policy. Variations in the method of payment for whole life insurance are available. For example, you might obtain a policy that requires annual premiums for 20 years. At the expiration of the 20-year period, the policy continues in effect for the balance of your life, but you do not have to continue paying the premiums. It is even possible for you to purchase a policy by making one large initial premium payment.

Regardless of how you pay for the policy, whole life insurance provides coverage for the rest of your life (as long as you have paid all the required premiums).

Universal life, *variable whole life*, and *variable universal life* are different types of permanent life insurance in which you have the option to vary (within the terms of the contract) the amount you pay in premiums from year to year and how your policy's cash reserves grow. Typically the cash value reserves held by the insurance company are invested in stocks, bonds, or mutual funds. You, as the policyholder, are able to select the investment from a menu offered by the insurance company. Some policies have guaranteed minimum returns on your investment; others allow you to borrow against the cash value during your life. How much your beneficiary would receive at your death depends on many factors, including the terms of the policy, the amounts paid in premiums, and the investment success of the insurance company.

Term insurance, on the other hand, provides insurance coverage only for a specified length of time. You might purchase a policy that provides coverage for five, ten, or twenty years. The annual premium for term insurance is substantially less than the annual premium for whole life insurance. The cost of purchasing the same amount of coverage gradually increases with the age of the purchaser. Many term life insurance contracts provide that the policy may be renewed at the end of the term without providing further proof of insurability. The premium for the renewed term will most likely be higher than for the original term because you would be older. Other term policies provide that they may be converted, within a certain time frame, into a permanent type of life insurance without proof of insurability. Once again, the premium would be adjusted.

While you were employed, your employer may have provided you with group term insurance. Typically, this type of insurance is intended to replace some of your family's income should something happen to you while you are employed. You may be given the option to continue that coverage at the time you retire, if you want to make the premium payments on your own. In making that decision now that you are retiring or retired, consider whether you need this coverage and if another insurance policy or investment option would better suit your new circumstances.

✓ Update the beneficiaries on your life insurance

Now is a good time to review each life insurance policy to make sure you have listed the names of those you want to receive the policy proceeds. You want to keep your list of beneficiaries up to date. Circumstances may have changed since you initially named the beneficiaries on your policies. For example, you probably don't want to have a former spouse as a beneficiary (unless you are required to maintain a policy under a divorce decree). Your family may have changed with marriages, divorces, or births of children and grandchildren. A beneficiary you named several years ago may now be deceased.

You can name one person, your estate, or multiple people as your beneficiaries. It's a good idea to name successor or secondary beneficiaries in case a primary beneficiary dies before you do. If you want to name more than one beneficiary, you should indicate the percentage that each is to receive. For example, you could name your spouse as the primary beneficiary to receive 100 percent of the policy and name your three children as secondary beneficiaries, with each receiving 33 percent if your spouse dies before you do.

✓ Review your health, disability, and Medicare insurance

Health insurance provides a means to pay doctor, hospital, and other medical expenses if you become sick or are in an accident. Many different types of accident and illness insurance policies exist. Some are very limited in scope and pay out only if you develop a specific type of illness, such as cancer. *Medical expense reimbursement policies* range from a policy that pays a fixed amount for each day you are hospitalized to one that covers almost every medical expense that the policyholder could incur. Because the coverage varies to such a great extent, the cost of medical coverage varies greatly. Be sure to review what coverage you have now and comparison shop for different coverage if your health, employment, or family circumstances have changed. Before purchasing any type of health insurance, be certain you understand what is and is not covered.

Most people get health insurance as an employee benefit where they work. Some people can continue to get health coverage through their former employer's health plan after they retire. Employers don't have to provide *retiree health insurance,* and they can change or eliminate those benefits. Before you retire, or if you are retired, be sure you know what health benefits are available to you. Get this information from your employer's benefit coordinator.

If you, your spouse, or children lose health coverage you've been getting through your work because you are planning to retire, you may be able to get coverage through the *Health Insurance Marketplace* in your state. Go to healthcare.gov for more information on coverage and how to enroll. The marketplace is a way to obtain health insurance that allows side-by-side comparison of the benefits and costs of approved health plans. All health plans sold in the marketplace must cover basic health benefits, including doctor visits, hospitalization, mental health services, and prescription drugs. People shopping for insurance in the marketplace can pick among several levels of coverage. Financial assistance to pay the premiums may be available, depending on income. Those who are eligible for insurance through the marketplace and do not buy it will be subject to a penalty.

Disability insurance is intended to provide you and your family with financial stability if you are no longer able to work because of an accident, injury, or illness. Some employers, unions, and professional associations provide disability insurance for their employees or members. Policies can vary in the amount of your income that would be replaced, how long you can receive the payments, and what types of disabilities you need to have before you can receive the benefits.

Medicare

Once you reach age 65 you are eligible for Medicare, whether you are still employed or retired. You'll need to understand all the costs, component parts, how they fit together for fuller coverage, and what to do if you need help figuring out Medicare claims. If you are still working and covered by your employer's health plan, or receiving retiree health coverage through your former employer, a big challenge is understanding how Medicare and any other health coverage you have work together.

Medicare is the federal health insurance program for people who are age 65 and over, for some younger people with disabilities, and for people with end-stage kidney disease. The Medicare program has several parts that provide different benefits. *Part A* helps pay for inpatient hospital care, as well as preventive screenings, hospice care, some home health care, and a limited amount of skilled nursing care. Most people don't pay premiums for Part A coverage because they have already been paid for through payroll taxes. For those who need to purchase Part A, the monthly premium is $411 (as of 2016).

Part B helps pay for part of the costs for doctor visits, some home health care, medical equipment, preventive services, outpatient hospital care, rehabilitative therapy, laboratory tests, X-rays, mental health services, ambulance services, and blood transfusions. Those who turn age 65 are automatically signed up for Part A and Part B if they are receiving Social Security or Railroad Retirement benefits.

Medicare beneficiaries pay a premium for Part B. In 2016, the premium is $104.90 each month for people with income under $85,000 for an individual or $170,000 for a married couple filing jointly and who get a Social Security benefit. For those not on Social Security, the premium is $121.80. People who earn more pay premiums between $170.50 and $389.89 (2016). This additional premium, called the income-related monthly adjustment amount or IRMAA, is based on the modified adjusted gross income reported on the income tax return filed the previous year. For example, the 2016 premium would be based on the income tax return filed in 2015 for 2014 income. The premium can be adjusted if your income has significantly decreased due to a life-changing event such as death of a spouse, marriage, divorce, or work stoppage. If you think you should not be paying an increased premium, make an appointment to speak with a claims representative at your local Social Security office or file form SSA-44, available at ssa.gov/forms/ssa-44.pdf.

For those taking Social Security, the Part B premium is automatically deducted from the monthly Social Security benefit. Those not receiving Social Security can sign up for Medicare Easy Pay at medicare.gov/your-medicare-costs/paying-parts-a-and-b/medicare easy-pay.html to have the Part B premiums automatically deducted from a bank account. In my experience, Medicare took many months to get the autopay started. I continued to write a check each month until I got the notice that my premium was being deducted.

You can decide not to have Part B if you are covered by another policy, such as your employer's plan. Many retiree health plans, however, require that you be enrolled in Part A and Part B. If your employer or retiree coverage ends, you have eight months to sign up for Part B. Most likely, you'll want to sign up for Part B promptly. After that eight-month deadline, you will have to pay a penalty of 10 percent more in premiums for each 12-month period that you could have had Part B but didn't sign up for it. You have to pay that premium hike every year.

Part C is now known as Medicare Advantage. Medicare Advantage plans are offered by private companies. Purchasing Medicare Advantage coverage is an option. These policies pay for the same services as Parts A and B and may offer other benefits such as drug, dental, or vision coverage. In most Medicare Advantage plans, participants can go only to doctors, specialists, and hospitals that are on the plan's list of providers. During the annual Medicare open enrollment periods (between October and December) people already on Medicare can change Medicare Advantage plans or select original Medicare (Part A and Part B).

Part D helps pay for prescription drugs. Like Medicare Advantage plans, Part D drug coverage is optional and offered through private insurance companies approved by Medicare. People already on Medicare Parts A and B can choose from many drug plans offered by many companies. The benefits and costs vary among insurance companies and each company's several plans. Your first opportunity to elect to purchase Part D drug coverage is when you become newly eligible for Medicare; wait too long, and there will be a late enrollment penalty. Participants can switch to a different prescription drug plan or sign up for a Part D plan during the annual Medicare open enrollment period (October through December). Those with higher income (over $85,000, or $170,000 for a couple filing a joint return) will have to pay an additional $12.70 to $72.90 (as of 2016) to Medicare on top of the regular Part D premium paid to the plan.

As with most other insurance plans, Medicare has an annual deductible, coinsurance, and copayments. And it doesn't pay for all types of health care costs. The most commonly misunderstood example of what Medicare doesn't cover is long-term care. To cover the gaps in Medicare, Medicare supplemental insurance, called Medigap insurance, is available. Medigap insurance covers some of the costs that Medicare does not pay—but not for long-term care. This private health insurance is offered by Medicare-approved insurance companies that can offer up to 11 standardized plans. Each standard plan offers a different set of benefits, fills different gaps in Medicare coverage, and varies in price. The standardization of plans makes it easier to compare policies among companies.

If your employer provides health benefits for retirees, you need to know what the health plan covers and how it works if you also have Medicare. For those of you under 65 when you retire, your retiree health plan will be your primary coverage. Check with your human relations department for the details about spouse and family coverage, premium amounts, and health services that are offered, including dental and vision. For those of you 65 and older and eligible for Medicare along with a retiree plan, you may have additional questions. I know I sure did.

Your experience may be different, but I found the process of getting on to and accustomed to my new health coverage rather daunting. According to my employer's plan, I needed to sign up for Medicare Part A and Part B three months before retiring. I had already signed up for Part A when I turned 65, so I knew that to sign up for Part B I had to go to Social Security. Still, the online form on ssa.gov for Medicare is for when you want to start an application, not when you need to add Part B. To add Part B takes a separate form (CMS 40-B) that you have to download and mail or take to a Social Security office. So I downloaded the form, filled it out, and headed out for my nearest Social Security office early one morning. I knew I wanted to be early to avoid waiting. But I wasn't early enough;

the line was out the door when I arrived. Luckily, I got processed rather quickly because I was only turning in a form, but unluckily, I'd locked my keys in my car!

A good reference on the intricacies of Medicare plans is AARP's *Medicare for Dummies* by Patricia Barry, available through aarp.org/MedicareForDummies or bookstores. Get answers to many of your Medicare questions at aarp.org/medicareqa. Compare the various Medicare plans, including prescription drug, Medicare Advantage, and Medigap at medicare.gov/find-a-plan. To sign up for Medicare, go to ssa.gov/medicare/apply.html. To readily track Medicare claims and payments, sign up for a personal account at MyMedicare.gov.

If you need help paying the Part A deductible, coinsurance, and copayments and Part B premiums and deductible, check out the Medicare Savings Programs. Depending on your income, you may qualify for state programs that pay some of the premium or deductibles even if your income and resources are higher than the state limits for Medicaid. A good place to get personal help understanding Medicare and Medicare Savings Programs is your local State Health Insurance Assistance Program (SHIP). To find the SHIP in your state, go to shipnpr.acl.gov.

I now have my Medicare card, my health plan card, and my prescription drug plan card. Each time I go to the doctor or pharmacy, I have to make sure they have my new plan information and numbers. For me, Medicare is primary; my retiree coverage is secondary. This means that the doctor or pharmacy must first bill Medicare, and then my retiree health plan. Generally the health plan pays some or most of what Medicare didn't cover. I haven't yet figured it all out. My advice to you is to pay very close attention to the doctor's bill or statement, the Medicare Summary Notice, and the insurance company's claim form for each visit (which all come at different times); compare the three and be ready to call the doctor's billing office, Medicare, or the insurance company if something doesn't look right. The Medical Claims Tracker Checklist in this chapter is a handy tool to organize your claims information.

Once you are on Medicare, pay close attention to the *Medicare Summary Notices* (MSN), which explain Medicare's action on claims that health care providers have filed to your account. MSNs come by mail, or you can set up an account at MyMedicare.gov, where claims are posted within about a day of being processed. The MSN, which prominently says "This is not a bill," contains important information about the provider that filed a claim; the service provided; the amount Medicare paid; and the amount, if anything, the provider can bill the patient. If you have a Medigap plan that covers deductibles and copayments, Medicare will automatically forward the claim notice to the plan for processing. For help understanding the information in a Part A or Part B MSN, go to aarp.org/decoders.

You should carefully compare all billing statements from the health care provider with the MSN to make sure the information matches: same provider, service or procedure, amount of claim, amount paid by Medicare, and amount the provider can bill. If, for example, you paid a doctor a higher copayment than Medicare calculated, contact the provider. If you see anything that doesn't look right, first contact the provider. It could be a simple mistake that the provider can correct. For bigger problems or suspected fraud, contact Medicare at 800-663-4227.

✓ Review insurance coverage for residences

Originally, fire insurance was about the only type of insurance that homeowners could obtain on their residence. Now you can get insurance to protect against windstorm, hail, flood, explosion, riot, or smoke damage. Insurance is also available for the contents of your home, as well as your garage or any outbuildings.

Today, most homeowners purchase a homeowners policy that combines fire and extended insurance coverage that also includes protection for your personal property, additional living expenses if you can't live in your home because of damage, and comprehensive personal liability. This personal liability coverage would make medical payments to guests who get injured in your home and pay for some damage to the property of others. Rather than having to purchase separate policies to cover each of these various risks, the homeowners policy combines them into one policy.

Similar types of policies are available to condominium owners and renters that cover your personal property due to damage to the unit. You can also add *riders* to your policy to fit specific needs, or to insure special items such as antiques or jewelry.

Many insurance companies offer additional insurance liability protection through an *umbrella policy*, which provides insurance coverage in excess of your regular automobile, personal liability, and other liability coverage. It is usually sold in multiples of $1 million and is a low-cost method of buying substantial protection.

Do you have valuable items that need to be specifically insured so their full value is covered in the event you need to make a claim? This might include jewelry, art work, musical instruments, furs, coin collections, and other costly items. This *scheduled personal property coverage* can be added to you homeowners policy for an additional premium. If you already have scheduled property coverage, is the listing of what you want insured current? If you sold the antique table to acquire a contemporary painting, have the agent amend your schedule.

If you've been living in the same home for a number of years, you may not have thought to check over this policy. Has there been a significant change in the value of your property, resulting in either too much or too little coverage? Keep in mind that replacing an existing home from scratch could cost more than current market value. Is there a cap on the maximum amount of reimbursement you would get if there was major damage to your house, or does the policy provide enough coverage to replace it at today's prices for materials and labor? Know that there are three types of coverage: guaranteed replacement, replacement cost, and cash value. Guaranteed replacement coverage, the priciest, will pay all of your repair or rebuilding costs if you need to replace your home if it is destroyed. The most you'll get with replacement cost coverage is whatever the policy states is the maximum amount. A cash-value policy will cover the cost of the house's replacement minus any wear and tear. Although this is the least expensive, most likely you will not get enough money to completely rebuild. Sit down with your insurance agent to go over your current policies so you understand what is or is not covered. I'm glad I did. The policy coverage on our home we bought 40 years ago had not kept pace with market changes. What was adequate coverage then would scarcely replace a fraction of our house now.

If you have a second residence, such as a beach house or lakefront property, review those policies with your agent, too. Do you have adequate flood coverage? Ask if you need special coverage if it is not occupied all the time.

✓ Keep vehicle insurance current

If you own a motor vehicle—car, truck, motorcycle, motorboat, snowmobile, or other recreational vehicle—you probably have vehicle insurance. In fact, many states require all drivers to be insured for liability to other persons for damages resulting from an automobile accident. Regardless of the law in your particular state, it makes good sense to insure yourself against the claims by others and against any expenses that might result from a collision or fire, or if your vehicle is stolen.

Review your policies to make sure the coverage is accurate. When I retired and stopped commuting to my office every day, I started driving many fewer miles. (Hooray, one of the biggest perks of retirement!) I explained the change in my driving routine to my insurance agent and got a discount by switching from commuter use to personal use. My agent found other places to save by eliminating the collision coverage on my husband's old junker we hardly ever use, along with adding a discount as an older driver. I appreciated the savings on my premiums. Maybe I can talk my husband into just getting rid of that car.

✓ Weigh the pros and cons of long-term care insurance

To help cover potential long-term care expenses, some people choose to buy long-term care insurance. Deciding whether long-term care insurance is right for you can take a significant amount of time and research, but making the effort will be time well spent.

Policies offer many different coverage options. Since you can't predict what your future long-term care needs will be, you may want to buy a policy with flexible options. Depending on the policy options you select, long-term care insurance can help you pay for the care you need, whether you are living at home or in an assisted living facility or skilled nursing facility. The insurance might also pay expenses for care coordination and other services. Some policies will even help pay costs associated with modifying your home so you can keep living in it safely. Here are some of the factors you should consider when thinking about whether to purchase long-term care insurance.

Your age and health. Policies cost less if purchased when you're younger and in good health. If you're older or have a serious health condition, you may not be able to get coverage—and if you do, you may have to spend considerably more. Insurers often turn down applicants due to preexisting conditions. If a company does sell a policy to someone with preexisting conditions, it often withholds payment for care related to those conditions for a specified period of time after the policy is sold. Make sure this period of withheld payments is reasonable for you. If you fail to notify a company of a preexisting condition, the company may not pay for care related to that condition.

The premiums. Will you be able to pay the policy's premiums—now and in the future— without breaking your budget? Premiums often increase over time, and your income may go down. If you find yourself unable to afford the premiums, you could lose all the money you've invested in a policy.

Your income. If you have difficulty paying your bills now, or are concerned about paying them in the years ahead, when you may have fewer assets, spending thousands of dollars a year for a long-term care policy might not make sense. If your income is low and you have few assets when you need care, you might quickly qualify for Medicaid. (Medicaid pays for nursing facility care; in most states it will also cover a limited amount of at-home care.) Unfortunately, to qualify for Medicaid you must first exhaust almost all your resources and meet Medicaid's other eligibility requirements.

Your support system. You may have family and friends who can provide some of your long-term care should you need it. Think about whether or not you would want their help and how much you can reasonably expect from them.

Your savings and investments. A financial adviser or a lawyer who specializes in elder law or estate planning can advise you about ways to save for future long-term care expenses and the pros and cons of purchasing long-term care insurance.

Your taxes. The benefits paid out through a long-term care policy are generally not taxed as income. Also, most policies sold today are "tax-qualified" by federal standards. This means if you are 65 or older, itemize deductions, and have in excess of 7.5 percent of your adjusted gross income, you can deduct the premium cost from your federal income taxes. (For those under 65, you need to have medical costs in excess of 10 percent to get the federal deduction.)

You have a variety of ways to shop for long-term care insurance. Most people buy an individual long-term care policy through an insurance agent or broker. If you go this route, make sure the person you're working with has had additional training in long-term care insurance (many states require it) and check with your state's insurance department to confirm that the person is licensed to sell insurance in your state.

Some employers offer group long-term care policies or make individual policies available at discounted group rates. A number of group plans don't include underwriting, which means you may not have to meet medical requirements to qualify, at least initially. Benefits may also be available to family members, who must pay premiums and might need to pass medical screenings. In most cases, if you leave the employer or the employer stops providing the benefit, you'll be able to retain the policy or receive a similar offering if you continue to pay the premiums.

A professional or service organization you belong to might offer group-rate long-term care insurance policies to its members. Just as with employer-sponsored coverage, study your options so you'll know what would happen if coverage were terminated or if you were to leave the organization.

Regarding Medicaid, if you purchase a long-term care insurance policy that qualifies for the State Partnership Program, you can keep a specified amount of assets and still qualify for Medicaid. Most states have a State Partnership Program. Be sure to ask your insurance agent whether the policy you're considering qualifies under the State Partnership Program, how it works with Medicaid, and when and how you would qualify for Medicaid. You can find out more about this program at longtermcare.gov/medicare-medicaid-more/ state-based-programs. If you have more questions about Medicaid and the partnership program in your state, check with your SHIP.

Joint policies let you buy a single policy that covers more than one person. The policy can be used by a husband and wife, two partners, or two related adults. Typically, a total or maximum benefit applies to everyone insured under the policy. For instance, if a couple has a policy with a $100,000 maximum benefit and one person uses $40,000, the other person would have $60,000 left for his or her own services. A downside is that with such a joint policy, you run the risk of one person depleting funds that the other partner might need.

Make sure you buy a policy that covers the types of facilities, programs, and services that you'll want and are available where you live. With some insurance policies, you must use services from a certified home care agency or a licensed professional; other policies allow you to hire independent or non-licensed providers or family members. Companies may place certain qualifications—such as licensure, if available in your state—or restrictions on facilities or programs used. (If you move to another area, check your policy. Moving might make a difference in your coverage and the types of services available.) Policies may cover the following care arrangements:

- **Skilled nursing facility**: A facility that provides a full range of skilled health care, rehabilitation care, personal care, and daily activities in a 24/7 setting. Find out whether the policy covers more than room and board.

- **Assisted living**: A residence with apartment-style units that makes personal care and other individualized services (such as meal delivery) available when needed.

- **Adult day care services**: A program outside the home that provides health, social, and other support services in a supervised setting for adults who need some degree of help during the day.

- **Home care**: An agency or individual who performs services, such as help with bathing, grooming, chores, and housework.

- **Home modification**: Adaptations, such as installing ramps or grab bars, to make your home safer and more accessible.

- **Care coordination**: Services provided by a trained or licensed professional who assists with determining needs, locating services, and arranging for care. The policy may also cover the monitoring of care providers.

- **Future service options**: If a new type of long-term care service is developed after you purchase the insurance, some policies have the flexibility to cover the new services. The "future service" option may be available if the policy contains specific language about alternative options.

Long-term care policies can pay different amounts for different services (such as $50 a day for home care and $100 a day for skilled nursing facility care), or they may pay one rate for any service. Most policies limit the amount of benefits you can receive, such as a specific number of years or a total dollar amount. When purchasing a policy, you select the benefit amount and duration to fit your budget and anticipated needs. "Pooled benefits" allow you to use a total dollar amount of benefits for different types of services. With this coverage option you can combine services that meet your particular needs.

To determine how useful a policy will be to you, compare the amount of your policy's daily benefits with the average cost of care in your area and remember that you'll have to pay the difference. As the price of care increases over time, your benefit will start to erode unless you select inflation protection in your policy.

Inflation protection is an important option to consider, too, since many people purchase long-term care insurance 10, 20, or 30 years before receiving benefits. Indexing to inflation allows the daily benefit you choose to keep up with the rising cost of care. You can increase your benefit by a given percent (5 percent is often recommended) with either compound or simple inflation protection. If you're under age 70 when you buy long-term care insurance, it's probably better to have automatic "compound" inflation protection. This means that the amount of your daily benefit increase will be based on the higher amount of coverage at each anniversary date of the policy. "Simple" inflation protection increases your daily benefit by a fixed percentage of the original benefit amount. Typically, the simple option won't keep pace with the price of services.

In lieu of automatic increases, some policies offer "future-purchase options" or "guaranteed-purchase options." These policies often start out with more limited coverage and a corresponding lower premium. At a later, designated time, you have the option of increasing your coverage—although at a substantially increased premium. If you turn down the option several times, you may lose the ability to increase the benefit in the future.

Be sure you understand what has to happen before you can start collecting benefits under a policy. "Benefit triggers" are the conditions that must occur before you start receiving your benefits. Most companies look to your inability to perform certain activities of daily living (ADLs) to figure out when you can start to receive benefits. Generally, benefits begin when you need help with two or three ADLs. Requiring assistance with bathing, eating, dressing, using the toilet, walking, and remaining continent are the most common ADLs used. You should be sure your policy includes bathing in the list of benefit triggers because this is often the first task that becomes impossible to do alone.

Pay close attention to what the policy uses as a trigger for paying benefits if you develop a cognitive impairment, such as Alzheimer's disease. This is because a person with Alzheimer's may be physically able to perform activities but is no longer capable of doing them without help. Mental function tests are commonly substituted as benefit triggers for cognitive impairments. Ask whether you must require someone to perform the activity for you, rather than just stand by and supervise you, to trigger benefits.

All policies exclude coverage for some conditions. Ask the agent to review these exclusions with you. Most states have outlawed companies from requiring you to have been in a hospital or nursing facility for a specific number of days before qualifying for benefits. Still, some states permit this exclusion, which could keep you from ever qualifying for a benefit.

Coverage exclusions for drug and alcohol abuse, mental disorders, and self-inflicted injuries are common. Be sure that Alzheimer's disease and other common illnesses, such as heart disease, diabetes, or certain forms of cancer, aren't mentioned as reasons not to pay benefits.

Most policies include a waiting or elimination period before the insurance company begins to pay. This period is the number of days after you are certified as "eligible for benefits," once you can no longer perform the required number of ADLs. You can typically choose from zero up to 100 days. Carefully calculate how many days you can afford to pay on your own before coverage kicks in. (The shorter the period, the higher the price of the policy.)

Many policies allow you to stop paying your premium after you've started receiving benefits. Some companies waive premiums immediately while others waive them after a certain number of days. Being able to continue to afford the premiums after retirement is a barrier for many people thinking about getting long-term care policies. Companies can't single you out for a rate increase, but they can increase rates on all similar policies sold in your state. Most premiums do increase over the life of the policy.

If you stop paying your premium or drop your benefit, a "nonforfeiture option" will allow you to receive a reduced amount of coverage based on the amount of money you've already paid. Some states require policies to offer nonforfeiture benefits, including benefit options with different premiums. Since nonforfeiture provisions vary by location, check with your state's insurance department or your state's listing at your SHIP before dropping your policy. If your policy doesn't have a nonforfeiture option and you stop paying the premiums, you'll lose all the benefits for which you have paid.

Long-term care policies are "guaranteed renewable," which means that they cannot be canceled or terminated because of the policyholder's age, physical condition, or mental health. This guarantee ensures that your policy won't expire unless you've used up your benefits or haven't paid your premium.

If you've determined which long-term care insurance options best meet your needs and you're ready to buy a policy, do the following:

- Ask your state insurance department for a list of companies approved to sell long-term care insurance policies in your state. Find out whether there were complaints about any of the companies that sold them.

- Check the stability of the company and be sure it has a long history with this type of insurance. You can check this information at websites for companies, including Moody's Investors Service, Standard and Poor's and A.M. Best.

- Compare information and costs from at least three major insurance companies. Ask how often and by how much the companies have increased their premiums.

- Get a written copy of any policy you're considering. Review it carefully, with the assistance of your attorney or financial adviser. Write out your questions, and have a representative of the insurance company respond to your questions in writing.

- Never let anyone pressure or scare you into making a quick decision.
- Never pay any insurance premium in cash, and always make your check payable to the company and not an individual.

Nearly all states require insurance companies to give you 30 days to review your signed policy. During this time, you can return a policy for a full refund if you change your mind.

Still have questions or concerns? Contact the agency listed for your state at your SHIP.

Insurance Action Checklists

The following Action Checklists are in Chapter 10:

❑ Annuity

❑ Life Insurance

❑ Health, Disability, and Medicare Insurance

❑ Medical Claims Tracker

❑ Homeowners and Renters Insurance

❑ Umbrella Insurance

❑ Vehicle Insurance

❑ Long-Term Care Insurance

Annuity

I have an annuity with the following policies and companies:

Insurance company: _____

Agent: _____

Phone: _____ Fax: _____

Address: _____

_____

E-mail: _____ Website: _____

Policy #: _____

Terms:_____

Beneficiary/beneficiaries: _____

Policy location: _____

Insurance company: _____

Agent: _____

Phone: _____ Fax: _____

Address: _____

_____

E-mail: _____ Website: _____

Policy #: _____

Terms:_____

Beneficiary/beneficiaries: _____

Policy location: _____

Life Insurance

I carry life insurance with the following companies:

Insurance company: _____

Agent:_____

Policy #: _____

Face amount: _____

Beneficiary/beneficiaries: _____

Phone: _____ Fax: _____

Address: _____

_____

E-mail: _____ Website: _____

Policy location: _____

Insurance company: _____

Agent:_____

Policy #: _____

Face amount: _____

Beneficiary/beneficiaries: _____

Phone: _____ Fax: _____

Address: _____

_____

E-mail: _____ Website: _____

Policy location: _____

Health, Disability, and Medicare Insurance

I carry health insurance with the following policies and companies:

- ❑ Dental
- ❑ Disability
- ❑ Hospitalization
- ❑ Long-term care
- ❑ Major medical
- ❑ Medicare
- ❑ Medicare Advantage
- ❑ Medicare Part D Prescription Drug Insurance
- ❑ Medicare Supplemental Insurance (Medigap)
- ❑ Surgical
- ❑ Travel accidental death
- ❑ Vision
- ❑ Other

Insurance company: _____

Type of policy: _____

Policy #: _____

Group #: _____

Policy premium due date: _____

Agent:_____

Phone: _____ Fax: _____

Address: _____

_____

E-mail: _____ Website: _____

Insurance company: _____

Type of policy: _____

Policy #: _____

Group #: _____

Policy premium due date: _____

Agent:_____

Phone: _____ Fax: _____

Address: _____

_____

E-mail: _____ Website: _____

Insurance company: _____

Type of policy: _____

Policy #: _____

Group #: _____

Policy premium due date: _____

Agent:_____

Phone: _____ Fax: _____

Address: _____

_____

E-mail: _____ Website: _____

Insurance company: _____

Type of policy: _____

Policy #: _____

Group #: _____

Policy premium due date: _____

Agent:_____

Phone: _____ Fax: _____

Address: _____

_____

E-mail: _____ Website: _____

Insurance company: _____

Type of policy: _____

Policy #: _____

Group #: _____

Policy premium due date: _____

Agent:_____

Phone: _____ Fax: _____

Address: _____

_____

E-mail: _____ Website: _____

Insurance company: _____

Type of policy: _____

Policy #: _____

Group #: _____

Policy premium due date: _____

Agent:_____

Phone: _____ Fax: _____

Address: _____

_____

E-mail: _____ Website: _____

Medical Claims Tracker

Date of service	Provider	Service (office visit, lab, etc.)	Medicare paid	Other insurance paid	Patient owes	Date paid	How paid (check, credit card)	Round trip mileage	Parking	Notes

Homeowners and Renters Insurance

I have homeowners, renters, condominium, or second residence insurance policies with the following companies:

Insurance company: _____

Policy #: _____

Agent: _____

Phone: _____ Fax: _____

Address: _____

_____

E-mail: _____ Website: _____

Description of coverage: _____

_____

_____

_____

Insurance company: _____

Policy #: _____

Agent: _____

Phone: _____ Fax: _____

Address: _____

_____

E-mail: _____ Website: _____

Description of coverage: _____

_____

_____

_____

Umbrella Insurance

I have umbrella insurance with the following companies:

Insurance company: _____

Policy #: _____

Group #: _____

Type of policy: _____

Policy premium due date: _____

Agent:_____

Phone: _____ Fax: _____

Address: _____

_____

E-mail: _____ Website: _____

Insurance company: _____

Policy #: _____

Group #: _____

Type of policy: _____

Policy premium due date: _____

Agent:_____

Phone: _____ Fax: _____

Address: _____

_____

E-mail: _____ Website: _____

Vehicle Insurance

I carry vehicle insurance on the following vehicles, including cars, airplanes, boats, motor-cycles, and snowmobiles, with the following companies:

Vehicle: _____

Year purchased: _____ Purchase price: _____

Insurance company: _____

Agent:_____

Phone: _____ Fax: _____

Address: _____

_____

E-mail: _____ Website: _____

Policy #: _____

Vehicle: _____

Year purchased: _____ Purchase price: _____

Insurance company: _____

Agent:_____

Phone: _____ Fax: _____

Address: _____

_____

E-mail: _____ Website: _____

Policy #: _____

Vehicle: _____

Year purchased: _____ Purchase price: _____

Insurance company: _____

Agent:_____

Phone: _____ Fax: _____

Address: _____

_____

E-mail: _____ Website: _____

Policy #: _____

Vehicle: _____

Year purchased: _____ Purchase price: _____

Insurance company: _____

Agent:_____

Phone: _____ Fax: _____

Address: _____

_____

E-mail: _____ Website: _____

Policy #: _____

Vehicle: _____

Year purchased: _____ Purchase price: _____

Insurance company: _____

Agent:_____

Phone: _____ Fax: _____

Address: _____

_____

E-mail: _____ Website: _____

Policy #: _____

Long-Term Care Insurance

I have the following long-term care insurance policy:

Insurance company: _____

Policy #: _____

Agent:_____

Phone: _____ Fax: _____

Address: _____

_____

E-mail: _____ Website: _____

The policy has been reviewed by the following lawyer:

Name:_____

Phone: _____ E-mail: _____

Address: _____

_____

The policy contains the following terms:

- ❑ Triggers to begin claiming benefits
    - ❑ Inability to perform _____ activities of daily living (ADLs)
    - ❑ Evaluation by company's medical professionals
    - ❑ Documentation by primary physician
    - ❑ Moderate cognitive impairment
    - ❑ Required hospital stay of _____ days
    - ❑ Other: _____
- ❑ Waiting period between eligibility and benefit payment of _____ days
- ❑ Deductible: _____
- ❑ Total days/years of coverage: _____
- ❑ Benefit maximum: $_____
- ❑ Daily rate: $_____
- ❑ Joint coverage for _____ and _____
- ❑ Inflation protection: ❑ Yes   ❑ No
    - ❑ Compound
    - ❑ Simple
- ❑ Premium waiver when benefits begin: ❑ Yes   ❑ No
- ❑ Benefit payments are taxable income: ❑ Yes   ❑ No
- ❑ Nonforfeiture benefits: ❑ Yes   ❑ No

Coverage includes:

- ❑ Home health care expenses
  - ❑ Licensed professional required: ❑ Yes   ❑ No
  - ❑ Payment details: _____
- ❑ Assisted living expenses
  - ❑ Certified facility required: ❑ Yes   ❑ No
  - ❑ Payment details: _____
- ❑ Skilled nursing facility expenses
  - ❑ Medicare approved facility required: ❑ Yes   ❑ No
  - ❑ Payment details: _____
- ❑ Compensation of family caregivers: ❑ Yes   ❑ No
- ❑ Adult day care: ❑ Yes   ❑ No
- ❑ Care coordination: ❑ Yes   ❑ No
- ❑ Pooled benefits: ❑ Yes   ❑ No
- ❑ Reimbursement of home modification: ❑ Yes   ❑ No
- ❑ State Partnership Program to qualify for Medicaid: ❑ Yes   ❑ No
- ❑ Other coverage: _____

Coverage excludes:

- ❑ Conditions: _____
- ❑ Services: _____

CHAPTER 11
DEAL WITH LEGAL MATTERS

Retirement offers an ideal time to get your legal affairs in order, if you haven't already. Most of this chapter looks ahead to three big legal areas: your preferences should you become ill, your wishes at the end of your life, and how you want your estate distributed after your death. As personal as these decisions are, many legal details and documents have to be involved.

This may sound depressing, but truthfully, I've found that one of the kindest things that you can do for your family is to spare them the distress of facing decisions about your health care without knowing your wishes. You can do this by making those decisions yourself and sharing them in this book.

In addition to knowing your wishes for your health care, your family will need to make many decisions at the time of your death. Decisions concerning the care of your body, including whether you want to be cremated or embalmed, are time sensitive.

Your family also has to know promptly upon your death if you wish to be an organ donor or if you have already made arrangements with a medical school to donate your body for medical research. If you have pre-paid for any part of your funeral or burial, your family members need to know about the contract so they don't pay unnecessarily for anything you have already paid for.

You will also want to have in place various legal documents that set out your plans for how you want your estate distributed after your death and who will handle your affairs. In this chapter, I offer the basics about wills and codicils, living trusts, and powers of attorney. Do what I do: Rely on a lawyer experienced in estate planning to draft all your estate planning documents.

By indicating on the checklists in this chapter what you want and the plans you have in place, you will be giving your loved ones a precious gift as you relieve them of any uncertainty about your wishes. They will be able to act with confidence that they are doing the right thing.

My To-Do Checklist

Done   **Need to Do**

❑   ❑   Document your health care preferences

❑   ❑   Prepare an organ donor card

❑   ❑   Plan the disposition of your body

❑   ❑   Let family know your funeral wishes

❑   ❑   Consider options for paying for your funeral

❑   ❑   Know your veterans' burial benefits

❑   ❑   Create or review your estate plan

❑   ❑   Identify a source of funding for the costs to close your estate

❑   ❑   Select an agent to manage your financial affairs

❑   ❑   Discuss your advance planning with those who need to know

✓ Document your health care preferences

Any time you become seriously ill—whatever your age—many decisions have to be made about the medical care you receive. As long as you are able to communicate your wishes, health care providers look to you for answers about the treatment choices you want. When you cannot communicate your wishes, decisions still have to be made. Your family and health care providers want to respect your treatment preferences, but they need to know ahead of time how to make the decisions you want them to make. Advance health care planning involves thinking about what treatments and health care you do or do not want, communicating your thoughts to those who will be called upon to make decisions on your behalf, and putting those wishes down on paper in the appropriate legal forms.

More than seven in ten people say they have given a great deal or some thought to their wishes for medical treatment at the end of their lives, according to the Pew Research Center. But in a 2013 survey reported in the *American Journal of Preventive Medicine*, just over a quarter of the respondents said they actually had an advance directive. According to the 2011 report "Living Well at the End of Life: A National Conversation," produced by the *National Journal* and the Regence Foundation, most people state a clear preference for options that make the end of life better, not just longer, including spending quality time with family and friends, having their pain managed, and avoiding emotional and financial devastation for their family. Despite wanting to avoid financial devastation, 43 percent of Medicare patients end up spending more than the total value of their assets, excluding real estate, on end-of life care, while 25 percent spend all their assets, including any money from home or property. Overall, the average Medicare patient spends more than $38,500 out of pocket during their final five years. Seven in ten say they want to die at home, but

74 percent die in a hospital or nursing home. If you make your intentions clear, you can choose, for the most part, how you will be cared for at the end of your life.

Deciding what you may want for medical care in the future may not be a simple step. It can be hard to foresee what your medical needs or problems might be at some unknown time in the future. At this point, you may want to talk with your family, doctor, spiritual advisers, or others who might be helpful in talking through serious medical issues and what brings quality to your life. The Five Wishes form (agingwithdignity.org/five-wishes. php) may be helpful in starting and structuring important conversations about the medical care you wish to have. The American Bar Association also has a kit that is very helpful in discussing with doctors and family your spiritual values, personal priorities, and more at abanet.org/aging/toolkit.

Advance health care planning documents let your family and health care providers know the types of care you would want in the event you are unable to communicate and who you want to make decisions about that care when you cannot. The multiple advance planning documents can be confusing. Some states give the documents different names or combine them in various ways. The most generic term for the documents in which people express health care treatment preferences is an advance directive.

The first part of an advance directive is a *living will*, which outlines the treatments you would or would not want if you are unable to communicate and your death is imminent, or if you're permanently unconscious, in a vegetative state, or at the end-stage of a chronic condition, such as Alzheimer's disease. You may want to talk with your doctor about the specifics of these life-limiting conditions.

In most states, the law restricts the circumstances under which a living will is effective. Typically, you can use it to document your wishes concerning specific end-of-life treatments. While it is crucial that your family and doctors understand your preferences concerning life-prolonging treatments, such as use of respirators, cardiopulmonary resuscitation, or intravenous nutrition or hydration, you may want to include directions on who makes sure your preferences are carried out.

The second part of an advance directive is the selection of a health care agent who can speak for you if you are unable to do so. This is also referred to as selecting a health care proxy or signing a *durable power of attorney for health care*. You can give your agent broad authority to make any health care decision you specify, not about just life-prolonging treatments. You can set down any guidance or instructions you want your agent and your health care team to follow. And, perhaps more importantly, you have someone who will speak for you and get necessary information from your health care providers to make the decisions you would want to be made. By having in writing what your preferences are and who will speak up on your behalf, you can help your family make difficult decisions and make sure your personal values are respected.

Your agent should be someone who knows you and understands your wishes about medical treatments. You can authorize your agent to make decisions in situations you might not have anticipated. Your agent can talk with your health care providers about your changing medical condition and authorize treatment or have it withdrawn as circumstances change. In the sometimes bewildering medical system, it is good to have someone in charge who can advocate for you. If health care providers resist following your wishes, your agent can stand up for what you want and take any other necessary steps to see that your wishes are honored. This includes changing doctors or hospitals, if necessary, to get the care you want.

When selecting your health care agent, you should choose someone you trust and who will be there for you now and well into the future. You will need to feel comfortable talking with him or her about your end-of-life care and confident that he or she will follow your wishes even if they are not similar to his or her own. Your agent should be able to be assertive, if necessary, when talking with health care professionals. Your choice also needs to meet your state's criteria for health care agents. Most states exclude some categories of people from being able to serve as agents such as your doctor, the administrator of the nursing facility where you are living, or someone who works in your nursing facility.

The conversations you need to have with your health care agent are a critical part of your planning. Your agent needs to understand what is important to you for your quality of life and the kind of medical care you would or would not want to have. Think of your advance directive as a written record of the conversations you have had with your agent about how you want to live up until the moment you die. Having your preferences in writing can be backup support for your agent and give you the assurance that your wishes are known.

Your agent and your health care providers need to have copies of your advance directives. You may also wish to carry a wallet card that indicates you have an advance directive and how to get in touch with your agent.

You don't need a lawyer to create advance directives. You can find state-specific forms at aarp.org/advancedirectives and links to other information about advance directives at ambar.org/HealthCarePOA. Many elder law attorneys will help you prepare your advance directives as part of estate and advance care planning. Most hospitals, area agencies on aging, bar associations, and medical societies also provide free forms.

Unlike the health care powers of attorney that you prepare, you may want to talk with your doctor about special medical orders that could include do-not-resuscitate orders (DNR), out-of-hospital DNRs, and physician orders for life-sustaining treatment.

A do-not-resuscitate (DNR) order is an instruction in your medical record that directs the hospital medical team not to attempt to revive you in the event you stop breathing or your heart stops beating. The doctor enters a DNR only after confirming with you or your health care agent that not trying to restore breathing or heart rhythm is your preferred alternative.

Some states also have provisions for out-of-hospital DNRs (OOH DNRS). These are orders that direct emergency medical service (EMS) responders not to try to revive a patient. Under most circumstances and state laws, EMS teams responding to a 9-1-1 call are required to make all attempts to revive an unresponsive person. Even if the person has a living will that specifies otherwise, EMS responders cannot honor it. People living at home or in an assisted living facility may not want to be resuscitated, but because of their medical condition they cannot stop the EMR team from going ahead with cardiopulmonary resuscitation (CPR), defibrillation, or other life-sustaining treatments. To overcome this, you can request an OOH DNR. After the doctor enters the OOH DNR, you wear a special DNR medical alert bracelet. In those states with OOH DNR laws, EMS personnel are trained to look for the DNR bracelet and to know that legally they cannot try to revive you.

Another special kind of medical order allowed in most states is a physician order for life-sustaining treatment (POLST). Typically, a state-prescribed POLST form is prepared for very sick patients with multiple chronic conditions. Although the details vary from state to state, as does the name (medical order for scope of treatment, or MOST, for example, is used in Colorado), in general this protocol is an effort to encourage conversations among medical providers, patients, and families to understand and document the patient's current treatment preferences. A POLST complements, rather than replaces, an advance directive. It records in detail the patient's current preferences and puts those decisions into medical orders to be followed in a medical crisis. The form is printed on brightly colored paper so it can be readily seen, followed, and transferred with the patient from hospital to nursing facility and back to the hospital. EMS personnel must honor a POLST. To find out about the POLST protocol in your state, go to polst.org.

Hospice care and palliative care are very similar when it comes to the most important issue for dying people: the care they receive during their final days. Most people have heard of hospice care and have a general idea of what services hospice provides. Fewer understand that palliative care is the "comfort care" provided in most hospitals as well as through hospice. Both hospice and palliative care services call for patients to receive a coordinated approach where medications, symptom treatment, and day-to-day care are provided through a single program. Where palliative care programs and hospice care programs differ is in the care location, timing, payment, and eligibility for services.

Palliative care is usually administered in an institution such as a hospital, extended care facility, or nursing facility, although it also can be administered in the home. Palliative care teams are made up of doctors, nurses, and other professional medical caregivers, often at the facility where a patient is receiving treatment. The team administers or oversees most of the ongoing comfort care that patients receive. Patients can receive palliative care at any time, at any stage of illness, whether it be terminal or not.

Generally, a patient's hospice care program, overseen by a team of hospice professionals, is administered in the home. The hospice team brings to the home everything the patient might need, such as a hospital bed, bedside commode, medications, or bandages. Hospice often relies on family caregivers as well as visiting hospice aides and nurses. Others on the hospice team include a social worker, counselor or chaplain, and a volunteer. Some programs may also add psychologists, psychiatrists, home health aides, art or pet therapists, nutritionists, and occupational, speech, massage, or physical therapists. While hospice can provide round-the-clock care in a skilled nursing or a special hospice facility, this is not the norm. To be eligible for hospice under Medicare rules, two physicians must certify that the patient has life-altering conditions with an expected prognosis of six months or less. The aim of hospice is to provide the best quality of life during whatever time is left. Hospice can also offer follow-up grief support for the patient's family.

Because most hospice programs concentrate on the patient's comfort rather than aggressive treatment or life-prolonging procedures, Medicare will not cover a hospice patient's treatment, procedures, or medications intended to cure the patient of the underlying disease. A patient can choose to leave hospice to receive curing treatments. That said, Medicare has a new pilot program that allows some patients to continue pursuing curative treatments while under hospice care in more than 100 hospices across the country. Because there are no time limits on when patients can receive palliative care, it can be available for patients who want and need comfort at any stage of any disease, whether terminal or chronic. People in a palliative care program can receive life-prolonging therapies.

Whereas Medicare covers all the costs of hospice care, private insurance coverage for hospice can vary. On the other hand, because palliative care is administered through the treating hospital, it is likely to be covered by Medicare or other hospitalization insurance and billed like regular hospital and doctor costs. Check the details with your private insurance company, doctor, or hospital administration.

✓ Prepare an organ donor card

Do you wish to share the gift of your organs or tissues with someone needing a transplant? These donations have saved or improved thousands of lives, at absolutely no cost to the donor. Yet there is always a very long list of patients waiting for organ transplants. According to the US Department of Health and Human Services, eighteen patients die each day because of the shortage of available donated organs.

If you do wish to give this gift, you need to sign and carry an organ donation card. In some states, you can indicate your wish to be an organ donor on your driver's license. Most, but not all, states have an organ donation registry. You can find out if your state does at organdonor.gov/becomingdonor/stateregistries.html. Sign up on your state's registry so your wishes can be honored.

Most organ donations are made after a person has been declared brain dead following an accident, heart attack, or stroke. The organs or tissues are removed through a surgical procedure. Most transplanted organs must be used within hours of the donation, while tissue donations of corneas, heart valves, skin, and bones can be preserved and stored in tissue banks. After the removal procedures, your body can be buried or cremated as though it were intact.

If you wish to make a *whole body donation* to a medical school or research facility, you need to make arrangements with the school or research entity before you die. You can find a list of anatomical research programs and learn more about what you need to do to make these arrangements at med.ufl.edu/anatbd/usprograms.html. Be sure to talk with your family members about your donation wishes so they will know the specific instructions for how to transfer your body. Typically, the facility will cremate your body at no expense and deliver your ashes as you instruct.

✓ Plan the disposition of your body

What do you wish to have done with your body after your death? This is a topic that people try to avoid, but again, making your wishes known will save your family the pressure of deciding for you and making decisions in stressful times. Do you want a natural burial, burial in a coffin in a cemetery or in a crypt in a mausoleum, or cremation? If you prefer cremation, do you want your ashes buried in an urn at a cemetery, placed in a columbarium, or scattered at the location of your choice?

More people are considering natural or "green" burials. With natural burial, your body would be promptly buried, without embalming, in the ground in a biodegradable coffin made of cardboard or bamboo, or in a shroud. You could have a tree or shrub planted instead of a stone grave marker, or request that instead of flowers, gifts could be made to your favorite charity. Those of the Jewish faith may have special rituals for washing the body, staying with the body until burial, and burying the body promptly without embalming.

People who wish to be cremated can also forego embalming. With direct cremation, your body would go directly from the place of death to the crematory. Before cremation, an official will need to prepare a death certificate and obtain a cremation permit. Typically, your spouse or next-of-kin will need to sign a consent about the disposition of your body. You may want to sign a pre-need authorization for cremation, especially if you have no spouse or close family. In this document, you appoint the person you want to consent to your cremation and to receive your ashes. A funeral home or crematory should be able to give you a form for you to sign so you can make sure your wishes to be cremated are carried out.

Every state has regulations concerning the scattering of ashes, so check with your state agency that regulates burials. The scattering of ashes at sea must be done at least three nautical miles from land and the Environmental Protection Agency needs notice within 30 days of the burial.

If you wish your body to be buried, you will need to purchase a lot at a cemetery or a niche in a mausoleum. You can purchase just a single lot or a number of lots in a block where other family members would also be buried. When purchasing a cemetery lot, ask about any additional charges for the opening, closing, and perpetual care of the gravesite. You should receive a deed to the land, or plot, that you have purchased. The cost of cemetery lots varies significantly depending on where you wish to be buried. It is essential your family knows if you have purchased a cemetery plot or place in a mausoleum so they can make the correct arrangements. Be sure to record that information on the Burial Checklist.

Because of the many options, be sure your family knows of your wishes by filing out the various checklists in this chapter.

✓ Let family know your funeral wishes

How do you wish your death to be commemorated? Depending on your family and cultural or religious traditions, you may wish no service or ceremony, a lively gathering of family and friends to celebrate your life, a memorial service, a viewing at a mortuary, a wake, or a religious service in your place of worship. You may want a simple ceremony that celebrates your life or a more elaborate memorial service. If you are a veteran, you may want a military bugler with burial in a national cemetery. Many people have firm opinions about whether a casket should be open or closed. Others have special organizations they want to receive memorial donations or ideas about what should be included in their obituary. Whatever your wishes, put them in writing and share them with your loved ones.

A funeral director can help you plan for whatever type of commemoration you wish. You can discuss ahead of time the type of casket you would prefer, as well as other arrangements for any service or ceremony. Funeral directors must give you written price lists that tell you the costs for body preparation and transportation, caskets or urns, grave liners or "outer burial containers," and other services.

With the price lists in hand, you can comparison shop among several funeral homes to make sure you get the arrangements exactly as you desire and have a better idea about the range of costs. Keep in mind that you can choose where you purchase your casket. You can even shop for one online.

A funeral director can also help you make arrangements for the type of grave marker or headstone you prefer. Headstones typically extend above the ground to identify the person buried. Grave markers lay flat on the ground. Some cemeteries or memorial parks require grave markers to make it easier to care for the grounds. You can also indicate on the Burial Checklist the inscription you want on your headstone or grave marker.

✓ Consider options for paying for your funeral

Many funeral establishments let you now pay a fixed price for your funeral. Prepaying fixes the costs at today's prices for your choice of a coffin and other services that may cost more in the future. Equally important, making your own financial arrangements gives you the peace of mind that your family will not have this financial burden.

Before pre-paying for your funeral with a funeral director, get confirmation in writing about how your financial investment will be protected. You want to be assured that your money is in safe hands and your pre-need contract will be honored a decade or more in the future. With most pre-need contracts you turn over a sum of money, either a lump sum or in installment payments. Your money is then placed in trust held by a third-party trustee or used to purchase an insurance policy. The trustee or insurance company is responsible for managing the money until it is time to pay the funeral home for the goods and services you listed in your contract. Ask whether your funds will be securely placed in a trust held by a financially sound third party or used to purchase an insurance policy. Also find out exactly what it covers and what you will pay for later. Does it include a religious leader officiating? The procession from funeral home to cemetery? The marker and inscription?

You will also want to inquire about the portability of your contract if you should move to another location and no longer want your funeral where you used to live. If your plans change or the funeral home changes hands, you'll want to be able to transfer the contract to a different funeral home.

Before paying for a pre-need contract, check with your state's attorney general or board of funeral directors to learn how pre-need contracts are regulated in your state. Also, if you have pre-paid for any part of your funeral or burial, your family needs to know about the contract so they don't have to pay unnecessarily for anything you have already paid for. Be sure to include the details on the Funeral/Memorial Service Checklist.

There are other options for making sure your family is not saddled with the expenses for your funeral. Funerals are expensive—on average $7,000—along with the emotional toll when someone dies. You may wish to purchase a life insurance policy that would cover the anticipated funeral costs, or invest your money in a certificate of deposit or in a savings account designated to cover these expenses. With options like these, you will know that the money will be available to your family, but you remain in control of the money as your plans for your final arrangements change.

✓ Know your veterans' burial benefits

If you are an eligible US military veteran, the US Department of Veterans Affairs (VA) provides a bundle of benefits at the time of your burial. The available benefits depend upon your length of service, the era during which you served, whether you are disabled, whether the disability was caused by active service, and many other criteria. Be sure to indicate on the Veteran's Burial Benefits Checklist if you want any of these benefits.

Family members applying for VA benefits need a copy of your service record, or your DD-214. The DD-214 will specify that you were on active military duty and show that your release from active duty was under other than dishonorable conditions. You can get this very important record at archives.gov/veterans/military-service-records. Here are some of the available benefits.

Burial Flag

A US flag may be issued to drape over your casket. After the funeral service, the flag will be given to your next of kin or close friend or associate. Flags are issued at any VA office and most local post offices. A Presidential Memorial Certificate is also available at no cost to the family.

Burial in a National Cemetery

Burial in a national cemetery is open to all members of the armed forces and veterans who have met minimum active service duty requirements and were discharged under conditions other than dishonorable. Your spouse, widow or widower, minor children, and, under certain conditions, unmarried adult children are also eligible for burial in a national cemetery. In most cases, one gravesite is provided for the burial of all eligible family members and a single headstone or marker is provided. When both you and your spouse are veterans, you can request two gravesites and two headstones or markers. Certain members of the armed forces' reserve components may also be eligible for burial. In each instance, space must be available. There is no charge for the grave plot, its opening and closing, a grave liner, or perpetual care.

Headstone or Marker

Eligible veterans can receive a government headstone or marker to be placed at their grave, whether at a national cemetery or elsewhere, at any cemetery around the world. Even if the grave was previously marked, you can obtain a government headstone. A headstone or marker is automatically furnished if burial is in a national cemetery. Otherwise, you must apply to the VA. The VA will ship the headstone or marker, without charge, to the person or firm designated on the application. The VA will also furnish a medallion, on request, to place on an existing headstone or marker that indicates that the person was a veteran. You must pay the cost of setting the headstone or marker, or attaching the medallion.

Military Honors

By law, every eligible veteran may receive a military funeral honors ceremony, to include folding and presenting the US burial flag and the playing of "Taps." A military funeral honors detail consists of two or more uniformed military persons, with at least one being a member of the veterans' branch of the armed forces. The US Department of Defense "Honoring Those Who Served" program calls for funeral directors to request military funeral honors on behalf of the family. Veterans' organizations may assist in providing military funeral honors. In support of this program, VA national cemetery staff can help coordinate military funeral honors either at a national or private cemetery. For more information go to cem.va.gov/military_funeral_honors.asp.

Reimbursement for Funeral or Burial Expenses

The VA is authorized to pay an allowance toward veterans' funeral and burial expenses. If it was a service-related death, the VA will pay up to $2,000 toward your burial expenses. If you are to be buried in a VA national cemetery, some or all of the cost of transporting your body to the cemetery may be reimbursed. For a non-service-related death, the VA will pay up to $300 toward your burial and funeral expenses and a $300 plot-interment allowance. If the death happens while you were in a VA hospital or under VA-contracted nursing home care, some or all of the costs for transporting your remains may be reimbursed.

✓ Create or review your estate plan

Your estate is everything that you own at the time of your death. Do you have a clear idea of who you want to get your estate after your death? Do you need help understanding all the legal nitty-gritty of how you make certain your estate plan will be carried out? Divvying up what you have involves a lot of confusing legal details and an assortment of legal documents to get it right.

My husband and I have done much of our estate planning using a variety of legal documents other than our wills. By signing the deed to our home as joint with right of survivorship, we did part of our estate planning because the surviving spouse will automatically get the house. When my husband inherited some land in New Hampshire, he did estate planning by deeding that out of-state property to a trust that named our son as the person to have that land. When I retired, I named my children as the beneficiaries of my life insurance so they will receive the money in that policy after my death. With each of those legal steps, we created parts of our estate plans. Through our wills, we distribute what's left over. It may be confusing, but a will covers the distribution of only those assets you have not otherwise distributed through other legal documents.

To ease you into estate planning, here's a cheat sheet on the basics you need to understand. You'll want to consult with estate planning experts who can guide you through the process. See Chapter 4 for tips on how to select someone.

What you own at the time of your death can be grouped into different categories depending on various factors:

- Your *overall estate* is everything you own at the time of your death.
- Your *probate estate* includes those things that will be distributed according to your will or, lacking that, your state's law of probate distribution.
- A *trust estate* is anything you have put in a trust (more on that later in this chapter).
- Your *taxable estate* includes those assets that the federal government or your state can tax.

Not everything in your estate is part of your probate estate, and not everything in your estate is subject to taxes.

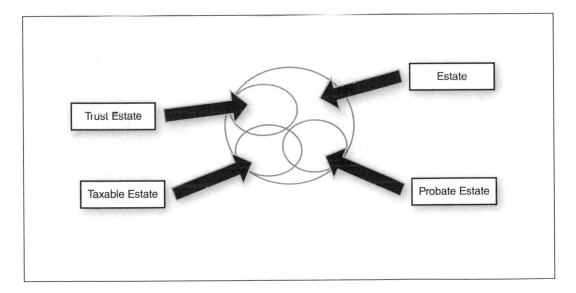

The first step to getting your estate plan in order is to identify everything you own, including bank accounts, investments, personal property, and real estate. The total package is your overall estate. Then, figure out if these items are in your probate estate or trust estate. To do that you need to understand some of the legal details of probate, wills, and trusts.

You figure out what assets are in your probate estate by determining what other actions you have taken to direct how specific assets are to be distributed on your death. You could do this by owning property jointly with right of survivorship; by transferring property into a trust; and by indicating a beneficiary of your life insurance, annuity, investment and bank accounts, or retirement fund. What is remaining is your probate estate. Your probate estate will be distributed according to the directions in your will or, if you have no will, according to the distribution laws in your state. If you have a will, you die *testate*; without a will you are said to have died *intestate*.

"Probate" is the court procedure that determines the validity of your will (if any), identifies who will be in charge of settling your affairs, identifies your heirs, inventories your probate assets, resolves claims against your estate, calculates any taxes to be paid, and makes sure the remaining proceeds are distributed to the proper persons. In your will, you establish who gets what and how much. If you don't have a will, your state's intestacy law does that for you. In effect, the probate court makes sure that your wishes are carried out, supervises how your estate is distributed, adjudicates any disputes over the terms of your will or claims against your estate, and sorts out family disagreements.

Last Will and Testament

A will, or last will and testament, is one of the key legal documents of your estate plan. In your will you determine who you want to receive your probate property. If you have a friend, domestic partner, or significant other who is not related to you that you want to receive any part of your estate, you must have a will. In essence, your will can also stipulate who you don't want to inherit your property, even if they're next of kin (but not your spouse).

In your will, you set out what you want your beneficiaries to receive. You can make gifts in your will of specific items, such as your car or wedding ring; a set dollar amount; or percentages divided among several friends or family members. (Another way to establish who is to get some of your personal property is through a letter of instruction, explained later in this chapter, which is separate from your will.) Your last will and testament can also indicate donations to the charities, schools, or religious groups you support, letting you take advantage of tax laws that encourage private philanthropy.

In your will, you name the person you want to be in charge of managing your estate, and the court will appoint that person as your *executor*. If you have not nominated an executor in your will, the court will appoint an *administrator* for you. The duties of the executor or administrator—also called a *personal representative*—are the same.

You should choose your personal representative with care, because that person has many responsibilities. It can be a big task that requires good financial skills, attention to detail, patience, and probably a dose of diplomacy. Your personal representative must inventory your assets, have them appraised, pay bills, publish legal notices, prepare your final income tax return, work with financial institutions to close out accounts, record documents to sell or transfer real estate, find and notify beneficiaries, file any estate tax returns, and file inventories and accountings with the court. All the while, your personal representative must keep happy the anxious and impatient debtors and beneficiaries of your estate.

If you have minor children, you need to name who you want to be their guardian until they reach the age of majority. If you wish to leave assets to any minors, such as your grandchildren, you'll want to create a testamentary trust so their inheritance can be managed until they reach the age you select when remaining funds are turned over to them. A testamentary trust is set up and funded as part of your will and comes into effect after your death. Be sure you have talked with those you want to serve as your children's guardian and any minors' trustee to make sure they are willing and able to take on these responsibilities.

It is a good idea to review your will every few years, especially when your personal or family circumstances or the tax laws change. Consult with your attorney to make sure your will continues to express your estate plan.

Codicil

A *codicil* is a document that amends your will. As circumstances change, such as a death, divorce, or birth in your family, you may need to change a part of your will. You may want to add a bequest for a new grandchild, or change whom you want as your executor. I've revised my will using codicils several times: when the person I originally named as my executor died, when my children got married, and when grandchildren came along.

It can be easier to draft a codicil rather than rewriting your entire will. But this is not a do-it-yourself project. Never make any changes directly on your will. Strike outs, erasures, and any other markings on your will can have the devious effect of invalidating your will. A codicil must be executed with the same formality, number of witnesses, and notary requirements as your will.

Living Trust

A living trust is a legal arrangement in which you transfer your interest in property so it can be managed for you. It is called a living trust because you create it while you are still alive. The trustee you select manages your trust assets while you are living as well as after your death. In addition to creating the trust document, you must also "fund" the trust by preparing deeds, retitling assets, reassigning brokerage accounts, or taking other steps to transfer ownership of the property you want in the trust. Because you must transfer legal ownership to the trust, the property in the trust no longer legally belongs to you and, therefore, is not part of your probate assets.

Every trust has three parties—the creator, the trustee, and the beneficiary or beneficiaries—although the same individual can be all three at the same time. For example, you can name yourself as the trustee if you want to manage the trust as long as you can. You can also name a successor trustee who takes over the trust management when you are no longer willing or able to be the trustee and then after your death. You can also name yourself as the principal trust beneficiary so you can receive the trust proceeds to support yourself while you are living. You would also name secondary beneficiaries with instructions on when and how the trust assets are to be managed and distributed after your death. In this way, your trust serves a very similar purpose to your will in identifying how any trust assets are distributed to the beneficiaries you have named. Because any assets you have transferred to the trust are not part of your probate estate, your trust, rather than your will, controls how those assets are distributed.

A trust can be an important component to your estate plan. Whether you should have a trust, in addition to your will, depends on many personal factors. If you have substantial property that you may not be able to manage if you become incapacitated, you may want to set up a trust. If a trustee manages your assets, your family may not need to have a guardian appointed to oversee your estate if you become mentally or physically unable to do so yourself. By placing real estate that you own in another state into a trust, you may be able to avoid going through probate in the other state.

You should discuss with your estate planner whether a trust would be appropriate in your circumstances and what assets might best be placed into a trust. Be sure to find out if placing your home in a living trust would jeopardize any homestead exemption, impact eligibility for Medicaid, or increase your property taxes. Putting assets into a living trust does not reduce your income or estate taxes. It also does not protect your property from creditors. Because not all your property will be held by your trust, you will probably need to have a will to direct the distribution of any property that is not in your trust and that you have not otherwise planned for how it is to be inherited.

You may want to consider setting up a special trust to provide for the care of your pets. According to the American Veterinary Medical Association, 44 states have adopted pet trust laws. These laws specifically allow you to name your pet as a beneficiary of a trust so you can ensure that funds are available for its care.

You'll want to consult a tax adviser as you think through your estate plan and prepare your documentation. Even if your taxable estate is well below the lifetime federal estate tax exemption ($5.43 million in 2015 or $10.86 million for married couples), there may be tax consequences to you and your heirs that you'll need to consider. Your tax adviser also can review your major financial gifts and work with you on a gifting plan if you are in the fortunate position of needing to reduce the size of your taxable estate. Gifts can also complicate your eligibility for Medicaid.

How can gifts complicate your eligibility for Medicaid? Medicaid is another very complex area, primarily because the laws frequently change and the details can vary from state to state. To simply summarize current law, before you can be eligible for Medicaid assistance in paying for your medical care in a long-term care facility, you have to demonstrate your need. Part of that assessment looks at gifts ("transfers for less than fair market value") in the five years prior to your application for Medicaid. As with the gift tax laws, there are permissible ways to make gifts under Medicaid rules, but they are similarly complex. I highly recommend that you get expert advice from an elder law attorney before making any substantial gift.

Tax and Medicaid laws change frequently, so check with a tax adviser or an estate planning elder law attorney for current tax and Medicaid provisions.

Letter of Instruction

A letter of instruction serves as guidance to your personal representative and your family about matters they must attend to after your death and how you want specific personal possessions divided. This informal document can be attached to your will but is not an official part of it. You don't need an attorney to prepare it. Although it doesn't carry the legal weight of a will and is in no way a substitute for one, a letter of instruction clarifies any special requests you want your family to carry out when you die. Think of it as a flexible, informal supplement to your will that covers information that is more personal than what is typically included in a will. You can easily change it as your circumstances or wishes change. All you need to do is sign and date your new letter.

Your letter of instruction can have two parts that do two different things. One part helps your family know how to find the information necessary to plan your funeral. You might include instructions about the type of funeral or memorial service you want, who should officiate, whom you want as pall bearers, or what songs should—or should not—be sung. You need to let your family know about your plans with the funeral home and whether you have already paid for any of the arrangements. Describe the location of your pre-purchased burial plot or crypt and where you keep the plot deed. If you want to be cremated, your family needs to know where you want your ashes placed. Much of this information can be detailed in Chapter 10 of this book.

The other part of your letter of instruction may help eliminate any family feuds over who you want to receive your personal items. We all have heard stories of family fights erupting over how to divide family pictures, necklaces, the stamp collection, or the wedding gift from Aunt Sue. The items may not have monetary value, but getting them to the right person can make a big difference to you and to them.

If you want to make sure that your granddaughter gets the pearl necklace you got for your high school graduation, or you have already promised your best friend she'd get your figurine collection, put your wishes in your letter. If you have other ideas or preferences as to who should get what, write it down. Be sure to leave instructions about care for your pets.

You can make your letter personal, too. You can use it to send important messages to your survivors. You might include special hopes you have for your grandchild's education, or the important values you want to pass on. This could be the place to tell your family something you never got around to saying. It can be whatever you want it to be.

Your wishes can change over time. It is easy to revisit your instructions every couple of years or when your circumstances change. You don't have to follow any legal format. Always sign and date each revision to eliminate confusion over which is your most current statement. Just make sure your latest instructions are clear. Discard any older versions so there's no confusion about which version is the right one.

✓ Identify a source of funding for the costs to close your estate

Much has been written about the cost of probate, with some people suggesting that probate is a detrimental process that should be avoided at all costs. In reality, going through probate simply means settling your estate. Settling your estate does incur fees and costs that cannot be avoided, but you can control some of the expense through advance preparation and planning. Some minor costs of the probate process include filing fees to open the probate case and publishing legal notices in newspapers. Some states may also charge other filing fees for the inventory or accountings.

The major expenses in settling your estate—with or without probate court involvement—could be professional fees for an attorney, real estate agent, appraiser, accountant, and tax preparer. The attorney for your estate advises your personal representative (also called the executor of your will, or, if you don't appoint someone in your will, the administrator of your estate), assists in filing court documents and represents your estate in any disputes. These professional fees will be paid as an expense of your estate. The more complex your financial affairs are, the higher your professional fees will be. Also, the less clear your wishes, the higher the professional fees.

The other major expense in settling your estate is compensation for your personal representative. Depending on the laws of your state, your personal representative will be paid a percentage of the inventory value of your estate, a set fee determined by the judge, or the amount you say in your will. States that use a percentage to calculate the fee typically use a sliding scale. As the size of the estate increases, a smaller percentage is taken from the greater portions of the estate. For example, a personal representative might be entitled to a fee of 5 percent on the first $10,000 of an estate, 4 percent of the next $25,000, 3 percent of the next $50,000, and 2 percent of anything over $85,000.

In the other states, the personal representative's fee is based on what would be "just and reasonable" compensation for the amount of work the representative has to do. The amount of work involved for two personal representatives can differ considerably even for estates of the same value. It is much simpler to administer an estate if assets can be readily found, no claims against the estate need to be resolved, and no family squabbles need to be negotiated. You can make your personal representative's job much easier—and less expensive to your estate—by completing the checklists in this book. The more advance work you do, the less time and expense your personal representative has to incur. Of course, you can say in your will that your executor is not to be paid, but before adding that provision, think about all the work he or she will need to do.

✓ Select an agent to manage your financial affairs

A financial power of attorney can be one of the most useful documents you can prepare, but it is effective only during your lifetime. By creating a power of attorney while you have the capacity to do so, you select the trustworthy individual—called your agent or attorney-in-fact—you want to manage your financial affairs if you become unable to do so yourself. A power of attorney can give you peace of mind that if you should become unable to take care of your business details for any reason, the person you choose will have the authority to start acting on your behalf.

You determine your agent's responsibilities and duties. You may want to give your agent general powers to do everything that you could do, or you may want to give specific powers. Among the powers that you can delegate to another are the responsibility to manage your investments, pay your bills, collect your debts, sue on your behalf, sell your real estate, negotiate with insurance companies, sell your car, or have access to bank accounts. You may want your agent to sign your income tax returns, apply for benefits on your behalf, or make gifts to your favorite charities. If you want your agent to be able to make gifts of your money, you need to be very specific about how those gifts are to be made. You should design your power of attorney to fit your anticipated needs.

Powers of attorney can differ depending on when you want your agent to be able to act for you. A *durable* power of attorney begins when you sign and stays in effect for your lifetime—even after you become incapacitated—unless you cancel it. In most states you must put specific words in the document stating that you want your agent's powers to stay in effect even if you become incapacitated. If you want this feature, it's very important that you have these words in your document. In those states that have adopted the Uniform Power of Attorney Act, you do not need to be concerned about including the "durable" language; the law presumes that you want your agent to act after you become incapacitated. Check with an attorney in your state.

You can also state in your power of attorney that you want to delay the time when you want your agent to begin to act. This is called a *springing* power of attorney because the effectiveness of the document springs into effect at some time after you have signed the document. Your attorney must carefully draft a springing power of attorney to avoid any difficulty in determining exactly when the springing event has happened.

Even if you sign a power of attorney, you can still manage your own affairs. You are not giving up anything. Think of a power of attorney as an extra set of car keys that you give to someone else. You have your own keys and control when that extra set of keys can be used. When you can't or don't want to drive yourself, someone else has the keys to do the driving for you.

You can cancel, or revoke, a power of attorney at any time by tearing it up, signing a new one, or writing on it that you want to cancel it. You don't have to give any reason. If you do cancel, be sure to let your agent and anyone your agent has been dealing with know that you have cancelled your agent's authority. Just like your will, it is important to review your power of attorney every few years or when your circumstances change. If you move to a new state, it's a good idea to have any attorney in that state review your powers of attorney.

All powers of attorney come to an end at your death. Your agent will have no authority to make any decisions after you die. Likewise, the executor you name in your will has no authority to act before your death.

Before deciding what powers you want your agent to have, carefully consider whom you want to be your agent. Select someone you trust completely and who can do the job. It is best to avoid someone who is ill, inexperienced in financial matters, has a hard time managing his or her own money, or who, for some other reason would not be able to carry out the responsibilities. Remember you are giving your agent the opportunity to act for you at a time when you may not be able to keep tabs on what the agent is doing. You may want to add ways for other people to check up on what your agent is doing when you cannot.

If you want your agent to have access to your bank account, be sure to get your bank's authorization forms and a signature card for your agent. Typically, a bank has its own form it wants your agent to sign before giving your agent access to a particular account. If you and your agent do not contact the bank before you become incapacitated, the bank may not honor checks or withdrawals your agent signs.

Giving your agent the authority to access your bank account is not the same as making someone a joint owner of the account. You'll want to make sure that you create the right kind of account so your agent has access to your funds to pay your bills but is not listed as an owner. Your bank may call this an agency, fiduciary, or convenience account.

✓ Discuss your advance planning with those who need to know

Be sure you have talked with those you want to serve as your health care agent, financial agent, executor, successor trustee, children's guardian, and minors' trustee, to make sure they are willing and able to take on these responsibilities. While you may be honoring those individuals with the responsibilities you've given them, these are tough jobs. Don't make it a surprise.

Talk with each person about why you've selected them and why you think they are the right person with the right skills to do the job. Also tell them your expectations for how they carry out their responsibilities. Your health care agent needs to know about any health care complications that would impact the medical decisions made on your behalf. Financial agents need to know the background of any important financial decisions. Executors need to know all of your assets and debts and how you want your estate to be distributed. Even though they may not have been in your shoes, they will need to walk in those shoes in the future.

Be sure your loved ones know where all your documents are located. Some documents will be with your attorney, others will be in your safe deposit box, and some will need to be on hand where your family can find them when decisions need to be made on your behalf. Indicate on the Where I Put It Checklist where you are safekeeping the documents discussed in this chapter. Use the checklists throughout this book to organize the information they'll need.

Legal Matters Action Checklists

The following Action Checklists are in Chapter 11:

- ❑ Health Care Directives and Medical Orders
- ❑ Final Wishes Summary
- ❑ Organ and Tissue Donation
- ❑ Whole Body Donation
- ❑ Cremation
- ❑ Burial
- ❑ Entombment
- ❑ Funeral/Memorial Service
- ❑ Veterans' Burial Benefits
- ❑ Will
- ❑ Codicils
- ❑ Living Trust
- ❑ Pet Care
- ❑ Letter of Instruction
- ❑ Financial Power of Attorney

Health Care Directives and Medical Orders

❑ I have a living will.

❑ I have a durable power of attorney for health care.

Health care agent's name: _____

Phone: _____ E-mail: _____

Address: _____

_____

Location of my advance health care directive: _____

❑ I have talked with my health care agent about my medical preferences.

❑ I have talked with my health care agent about palliative and hospice care.

❑ I have talked with my doctor and health care agent about do not resuscitate orders.

❑ I have an out of hospital do not resuscitate order.

❑ My doctor has entered medical orders for life-sustaining treatments.

Final Wishes Summary

I wish to:

- ❏ be embalmed
- ❏ be cremated (see the Cremation Checklist)
- ❏ be an organ donor (see the Organ and Tissue Donation Checklist)
- ❏ have my body bequeathed to a medical school (see the Whole Body Donation Checklist)
- ❏ have my body buried in the earth (see the Burial Checklist)
- ❏ have my body entombed in a mausoleum (see the Entombment Checklist)
- ❏ other: _____

I wish to have:

- ❏ funeral service (body present) (see the Funeral/Memorial Service Checklist)
- ❏ memorial service (body not present)
- ❏ celebration of life service
- ❏ no service
- ❏ graveside service
- ❏ I would like a US flag covering my coffin
- ❏ I would like to have military funeral honors (see Veterans' Burial Benefits Checklist)
- ❏ other: _____

My preferences are as follows:

_____

_____

_____

_____

_____

_____

_____

_____

_____

Organ and Tissue Donation

❑ I wish to donate any needed organs or tissues.

My blood type is _____

❑ I wish to donate only the following organs or tissues:

Organs:

❑ Heart

❑ Kidneys

❑ Liver

❑ Lungs

❑ Pancreas

❑ Other:_____

Tissues:

❑ Blood vessels

❑ Bone

❑ Cartilage

❑ Corneas

❑ Heart valves

❑ Inner ear

❑ Intestines

❑ Skin

❑ Other:_____

❑ I have not prepared a uniform donor card.

❑ I have a uniform donor card.

❑ I have registered with my state's organ donation registry at this website: _____

_____

Location of uniform donor card: _____

Whole Body Donation

I have made the following prearrangements with the following medical school or research organization:

Medical school: _____

Address: _____

_____

Contact person: _____ Phone: _____

Research organization: _____

Address: _____

_____

Contact person: _____ Phone: _____

Cremation

❑ I want my body to be cremated.

❑ I want my body to be cremated followed by a memorial service.

❑ I want my body to be cremated followed by a celebration of life service.

I have made the following prearrangements for my cremation:

Company: _____

Address: _____

_____

Phone: _____ Website: _____

The contract is located _____

Following my cremation, I wish my ashes be distributed as follows:

❑ Scattered in the following places: _____

❑ Placed in an urn and buried or entombed: _____

❑ Other: _____

❑ Handled as my loved ones see fit.

Burial

The ownership of the cemetery lot is in the name of _____

Location of the lot:

Cemetery: _____

Section: _____ Lot: _____

Address: _____

_____

Other description: _____

_____

Location of deed: _____

- ❏ I would like to have a grave marker.
- ❏ I would like to have a grave marker furnished by the Department of Veterans Affairs.
- ❏ I would like to have a service medallion furnished by the Department of Veterans Affairs.

I would like the following words to be placed on my grave marker:

_____

_____

_____

I would like the following type of casket: _____

Other burial instructions: _____

_____

_____

_____

_____

_____

_____

_____

_____

_____

Entombment

The ownership of the crypt is in the name of _____.

Location of the crypt:

Church/Cemetery/Mausoleum: _____

Address: _____

_____

Space #: _____

Other description: _____

_____

Location of deed or contract: _____

I would like the following words to be placed on the crypt:

_____

_____

_____

Other instructions:

_____

_____

_____

_____

_____

_____

_____

_____

_____

_____

_____

_____

_____

_____

Funeral/Memorial Service

- ❏ I want a funeral.
- ❏ I want a memorial service.
- ❏ I want a graveside service.
- ❏ I have not made funeral prearrangements.
- ❏ I have a pre-need contract and have pre-paid for some or all of my funeral.

I have made the following funeral pre-need arrangements:

_____

_____

_____

_____

_____

_____

The pre-need contract is located _____.

I wish the commemorative service to be for:

- ❏ Friends and relatives
- ❏ Private
- ❏ Other: _____

I wish the graveside service to be for:

- ❏ Friends and relatives
- ❏ Private
- ❏ Other: _____

I want the casket to be:

- ❏ Closed
- ❏ Open

The urn with ashes should be present: ❏ Yes ❏ No

Location of the service:

Funeral establishment: _____

Address: _____

_____

Phone: _____ E-mail: _____

House of worship: _____

Address: _____

_____

Phone: _____ E-mail: _____

Religious leader/Officiant/Clergy: _____

Address: _____

_____

Phone: _____ E-mail: _____

Speakers/Readers:

_____

_____

_____

_____

Ushers/Pallbearers:

_____

_____

_____

_____

Favorite scripture, psalms, poems:

_____

_____

_____

_____

Special hymns, music, musicians, soloists:

_____

_____

_____

_____

Veterans' Burial Benefits

- ❑ I served in the US military.
- ❑ I or other family members may be eligible for veterans' benefits.
- ❑ I have a copy of my DD-214.
- ❑ I want a burial flag for my casket.
- ❑ I want burial in a national cemetery.
- ❑ I want a veteran's headstone.
- ❑ I want military honors at the burial.

Name I served under while in the military:

_____

     First   Middle   Last

Location of my DD-214: _____

Date entered active service: _____

Date separated from active service: _____

Branch: _____

Grade or rank: _____

National Guard: _____

Reserves: _____

Will

I have a will.

Executor's name: _____

Phone: _____ E-mail: _____

Address: _____

_____

Drafting attorney's name: _____

Phone: _____ E-mail: _____

Address: _____

_____

Witness's name: _____

Phone: _____ E-mail: _____

Address: _____

_____

Witness's name: _____

Phone: _____ E-mail: _____

Address: _____

_____

The original of my will is located _____.

Codicils

I have executed a codicil to my will.

Codicil date: _____

Attorney's name: _____

Phone: _____ E-mail: _____

Address: _____

_____

Executor (if changed): _____

Phone: _____ E-mail: _____

Address: _____

_____

Witness's name: _____

Phone: _____ E-mail: _____

Address: _____

_____

Witness's name:_____

Phone: _____ E-mail: _____

Address: _____

_____

My codicil is located with my will: _____

Living Trust

I have a living trust.

Trustee's name: _____

Phone: _____ E-mail: _____

Address: _____

_____

Drafting attorney's name: _____

Phone: _____ E-mail: _____

Address: _____

_____

Witness's name: _____

Phone: _____ E-mail: _____

Address: _____

_____

Witness's name: _____

Phone: _____ E-mail: _____

Address: _____

_____

The original of my living trust is located _____.

Pet Care

I have made the following arrangements for the care of my pets:

_____

_____

_____

_____

_____

_____

_____

_____

I have made the following financial arrangements for the care of my pets:

_____

_____

_____

_____

_____

_____

Letter of Instruction

I have a letter of instruction.

Location of my letter of instruction: _____

Date I last updated my letter of instruction: _____

Financial Power of Attorney

- ❏ I have a durable power of attorney for financial management.
- ❏ I have discussed my expectations with my agent.
- ❏ My agent has a copy of my durable power of attorney.

Agent's name:_____

Phone: _____ E-mail: _____

Address: _____

_____

CHAPTER 12

TAKE CARE OF YOURSELF

Exercising to have fun and stay fit. Eating better and managing stress to improve our health. Staying connected socially. When our parents retired, these priorities probably weren't top of mind. Compared to the previous generations, we have decades more to live and enjoy. And we are living well. According to the 2014 National Health Interview Survey, 54 percent of people age 45 to 64, 50 percent of those age 65 to 74, and 40 percent of people 75 and older say they are in excellent or very good health. And 56 percent of Americans 75 and older say they have no limitations on their ability to work or to live their lives. We want to sustain that level of good health and well-being.

Still, we all know people struggling with ailments of the body and mind. Two-thirds of people past age 65 say they cope with multiple chronic illnesses, according to the Centers for Disease Control and Prevention. The incidence of Alzheimer's disease and other debilitating conditions such as Huntington's and Parkinson's disease is rising as the population ages. What better motivation to take better care of ourselves in retirement?

To sustain the goal of longer, healthier, and happier lives, we have to take charge of our own health. This includes the activities we do, food we eat every day, and relationships we engage in. Staying active and socially connected allows us to live out our retirement dreams with confidence.

My To-Do Checklist

Done	Need to Do	
❑	❑	Exercise to stay strong
❑	❑	Eat the good (for you) stuff
❑	❑	Keep your spirits up and your stress low
❑	❑	Take advantage of preventive services
❑	❑	Carry with you a personal medication record
❑	❑	Know your family medical history

✓ Exercise to stay strong

Experts may not agree on just how much exercise we need to stay strong, but there is consensus that most of us could benefit from getting more. About 67 percent of Americans are overweight or obese. A third of those 65 and older reported they engage in no physical activity or exercise, according to America's Health Rankings in 2015. Our bodies work best when they move. Physical activity reduces the risk of Alzheimer's disease, osteoporosis, and other chronic conditions. When you were working and sitting at a desk all day, you might have used the excuse that you didn't have time to exercise. But now that you've retired, you have more free time to get that exercise you need.

Find simple ways to reengineer your life to incorporate movement into your days. Getting moving doesn't mean you have to commit to hours in the gym. Just 30 minutes of brisk walking every day will do you good. Some experts recommend 10,000 steps a day, which can be tracked using a pedometer. Park your car in the farthest, rather than closest, parking spot to add steps to your day. Take the stairs as much as you are able. Find a walking routine that you enjoy so you keep at it. This could include joining a mall-walking club that circuits the shopping mall before the stores open, recruiting a friend to join you in your evening walk, or volunteering to walk the neighbors' dog while they are on vacation.

Retirement is also the time to get better at the sports or activities you already do. Now you have the time to take lessons to improve your golf swing, tennis serve, or cross-country skiing. My skills in kayaking, ice skating, and downhill skiing have greatly benefited—and I have too—by having more time in retirement to work on my technique. With my senior pass at the nearest ski slope, I get to ski during the week when there are no weekend crowds, I don't have to dodge the snowboarders sitting right where I want to turn, and the snow is fresher. I might even join a masters swimming club to have some company and competition while I swim. Learn more at usms.org.

Share your skills with others by coaching a Little League baseball or softball team. Tackle that new sport you've put off doing. Have you always wanted to rock climb or run a 10K, marathon, or ultramarathon? You've got the time now to start training. Another great way to get exercise and explore the outdoors is to go geocaching (geocaching.com).

Dancing is another great way to get moving. Break out the Chubby Checker 45 to twist again, try ballroom dancing, or get on the floor to two-step. Whatever the style or tempo, dancing is a fun way to stay limber and energized. Check with your local gym, recreation center, or senior center for yoga, Pilates, or other exercise classes. My church even hosts yoga classes, both during the day and in the evenings.

More than just being fun, exercise is essential to staying healthy. Weight-bearing exercises, such as dancing, hiking, jogging, stair climbing, and tennis, are important to build and maintain bone density and stave off osteoporosis. Muscle-strengthening exercises, including yoga, elastic bands, or free weights, improve your agility, posture, and balance to increase ability and reduce the risk of falls. Whatever fits your interests, get moving!

✓ Eat the good (for you) stuff

What's in our diets accounts for about 80 percent of the health benefits we get from a healthy lifestyle. Research shows that what we eat has a big impact on our brains, hearts, and bodies.

Scientists have found that the right foods—and combinations of food—can help enhance memory, build new brain cells, and even ward off Alzheimer's. Eating plans, including the Mediterranean, DASH, and MIND, may help stave off cognitive decline and protect the heart and brain against disease. The Mediterranean diet features fish, fruit, vegetables, olive oil, nuts, a little red wine, and not so much meat and dairy. The DASH (Dietary Approaches to Stop Hypertension) diet helps people lower blood pressure and cholesterol, as well as lose weight, by centering on food that is rich in fruits, vegetables, and low-fat dairy, with reduced red meat, fats, and sweets. The MIND (Mediterranean-DASH Intervention for Neurodegenerative Delay) diet combines the strengths of the Mediterranean and DASH plans to focus on the foods that specifically affect brain health: green leafy vegetables, all other vegetables, nuts, berries, beans, whole gains, fish, poultry, olive oil, and red wine.

Doctors know how certain foods affect our bodies, so we can adjust our diet accordingly to stay healthy and lose weight. More than 80 percent of all cases of type 2 diabetes are related to weight. One out of every three cancer deaths is linked to excess body weight, poor nutrition, or physical inactivity. Moreover, your risk of dying prematurely increases even if you're just 10 pounds overweight.

A good diet can help prevent or delay heart disease, cancer, and diabetes. Dr. John Whyte, in *AARP New American Diet: Lose Weight, Live Longer*, draws on the findings from the 25-year NIH/AARP Diet and Health Study, the largest-ever survey of American diet and lifestyle. Whyte suggests we focus on fresh and colorful vegetables, fruits, whole grains, fish, low-fat dairy, and nuts, while avoiding highly processed foods, high-sugar foods and sodas, and saturated fats.

Moderation and balance are the key words used by most nutrition experts. Things to cut back on: salt, sugary drinks, red meats, processed meat, fried or fast foods, and desserts. Food to eat more of: leafy green vegetables, fruit, beans, nuts, root vegetables, and whole grains. Get a variety of foods every day so you get a natural combination of the good things for you. Being retired means I can spend more time in the kitchen trying out new recipes that include all the good-for-me foods and less time eating restaurant fare at lunch time. Now that I'm home more during the day, I have to make sure that my refrigerator is stocked with healthy snacks so I'm not tempted to forage for chips or cookies. The Eating Well Checklist can help you track what should be going into your shopping basket, as well as foods to avoid or cut back.

Along with eating the right stuff, the best medicine for staying healthy is drinking enough water. Other beverages don't hydrate us; in fact, they are more likely to dehydrate our systems. On my last visit my cardiologist said, for my height, weight, and age, I should drink at least eight cups every day.

✓ Keep your spirits up and your stress low

Retirement gives us time to focus not just on our physical but also on our emotional well-being. Identify what makes you feel happy and content. Make time to relax and do what brings you the most pleasure. Intentionally de-stress. This might be just closing your eyes and taking some deep breaths. Get up from your chair to wiggle your shoulders and stretch your arms. Go to a quiet spot to read a chapter in a book. Put on headphones or earbuds to listen to music. Learn meditation techniques. I've found that when I really get stressed out, I get relief if I methodically start thinking about relaxing my toes, then ankles, then knees, and on up through each part of my body. By the time I get to my head, I'm calmer.

Retirement brings many changes, and change can be unsettling. We may be faced with different routines, changed roles, new friends, and reduced finances. We may notice a decline in our eyesight, hearing, metabolism, and muscle tone, common as we age. We all have "senior moments" where we forget a name or a number. Counterattack these discomfiting changes with positive thinking and acting.

The normal ups and downs of life mean that everyone feels sad or has the blues from time to time. This is a normal reaction to life's struggles, setbacks, and disappointments. The changes that often come in later life—retirement, death of loved ones, decreased socialization, health problems—can lead to depression. Different people have different symptoms, but here is a list of the common signs of depression:

- Sadness
- Loss of energy or fatigue
- Loss of interest in favorite activities
- Social withdrawal or a reluctance to be with friends
- Weight loss or loss of appetite
- Difficulty falling asleep or sleeping too much
- Increased use of alcohol or other drugs
- Fixation on death
- Unexplained or aggravated aches and pain (arthritis, backache, or headaches)
- Feelings of hopelessness, helplessness, or worthlessness
- Anxiety
- Diminished ability to think, concentrate, or make decisions
- Memory problems
- Lack of motivation
- Slowed movement and speech
- Irritability or anger
- Neglecting personal care

Neither depression nor dementia, however, are an inevitable part of aging. Some of the signs of depression can be mistaken for dementia, may be the side effect of prescription drugs, or could be caused by medical problems. If you recognize these symptoms in you or someone you love, seek help from a medical professional.

Another way to improve your spirits and health is to stay connected with family, friends, and former co-workers. They can provide you with a strong support network, even a friendly shoulder to cry on, and keep loneliness at bay. Some activities that build social connections include joining a book club; volunteering at a school, hospital, or non-profit organization; or getting involved with your place of worship. You'll find many more ideas in Chapter 5. Technology is another way we can stay connected. Social media networks, blogging, and browsing for information about hobbies and interests have proven to be successful in creating connections, according to people who get technology training through the AARP Foundation's Connecting to Community program.

I take staying connected seriously. Research shows that isolation can have devastating health effects. The mortality risk from breast cancer, high blood pressure, heart disease, and other chronic diseases is about three times as high for isolated people—those who are not married, have few friends or relatives, or do not belong to a volunteer or religious organization—compared with those who have more sources of social contacts.

✓ Take advantage of preventive services

One of the best ways to stay healthy so you can get the most out of your retirement is to take advantage of preventive screenings and immunizations. Under the Affordable Care Act (ACA) and Medicare, many of these services are provided for little or no extra cost.

During the first year you are on Medicare Part B, you can get a "Welcome to Medicare" preventive visit. Although this is not a physical exam, it includes a review of your medical and social history, counseling about available preventive services, and referrals for other care you might need. When you make this appointment with a doctor who accepts Medicare, you should let the doctor's office know you are scheduling your "Welcome to Medicare" visit. The preventive benefit is free, but you may have to pay coinsurance on other tests and services the doctor conducts during the same visit, and the Part B deductible may apply. (Refer to the Medicare section in Chapter 10 of *AARP Medicare for Dummies* for more information about Medicare.)

Free yearly wellness visits are also covered by Medicare. During this visit, Medicare recipients fill out a health risk assessment and the doctor will develop or update your personalized preventive wellness plan. This visit is covered once every 12 months and you don't need to have had a "Welcome to Medicare" visit to qualify for the yearly wellness visit. Again, you may be charged for other services or tests your doctor provides outside of preventive care.

Women can get bone density screenings to watch for signs of osteoporosis, mammograms to screen for breast cancer, and screenings for cervical and vaginal cancer. Men can be screened for prostate cancer. In addition to the various cancer screenings, flu and pneumococcal vaccines are free once a year. At my last appointment, my doctor reminded me that there are now two different vaccines to prevent pneumonia that are given at least one year apart. What preventive services are available to you depends on your health insurance. Under the ACA, many preventive services, screenings, and immunizations are offered free or at very low cost. Refer to the current lists of all ACA-covered and Medicare-covered preventive services in this chapter and talk to your doctor about any screenings you should get. Depending on the type of screening, your doctor will need to determine which tests are appropriate for you. Some are available once a year, others every five years, and some just one time.

Some people may avoid getting screened because they think what they don't know won't hurt them. But early detection of most cancers saves lives. Every year Medicare mails *Medicare and You* to everyone with Medicare. Keep it handy as a reference for all that Medicare covers. Go to hhs.gov/healthcare to see what's covered under the ACA.

✓ Carry with you a personal medication record

Carrying with you at all times a record of the medications you are taking can be life-saving. If you should have a sudden illness, emergency responders need to know promptly what medications you have taken, any medical conditions for which you are receiving treatment, and any drug allergies you might have. Having all your medications and allergies on one form also comes in handy when you go to your doctors. I know every time I see a health care provider, I'm asked about the meds I'm taking. Although my list isn't long, it's convenient to have the list at my fingertips.

On your personal medication record, list your prescription drugs as well as any over-the-counter drugs, vitamins, or herbal or dietary supplements. Also include the reason you are taking each medication along with the pharmacy and prescribing physician, if any. If you are not sure why you are taking a prescribed medication, ask your doctor. You can also list the form of the medication, such as a pill, liquid, patch or injection, and dosage, for example, how many milligrams in each tablet. Note the frequency, too, such as "one pill at breakfast." In the last column, you can include any special directions, such as "with food." You can get a free personal medication record in a vinyl case from AARP.

✓ Know your family medical history

Knowing your family's medical history can shed some light on your own health. You can use this information to see if there are common illnesses or medical conditions in your family. This will help you and your family to identify possible risks for certain disease and take steps to recue or prevent those risks in the future. It may prove valuable in the diagnosis, early treatment, and, in some cases, prevention of certain hereditary medical conditions.

Take Care of Yourself Action Checklists

The following Action Checklists are in Chapter 12:

- ❑ Getting or Staying Fit
- ❑ Eating Well
- ❑ Personal Medication Record
- ❑ Medicare-Covered Preventive Services
- ❑ ACA-Covered Preventive Services
- ❑ Family Medical History

Getting or Staying Fit

I do now   **I'd like to do**

I do now	I'd like to do	Activity
❑	❑	Baseball/softball
❑	❑	Canoeing
❑	❑	Chair aerobics
❑	❑	Dancing
❑	❑	Exercise class
❑	❑	Fishing
❑	❑	Gardening
❑	❑	Geocaching
❑	❑	Golf
❑	❑	Hiking
❑	❑	Jogging
❑	❑	Karate
❑	❑	Kayaking
❑	❑	Pilates
❑	❑	Racquet ball
❑	❑	Rock climbing
❑	❑	Running
❑	❑	Sailing
❑	❑	Scuba diving
❑	❑	Skating
❑	❑	Skiing (cross country)
❑	❑	Skiing (downhill)
❑	❑	Snowboarding
❑	❑	Surfing
❑	❑	Strength training
❑	❑	Swimming
❑	❑	Tai Chi

I do now   **I'd like to do**

❏   ❏   Tennis

❏   ❏   Walking

❏   ❏   Yoga

❏   ❏   Other: _____

Eating Well

I eat now   **I will eat more**

☐   ☐   Beans

☐   ☐   Brown rice

☐   ☐   Dairy

☐   ☐   Fish

☐   ☐   Fruit

☐   ☐   Green tea

☐   ☐   Hummus

☐   ☐   Lean meats (just a few times a week)

☐   ☐   Lentils

☐   ☐   Nuts

☐   ☐   Oatmeal

☐   ☐   Olive oil

☐   ☐   Vegetables (green, leafy, colorful, root)

☐   ☐   Whole grains

I eat now   **I will eat less**

☐   ☐   Artificial sweeteners

☐   ☐   Fried food

☐   ☐   Fruit drinks

☐   ☐   High fructose corn syrup

☐   ☐   Meats with nitrates and nitrites (bacon, hot dogs, lunch meats)

☐   ☐   Processed foods

☐   ☐   Saturated fat

☐   ☐   Sodas (diet and regular)

☐   ☐   Sweets such as cakes, cookies, ice cream, and pastries

☐   ☐   White bread, pasta, and rice

Personal Medication Record

My Personal Information:

Name:_____

Date of birth: _____

Phone number: _____

Emergency Contact:

Name: _____

Relationship: _____

Phone number: _____

Primary Care Physician:

Name:_____

Phone number: _____

Website: _____

Pharmacy/Drugstore:

Name:_____

Pharmacist: _____

Phone number: _____

Website: _____

Other Physicians:

Name:_____

Specialty: _____

Phone number: _____

Website: _____

Name:_____

Specialty: _____

Phone number: _____

Website: _____

My Medical Conditions:

_____

_____

_____

_____

_____

My Allergies:

_____

_____

_____

_____

_____

My Notes:

_____

_____

_____

_____

_____

What	Reason	Form	Dosage	When	Notes

Be sure to include *all* prescription drugs, over-the-counter drugs, vitamins, and herbal or dietary supplements.

Medicare-Covered Preventive Services

I'm on Medicare and have received or need the following preventive services:

Screening or Service	Need	Date(s) Received
Welcome to Medicare visit	❑	_____
Yearly wellness visit	❑	_____
Flu shot	❑	_____
Pneumococcal vaccines	❑	_____
Hepatitis B shot	❑	_____
Abdominal aortic aneurysm screening	❑	_____
Bone density measurement	❑	_____
Breast cancer screening (mammogram)	❑	_____
Cardiovascular disease screening	❑	_____
Cervical and vaginal cancer screening	❑	_____
Colorectal cancer screening	❑	_____
Depression screening	❑	_____
Diabetes screening	❑	_____
Glaucoma test	❑	_____
Hepatitis C screening	❑	_____
HIV screening	❑	_____
Lung cancer screening	❑	_____
Obesity screening	❑	_____
Prostate cancer screening	❑	_____
Sexually transmitted infections screening	❑	_____
Alcohol misuse screening	❑	_____
Diabetes self-management training	❑	_____
Medical nutrition therapy	❑	_____
Smoking and tobacco use counseling	❑	_____

ACA-Covered Preventive Services

I'm not on Medicare but have received or need the following preventive services:

Screening or Service	Need	Date(s) Received
Abdominal aortic aneurysm screening	❏	_____
Alcohol misuse screening	❏	_____
Aspirin use	❏	_____
Bone density measurement	❏	_____
Blood pressure screening	❏	_____
Breast cancer screening (mammogram)	❏	_____
Cervical and vaginal cancer screening	❏	_____
Cholesterol screening	❏	_____
Colorectal cancer screening	❏	_____
Depression screening	❏	_____
Type 2 diabetes screening	❏	_____
Diet screening	❏	_____
Domestic violence screening	❏	_____
HIV screening	❏	_____
Obesity screening	❏	_____
Sexually transmitted infections screening	❏	_____
Syphilis screening	❏	_____
Tobacco use screening and cessation counseling	❏	_____
Hepatitis A vaccine	❏	_____
Hepatitis B vaccine	❏	_____
Human papillomavirus vaccine	❏	_____
Influenza vaccine	❏	_____
Measles, mumps, rubella vaccine	❏	_____
Meningococcal vaccine	❏	_____
Pneumococcal vaccine	❏	_____

Tetanus, diphtheria, pertussis vaccine	❑	_____
Tetanus vaccine	❑	_____
Varicella vaccine	❑	_____

Family Medical History

The following lists my family medical history. I, or any of my blood relatives (including parents, grandparents, sisters, brothers, uncles, aunts, and children), have had the following medical issues:

Yes		Who
❏	Alcoholism	_____
❏	Allergies	_____
❏	Alzheimer's disease	_____
❏	Arthritis	_____
❏	Asthma	_____
❏	Birth defects	_____
❏	Blood disorder	_____
❏	Cancer	_____
❏	Chromosomal disorder	_____
❏	Cystic fibrosis	_____
❏	Diabetes	_____
❏	Dementia	_____
❏	Eczema	_____
❏	Endometriosis	_____
❏	Epilepsy	_____
❏	Gallbladder problems	_____
❏	Gastrointestinal disorder	_____
❏	Glaucoma	_____
❏	Gout	_____
❏	Hay fever	_____
❏	Hearing loss	_____
❏	Heart disease	_____
❏	High blood pressure	_____
❏	High cholesterol	_____
❏	Infertility	_____
❏	Inflammatory bowel disease	_____
❏	Intellectual disability	_____

❑   Kidney disease   _____

❑   Learning disabilities   _____

❑   Lung disease   _____

❑   Lymphoma   _____

❑   Mental disorder   _____

❑   Miscarriage, stillbirth   _____

❑   Muscular dystrophy   _____

❑   Neurological disorders   _____

❑   Osteoporosis   _____

❑   Psoriasis   _____

❑   Sickle cell disease   _____

❑   Skin cancer: basal cell   _____

❑   Skin cancer: melanoma   _____

❑   Skin cancer: squamous cell   _____

❑   Stomach disorders   _____

❑   Stroke   _____

❑   Thyroid disorder   _____

❑   Ulcers   _____

❑   Vision impairment   _____

❑   Other   _____

❑   Other   _____

Notes about my family's medical history:

_____

_____

_____

_____

_____

_____

Notes

Notes

Notes

Notes

Notes

Notes

Notes

Notes